C000178363

No Ordinary Life

This book has a charitable philosophy.
Money from the sale of this book will be donated to charity and worthy causes, in the example and tradition of Grandma's Garden.

Diana Rhodes

© Diana Rhodes 2010

Published by Stand Sure Publishing

ISBN 978-0-9566815-0-8

A catalogue record for this book is available from the British Library.

Cover design by Clare Brayshaw

Prepared and printed by:

York Publishing Services Ltd
64 Hallfield Road
Layerthorpe
York YO31 7ZQ
Tel: 01904 431213

Website: www.yps-publishing.co.uk

Endorsements

Jane Goodall PhD, DBE Founder – the Jane Goodall Institute & UN Messenger of Peace www.janegoodall.org

Diana Rhodes is the ultimate example of the 'indomitable human spirit'. She has started a whole new movement "Seeds of Peace" that has inspired hope in people all around the world. She has created a magical garden in a most spiritually powerful part of the world (in Wales), Grandma's Garden. She has built a couple of businesses and a couple of homes. She has made contact with the like of Nelson Mandela, the Dalai Llama and HRH Prince Charles. She has helped many children overcome learning difficulties – and changed the attitude towards how to teach such children. And she has done all this despite the fact that she is afflicted with RA, causing frequent bouts of excruciating pain. And despite the fact that she was then diagnosed with the very rare condition, Sjogrens Syndrome – she has to receive all her nourishment through a tube and has been unable to eat or drink normally for over ten years. Perhaps the most extraordinary of all – she is still alive in defiance of her doctors' prognoses and her family's fears.

Indeed, Diana's body has suffered cruelly. But her mind, strengthened perhaps by adversity, as well as by contact with a number of wise and sometimes also very spiritual human beings, is immensely strong and her spirit seems invincible She has gained much wisdom, gathering unto herself an understanding of the human condition and of life beyond mortal death so that we may think of ourselves as dying into life

Her life is inspirational. Her courage is extraordinary. She is one of those people who make you realize how lucky you are to have been blessed by the gift of good health.

Diana has never lost her sense of humour – indeed, I doubt she could have survived without it. And she has not fought this battle alone. Her husband, Richard, is a true tower of strength, the partner she so clearly deserves. Together they made a home and raised a family. Together they faced "the slings and arrows of outrageous fortune".

I am certainly glad that I have been privileged to meet this remarkable couple. It was but twice, and we were surrounded by people – but there is – at least so I feel – a bond between us that goes beyond the fleeting physical moments we spent together.

I hope that her story will reach many, inspire many, and encourage them to work harder to achieve their own goals, and to think more deeply about the choices that we make each day, the thoughts that we think each day. For it is our combined actions and thoughts that will, in the end, heal and re-create the world we leave for our children and theirs.

David Bellamy OBE

'This is the story of a gentlewoman who found inner strength that allowed her to live two lives to an overflowing fullness.

Wife, Mother, Grandma and founding force of a holiday park where visitors spend quality time with families and friends, all set about with the local flora and fauna.

Diana's other driving force was and still is in the international arena of world peace.

From the boundless (for her) confines of a high tech wheel chair with Richard at her side, she travelled the world chiding Nations to speak the commonsense of peace unto Nations.

Back home this amazing lady is still creating a road map of themed gardens pointing the way ahead in what was once a grove of Oaks. Sacred places for the Roman Goddess Diana lady of wild creatures and revered as a symbol of strength in women.'

Dr Josh Dixey MD FRCP Consultant Rheumatologist

'Diana Rhodes describes how she has been able to remain so productive despite her own considerable disability with arthritis. Her philosophy to life which is positive and full of hope will bring inspiration to those with their own disabilities and Diana's words should become required reading for all health professionals and carers who are involved with long-term disability from whatever cause. Her lightness of touch means that there is much to smile about in this book and the reader will come away uplifted.'

Sharon G Mijares PhD

'Diana Rhodes is a remarkable woman. Despite the numerous and ongoing health challenges taking place in her own life, she has tirelessly attended to needs of children, women and men, wherever and whenever it is needed. Her remarkableness is not only in her caring, but also in her abundant creative spirit spreading seeds of peace in her numerous endeavours. Her creative stamp has been left in numerous places, including her writing. She has changed children's lives, brought education where it was needed, and basically done her part in bettering the human condition. Her own life is like the gardens she treasures, and the story of her strength and contributions is well worth reading. We were particularly pleased to have a chapter from her in our own book, A Power Such As the World Has Never Known, as her life is a living example of peaceful efforts and goodwill.'

Elinore Detiger, Founder of The Detiger Family Trust of the Netherlands.

'Diana is working in a unique way – inspired and also in a lovely spontaneous (yet tough, disciplined, dedicated way) which is so typical of so many women I have met and from all over the world. There is an open sharingness about what she does which has the stamp of 'the Mother' on it. We are also daughters and sisters of each other. And of the Divine.

Thank you Diana for being one of those beautiful but strong plants – first flowering but now growing into a tree, for being who you are and doing what you do.'

Acknowledgements

If I was to thank all those who have been instrumental in my life and writing there would not be room to include the book.

Maybe when Richard sees this book in print he will accept the part he played in persuading me to write it. My love and thanks for the role he has played in my life are expressed in every word, not least in my letter to him.

Jane, right hand, third sister, Angel of friendship. If I can't, she can and vice versa. We work and laugh as one. Thank you for being my close companion, I could not have wished for anyone more suited.

My friend Janet, without her help and encouragement I may never have put pen to paper. She has encouraged and inspired me in so many ways.

To the Doctors, Nurses and Carers who have helped me in my independence.

To my family, friends and everyone in the book and everyone I have ever known, without you there would not have been a story to tell.

Thank you all for being who you are.

Biography Diana Rhodes

Diana Rhodes is a devoted wife, mother and grandmother. She is a teacher and educator and a tireless worker for the peace process. Despite, or perhaps even because of, serious ongoing health challenges she has a passion for her work.

The knowledge she has acquired through both formal and personal study she practices in her day to day life. With the benefit of this knowledge she has gained wisdom, a wisdom that permeates her work and all relationships. Her work has involved the education of less able children and those in need of specific educational understanding. Her total commitment to linking millions of people around the world to work for peace and understanding has included an annual gathering and world prayer for peace and healing. She has compiled, edited and published three books of words of peace and encouragement from around the world. The Foreword for the third book being written and blessed by His Holiness the Dalai Lama. She is a published poet.

She, with her loyal and supportive husband, has created an Award winning Peace Garden and Sculpture

Park, Grandma's Garden, in the grounds of their natural arboretum. Despite her severe physical difficulties she has helped organize and attended peace initiatives around the world and continues to work with her garden raising money for local and national charity and worthy causes.

Contents

	Endorsements	iii
	Acknowledgements	vii
	Biography Diana Rhodes	ix
	Synopsis	xiii
	Foreword	xv
	Introduction	xvii
1	'You're Going to Die!'	1
2	Early Days	8
3	Richard – A Life After Life Partner	27
4	Trauma and the Gift of Life	33
5	Marriage and Young Love	38
6	Search for Spiritual Understanding	54
7	What is Death?	69
8	Moving On	80
9	Greaves Farm – The Good Life	89
10	Disaster! – Enforced Lifestyle Change	99
11	The Garth – A New Beginning in Wales	110
12	More Health Problems	125

13	Building the Business	139
14	Teaching and Learning – Who Teaches Whom?	156
15	Plas Dolguog – Destiny Presents Itself	190
16	A Decade of Change	203
17	Native American Sacred Sundance Ceremony	251
18	The Seed of Life Peace Foundation Gathers the World	276
19	The Work Continues	287
20	Grandma's Garden	326
21	Self Help	351
22	Plas Dolguog – Destiny Threatened	381
23	Creativity – It's Effects On Healing	388
24	The End or the Beginning of Another Beginning?	396

Synopsis

No Ordinary Life – Diana Rhodes

The inspirational story of a woman with severe physical disabilities who has made her mark as a wife, mother, grandmother, teacher, peace delegate to the United Nations and founder of the Seed of Life Peace Foundation and Grandma's Garden, a tourist attraction featured by both BBC and ITV, dedicated to raising money for charity.

From an early age, Diana always felt different. While her two sisters were strong and healthy, Diana was often sick and confined to bed. A sensitive child, she was attuned to the non-physical realms and no stranger to communicating with others who had died. She challenges our concepts of life and death and the role we each play in society and the kind of world in which we live.

Diana's own first brush with death came at age eighteen after an operation to remove part of her thyroid. After complications set in, four young doctors battled to save her life with an emergency tracheotomy.

None of this barred Diana from finding happiness with Richard, the love of her life, and they married when she was twenty. Three children followed, with more health problems along the way, but Diana has never lost her sense of humour and her story is peppered with funny, irreverent anecdotes and asides. These include a passionate search for spiritual understanding and tales of years devoted to teaching 'unteachable' children with severe dyslexia and other learning problems.

Fate led Diana and Richard to a magical part of Wales, where they first ran a caravan park from an ancient stone cottage with hardly a penny to their name. Hard work paid off, and they were able to extend their boundaries to include a small hotel. All the while, Diana's health was a rogue factor and at age thirty six she had another brush with death following a hysterectomy. Diagnoses of severe rheumatoid arthritis and Sjogrens syndrome were to come, and she began to use a wheelchair.

Through all of this, Diana's infectious sense of humour shines out to captivate her readers. When she had to give up teaching she set out to make a difference in another way, setting up the Seed of Life Peace Foundation to bring about one world vision and prayer. A Peace Gathering at Plas Dolguog attracted people from all over the world and Diana's work grew to the point where she was invited to attend the launch of the Earth Charter at The Hague in the Netherlands. This led to an invitation to attend the Millennium World Summit for Religious and Spiritual Leaders and the presentation of her Peace Scroll to the United Nations and the United Nations University of Peace, the Foreword to this book written by His Holiness the Dalai Lama.

Yet to come would be Diana's vision of a special garden at Dolguog dedicated to peace. Her work is tireless and now supports many different local and national charities. As her health has deteriorated, Diana's determination has grown. You will be amazed, uplifted and enlightened by her story.

Foreword

Without a doubt, Diana Rhodes is one of the most extraordinary and inspirational people I have ever met. Whilst most people would struggle to live with one illness, Diana has had years of living with two debilitating auto-immune diseases – rheumatoid arthritis and the rarer Sjogren's syndrome. Always reliant on oxygen and fed by a pipe into her stomach, most people would face the wall and curl up. But not Diana! With every physical setback and limitation, she has been able to tap into a deeper level of her spiritual essence from which she draws the most remarkable energy. It has long been known that whilst it is possible to break someone's body, it is much more difficult to break their spirit.

Diana is an indomitable and fearless lady who has devoted much of her life to raising money for charity and helping others. On top of all this she has also travelled extensively – something that almost anyone else with similar health problems and physical difficulties would not even contemplate. She puts many of us to shame with her quest and vision, her dynamism and inner energy.

This book is truly inspirational for all of us who are blessed with good health but is also essential reading for anyone whose life is affected by long-term chronic illness or disability. Thank you, Diana – you have touched my life with your kindness and wisdom. With this extraordinary story I know that you will reach out to many thousands more.

Matthew Manning
Suffolk, September 2010

Introduction

I have a story to tell. It spans many years and is still in the making. Each little piece of my jigsaw is slowly piecing together an immense and intricate picture. The exquisite threads that make up God's tapestry surely begin with small beginnings.

I cannot find a beginning to my story. The day we bought Plas Dolguog? No. The choice of life partner and husband? No. The day I was born? No. Even now I cannot find a logical time that I can start my story. It has no beginning – I suspect it has no end. It is timeless in a timeless universe. A No thing and yet all things. I now know that man's concept of time has no meaning even within our culture of time – past, present and future.

Just as a June bug lives out its entire life in a twenty four hour cycle can have no concept of a seventy, eighty, ninety year life span in humans, nor can we humans have a concept of a time cycle spanning millennia after millennia out into infinity.

I have known from even before I can remember that there was another way of living, another way of being, than the one that is so often presented by the world. As I searched for my beginning and for meaning my search led me on a very convoluted tour.

I think I digress, I hear you say – when will we get to the interesting part?

Chapter One

'You're Going to Die!'

'You're going to die!' screamed the doctor, now puce with rage. 'You're going to die tomorrow. You'll never survive the anaesthetic, never mind the operation!'

I was distressed. I had been rushed into hospital with pneumonia two weeks earlier. Now it was New Year's Eve, 1999, and it seemed I would never know the wonders of the new millennium. The whole world was celebrating, but I was on my way out and would not be around to see it.

At the time I was losing a pound a day and my weight had dropped to five and a half stone. During those two weeks in hospital I had received only fluid through an IV tube and my body was wasting away. I knew I desperately needed some nutrition.

I was unable to swallow – another story – and the decision had been made to fit a PEG (Percutaneous Endoscopic Gastrostomy), which is basically a permanent fitting through the stomach wall that connects to a feeding tube and pump, allowing liquid nutrition to be pumped directly into the stomach. Unbeknown to me, I discovered later, my Consultant had arranged for me to see the Head Psychiatrist of the area as they had decided I was anorexic.

This gentleman duly arrived at my bedside, insisting that he wanted me to go onto his ward, which was, of course, the psychiatric ward. We talked for some time and I kept saying to him,

'All I know is that I need some nutrition. I'm not going to live much longer unless someone decides to get nourishment into me somehow.' He insisted that I needed to go onto the psychiatric ward. His ward.

'If I come onto your ward, what will you do as far as feeding me is concerned?'

'Well,' he said. 'That will take time.'

'I don't have any time. So what are we going to do? If I come onto your ward and don't receive some nutrition, I'm not going to survive this situation.'

He kept insisting that I must go onto his ward and feeding would take time. In sheer exasperation I asserted,

'Look. I assume you watch the news. When we see third world countries where the people are dying of starvation, we don't send them psychiatrists. We send them food! I need food!'

At which point he strutted, tutted, and departed, red in the face.

Meanwhile, Richard had been in touch with our GP who told him

'Diana is becoming so low in body weight that, as in anorexia, no matter what we do, the point is fast approaching where we won't be able to pull her back. Something needs to be done.'

Richard arranged an appointment with the Consultant personally for the following Monday morning, only to turn up and be told that he had gone skiing for seven days. After an emergency meeting with his understudy, and with the help of our GP, Richard was told that if he got the five signatures required, they would go ahead and fit the PEG.

My dear husband spent the day running frantically from place to place. Because of our rural position and the peripatetic nature of our doctors, the traveling entailed a journey from Machynlleth to Llanidloes, Llanidloes to Aberystwyth, and Aberystwyth to Machynlleth, a round trip of nearly one hundred miles, in order to catch the different consultants and doctors to obtain their signatures. At the end of the day, he collapsed exhausted but triumphant, with the signatures in hand. The operation would take place the following day.

That afternoon the psychiatrist came to see me again.

'Well, well. And how are you feeling today?'

'Very relieved, but rather nervous.'

'Why?'

'Well, relieved that at last I will be getting a way to receive nutrition, but nervous about the operation.'

He went berserk. Jumped up from his seat and started to shout.

'I want you on my ward! There's no way you're going to survive this operation. If the anaesthetic doesn't kill you the procedure will.'

He pointed his finger and shook it at me.

'You are going to die! You are going to die!'

Over and over, he kept on shouting. The other patients in the ward were horrorstruck, sitting in bed with their mouths open. It would have been comical if it hadn't been so surreal.

Eventually I found my voice.

'Do you mind if I call the nurse. I don't think I understand.' I honestly felt as if I was in a nightmare, struggling to wake up. I rang the bell.

My visitor yelled,

'I've got twenty thousand patients in my care. I can't waste any more time on you!' And he stormed off down the corridor, leaving me bemused and distressed.

The nurse arrived. A lovely girl, who had won the Nurse of the Year Award for Wales, and I told her what had happened.

'No, no, of course you're not going to die tomorrow. I think you've misunderstood.' So did I.

She sat with her arm around my shoulders, trying to reassure and comfort me. The Head Psychiatrist loomed into view once more,

'What's going on here?'

The nurse responded,

'Mrs Rhodes seems to think you've told her she's going to die tomorrow morning. I'm sure you can tell her that's not what you meant.'

'Oh no I can't. That's exactly what I meant!'

And he proceeded to repeat what he had said to me, word for word. Just as well, for I'm sure nobody would ever have believed my story, had not the nurse promptly gone to record the whole incident in my notes.

During the course of that day, I do believe every doctor in the hospital must have come to visit me. Trainee doctors, junior doctors, senior doctors, all wanting to see the woman who had been told she was going to die. One after another they would walk up to the end of the bed and ask,

'Are you alright?'

I would nod, and assure them that I was. Nonetheless, that night I penned letters to Richard and our children. Richard's letter included the following:-

'For all the times I have made you sad –
I ask forgiveness.

For all the times I have been, or have made you angry –
I ask forgiveness.

For all the times I have wondered how I could ever live
without you – I bless you.

For your smile, for your precious blue eyes that whirl me
out of this world to understand lives beyond –
I bless you.

For our children and their children – I bless you.

For your honesty, integrity and loyalty – I bless you.

For knowing that we are one – I bless you.

For all this and more the word love is inadequate and yet
expresses all.

Until we meet again – I love you.

Release and move on –
relationships of love are never possessive.

You are my lotus blossom of love and always will be.'

The doctor who carried out the procedure was concerned that I was OK. Yes, the psychiatrist was sitting on my shoulder, but then again, yes, I was alright. Next morning, the operation was duly performed, I survived, and at last my body was able to receive the nutrition I so desperately needed. From that point on I started to gain strength and within a year I had gained a total of two stones, bringing me back to what was, for me, a near normal body weight.

Less than a week after the PEG was fitted I was transferred from the General Hospital to the small local hospital. When Richard asked why when I was so ill, the reply he received was,

'The Consultant is back from his skiing holiday. We all overrode him so it is better that Mrs Rhodes is gone, out of sight out of mind!'

Within two days of arriving at the local hospital I was surrounded by doctors and a Staff Nurse telling me I was being moved to a private ward. Oh dear, what had I said now? Hospitals appear to be no different to supermarkets. Loss leaders, buy one get one free. On my day of being in hospital the 'freebie' was MRSA. This has certainly aggravated and exacerbated my health problems over the years. A few years later I asked the doctor why I had such trouble with the PEG site. It was sore and often raw and I wanted to know how long before it healed properly. She looked at me a little embarrassed as she told me,

'The chances are it won't ever properly heal, at least not as long as the MRSA is active.'

For weeks before this latest upset I had been planning a secret, surprise party for Richard's sixtieth birthday, with sixty friends and family coming from all over the UK to celebrate and acknowledge all he had achieved in his life so far. Richard's birthday is 24th January and I was still in hospital after having the PEG fitted. The secret arrangements had to continue with help from the three boys, who were pledged not to tell their father.

The doctors gave permission for me to be 'let out' for an hour and my daughter-in-law came to the hospital to do my hair and help me dress. It was wonderful to see Richard's face as he entered the room and the lights went on to reveal the surprise guests all singing Happy Birthday. I hadn't realized how weak I was though, and one hour was more than enough for me to be there. I returned to the hospital with birthday cake for the nurses and left all the guests to their merriment, just happy to be alive and witness to such a lovely occasion.

This was not the first, or even the last time I was to have a close brush with death – maybe that's one of the reasons I'm so determined to get the most out of life, knowing how vulnerable we are and how short our life span.

Chapter Two

Early Days

Where did it all begin? What is it that determines the course of anybody's life? Are we here for a purpose I wonder, or do we have an agenda that may or may not become clear as we make our way the best we can through all the experiences life has to offer?

I was born in February 1943, during the Second World War. My Father was based in Ireland with the Air Sea Rescue Corps. He had not wanted to extend his family into a war-torn world but my Mother, along with many, could see no end to the dreadful situation in which most people found themselves, and was keen to add to the family. Five years was quite long enough between children. It was time Jillian had a playmate. I don't think anyone who did not experience those times could ever fully understand the uncertainties, even of life itself.

Daddy would post home six eggs from the local farm, packed as though his life depended on it. Mummy would tell us years later how she would cry when she found one was broken. These were more precious than gold in a time of severe rationing and a lack of fresh produce. Often Mummy's main meal of the day when carrying me would be mashed potato and a little Bisto gravy. My favourite dish was always mashed potato! She once sold her best shoes in order to have enough money to buy food for the rest of the week.

In April 1946, at the end of the war, another child was born. Another daughter in what would be a patriarchal home. Jillian, the eldest was a tomboy, frequently found up a tree and Janet, eight years later, would generally follow her in that role. I was different. I know I was a fey child, wyrd in the old meaning of the word weird, spiritually sensitive and afraid of my own shadow and painfully shy. At the age of three when Daddy returned from the war, I would stand hiding in Mummy's skirt, telling him to go away.

'Send that man away Mummy.' It would be many years later before I had the spiritual opportunity and experience to realise the forgiveness that was needed to heal the hurt of rejection that both of us must have felt, created by events beyond our individual conscious control.

Mummy told stories of being in the Doctor's surgery waiting room and someone giving me a bar of chocolate, what a prize in times of rationing, just because I was such a quiet well behaved child. I lived a lie, I was not well behaved just terrified of the world so I retired into my shell, my own world of non confrontation, with no need to face this unsought for alien world. I never did tell my parents but my fear stemmed from a very profound and undeniable internal or spiritual gnosis. I had been sent, not only to the wrong parents, but to the wrong planet.

There was no one whom I could tell. No-one who could help me. No-one who understood. This world was harsh, the colours, the noises, the crude communication were all somehow lacking in subtlety, in divinity, in unconditional love. And I knew I must learn slowly and painfully to adjust and live with it. Not only to cope with it but to transform myself and it into a life worth living. I must stress, I was born into a loving and caring home, to parents who did their best, which is all any parent can do, as I later found through experience, but that did nothing to alleviate my distress.

Perhaps I would be five or at the most six. Our house was renowned for its display of lupins. All the houses in the street had gardens with lupins but none could compare with ours. Everybody else had blue and pink and even that lovely purple shade but only one garden could boast a patch of yellow – that was ours. It would have won any competition for the way the colours blended in such a professional manner. Although as I reflect the realization dawns that nature had a lot more to do with it than my Father who to my small eyes was the God of Fairfield Grove. I was busy contemplating our colour scheme as I walked up our garden path. Two steps and a flat bit, two more steps and a rise …. There half way up the rise was a ladybird. The most beautiful thing I could ever remember seeing. The redness of the red and the blackness of the spots,

'Ladybird, ladybird, fly away home.' I thought, 'but not just yet. Let me look a little closer.' I couldn't get much closer, we were almost one, the sort of closeness children have when they are absorbed. Suddenly, out came its wings. Totally unexpected, as I am sure I did not realise it possessed them, despite the rhyme. My stomach somersaulted, the panic rose to my throat – I stamped on it.

A few seconds later a dejected child looked at the squashed ladybird, quite the opposite of beautiful. No colour now, just a squashed splurge on the path. What had I done? The panic had waned only to be replaced by a traumatic guilty conscience which I will never forget. What right had I to relieve this beautiful creature of its life? Who was I? to be afraid of a thing so tiny as, and possessing the same qualities as, a fairy. The responsibility was too great, the noise began to rise and the tears began to flow. Up the garden path to Mummy who, of course, was completely unaware that this small murderess was coming for consolation.

Later in the year came bonfire night. Our street was not 'made', it only had a very rough surface and therefore it was quite in order, said the grownups, to have our bonfire there. Many, many weeks were spent in chumping and hoarding suitable materials until the day of the wonderful night. The Guy was made by various members of various families with detail and patience usually reserved for some special work of art.

Literally everybody came out to build the monument that night – which naturally had to be the biggest and the best in the area. As night fell out came the chairs circled around the bonfire. Funnily enough, I cannot remember the ceremonial placing of the Guy, which I am sure would have taken place, or the lighting of the fire but only the heat generated, the hot, sooty tasting potatoes, the moggy (soggy ginger bread), the plot toffee – everybody ate everybody else's food. It just was not the done thing to eat one's own food, that was made to hand around and give away.

Jumping crackers, rockets, catherine wheels, roman candles, all these were made to last in those days, The whole evening seemed to last a week, whereas actually children were always in bed by 10.00 pm, only to rise again at 7.00 am the next day to re-kindle the flames and just burn up the little hoards, which had been hidden away especially for the purpose before the fire was lit.

Bonfires have never assumed any importance since we left this street even though I have sometimes struggled hard to recapture a little of the excitement we knew then.

Visits to the doctor were frequent and on doctor's orders I spent one day in ten in bed, in order to cope with the other nine. My tonsils, which often swelled to block my throat and threaten my ability to breathe, eventually won and I went to hospital to have them removed.

There must have been twelve of us, boys and girls mixed, about five years old. We were all given some form of pre-med and ushered into a side ward, where two old ladies were sitting in bed. Pink, frilly bedjackets, bowls of fruit, juice and chocolates stacked on lockers beside them. We were all desperately thirsty as a result of our pre-meds obviously.

'Now, nothing to eat or drink, you lot! Do you hear?' announced the nurse. Oh yes we heard alright but then not all of us were listening. The door had no sooner closed than the old ladies, clucking and cooing, proceeded to pass around the orange squash and chocolates to these poor little chickens who were being bullied by the big old nurse, I was probably the only one who didn't partake. Well behaved? Not at all, just the old fear of non understanding rearing its head again. I never did know how many children reacted to their pre-op feast, all I know is I was sick without the feast. No justice even at this young age.

Little did I know that the experience of having my tonsils out was just a precursor to something far more terrifying that would affect the rest of my life.

Childhood memories are few, I know my sisters retell memories that I can only remember with their retelling and sometimes not even then. I do not have a good recall of much of my childhood.

When I was about six or seven, my paternal grandmother, contracted Hodgkins Disease and died. I was not told of her death. As far as I was concerned she had just gone away and I no longer saw her. This was quite devastating when I had felt so close to her. She was a large bosomed lady, shall I say of ample proportions, homely and yet strict. Mummy told me that I was in fact, her favourite, I think because I was fairer than the other two with blue eyes and looked more like Daddy. Jillian was like Mummy to look at, dark hair and brown eyes, Janet also, with her brown eyes. I can remember one incident clearly. For some reason I had been left with Granny and Grandpa, just me not the other two. Grandpa gave me two walnuts and I sat on the back door step in the cold with these two walnuts trying to crack them, one against the other, as he had shown me. It never entered my head that this was strange to be sitting out in the cold, nor to make a fuss and demand re-entry until I was told to come in.

When Granny died Grandpa moved from their house. It was a council house like ours and he moved into a flat near Manningham Lane, Bradford. He visited us frequently. I would be about eleven I think when Grandpa died, he stepped onto a Zebra crossing and a lorry ploughed into him and killed him. The driver was fined five pounds and convicted of manslaughter. Again I was not told about his death, I presume Jillian being older would be, but not Janet and I who were considered too young to be confronted with the prospect of death. When I asked,

'What's wrong, something's wrong and nobody is telling me?' My Aunt's reply was that all was well and not to worry. Children were not involved in death so yet again he just disappeared as Granny had done.

My Maternal Grandmother, Granny Andy, had a shop selling ladies and children's clothing. Mummy spent a lot of time there altering garments to customer's requirements, Granny did not charge for this service. If a garment came back ten years later and needed altering due to the customer's weight loss or weight gain then this free service continued.

The cellars and attics of the shop were living accommodation and the ground floor was shop and alterations room, with a showroom and fitting room and bedroom on the third floor. The toilet was an outside 'midden', no shower or bath was available. As children we spent hours tearing newspaper into six inch squares and threading these with wool and a large needle into bundles to hang in the outside toilet as toilet paper. When a clothes delivery was made the tissue paper was ironed by Granny to be re-used to wrap sold garments and any spare meant the great luxury of tissue paper instead of newspaper in the toilet.

Mummy's sister Pat was a Catophile. Cats to her were the main reason for living. Many an hour was spent with a pipette, feeding a motherless kitten as it lay on a cushion on your lap as the urine came out faster than the milk went in. Janet when very young was found one day trying to flush a particularly aggressive cat down the outside toilet. It took Pat a long time to forgive her.

Pat often went off to the Warehouses in Leeds to buy or pick up stock and one day I nattered and nattered to go with her.

'You can go with pleasure, dear.' Granny said. I promptly burst into tears,

'I don't want to go with pleasure, I want to go with Pat.'

Pat was fifteen years younger than Mummy which put her more on a level with us, particularly with Jillian, than with Mummy, certainly in our eyes.

Granny suffered with flatulence, and I mean rip roaring flatulence.

'Bang goes sixpence.' she would calmly intone. It didn't matter who was in the shop or where she was, it never flustered her. We three sisters however would be scarlet with embarrassment.

Grandpa Andy had been severely affected during his time as a soldier in the 1st World War. Another soldier, whose boots were now in a state of total disrepair, found a good boot in a pile of rubble, the remains of a bombed building. As he pulled on the boot he found it contained a living leg. What he then proceeded to unearth, following the leg, was Grandpa who then went on to fight another day, only to have half his stomach removed due to gun shot wounds and shrapnel. He spent his time in the living area in the basement of their house and shop.

His meals were made up of tripe, poached in milk and his preferred beverage was whisky. What traumatic stress he must have suffered no one will ever know, but not surprisingly in retrospect he was a man with an unpleasant attitude to life, as children we were frightened of him.

Janet and I were sent one day to make a cup of tea, so we must have been old enough to be trusted with boiling water. The kitchen was made up of a sink, a cooker and a store cupboard, with a wall cupboard above, by today's standards not fit to be given the title of kitchen. Grandpa was huddled over the fire, listening to his beloved 'Gee Gees' as he called the horse racing. His days excitement was to place his bets. Anyway, the tea caddy was empty and between the two of us we managed to spill the contents of a quarter pound packet of loose tea. We stood looking at each other unmoving, until silently, like automated puppets and in total synchronicity we swept it under the rug, rescued enough to make the tea and fled, wordless. I have no idea who found this strange offering, left as if to the Gods, as it was never mentioned by anyone.

Because of Grandpa's penchant for the horses, Granny was very careful with her cash. We three grand-daughters each have a beautiful diamond ring, because as she said,

'If it's on my finger it can't go on the horses.'

By this time Granny had a second home in Morecombe, she had a dreadful accident when getting off a coach in Morecombe bus station. As she walked behind it to cross the road, the bus reversed, its double wheels running over both her legs and breaking all the bones in her feet and legs. It was not long after this that buses were fitted with reversing alarms. Mummy spent more and more time between home and the shop, caring for Granny and Grandpa and running the shop. Granny's medical prognosis was that she would never walk again. Wrong! I think it must be a family trait to prove the medical profession wrong as she not only walked but got back to being in the shop at least some of the time.

She lost all her hair during this ordeal and went for what she called 'sun treatment' at the hospital. Her hair came back, thick, black and shiny, the permanent hat was discarded. She took great delight when asked what she used to colour her hair by saying,

'Well, what you need to do is lie down in the road and let a bus drive over your legs .....'

I have always had a heightened sense of colour and sometimes I wonder if this particular sense was stimulated by the amount of time my sisters and I spent in Granny Andy's shop. There was a glass cabinet filled with cotton reels of every colour and hue you could imagine – a source of wonder and fascination to me. I would spend hours sorting the reels and feasting on the colours. Now, of course, I understand the therapeutic role of colour in healing, each has a frequency, or vibration, that can help to stimulate, align, balance and heal different parts of the body. No wonder I was so happy while engaged in this favourite pastime.

The second basement room was turned over to laundry, with a large boiler, a large fluted (I presume for strength) dustbin sized tub and a drain in the floor. Clothes were put to soak and then a posser, this was an inverted copper bowl with holes just above the perimeter and attached to a long wooden handle, was 'possed' up and down, pushing and squeezing the clothes with a washing machine type action to clean the clothes. I loved doing this, it was so satisfying to watch the soapy bubbles and hear the squelching, sucking noises as you pushed up and down and moved round the tub to include all the clothes.The clothes were then put through an old fashioned mangle and the hot soapy water caught and used again if it wasn't too dirty. This was an adult's job as it was heavy work and was carried out whilst also running up and down stairs to attend to shop customers.

Old people to children can often seem like a strange species. My Godmother, Aunt Ann, was a spinster lady and lived with her older sister Aunty Mary. I can clearly remember visiting with Mummy and Daddy. Janet and I were instructed to sit on a two seater sofa in the window of their cottage facing into the room, nothing to see, nothing to do.

'You must keep quiet and not do anything to disturb Aunty Mary. She is very sick and noise troubles her.'

Actually she had tinnitus but the way it was described to us was like some living hell and torture. The description, to us, didn't fit the lady, she always liked to be in control of a situation. I can remember sitting, occasionally meeting Janet's glance, perched on the edge of our seats waiting for this old lady to drop dead in front of our eyes. We can't have been very old perhaps five and eight.

When Aunt Anne died in her sixties, the murmurings were that looking after Aunty Mary, the sick one, had worn her out.

I am ashamed to admit that when Aunty Mary did die, some years later, I laughed uproariously before I took control of myself. I was a grandmother and Aunty Mary was ninety eight!

Another traumatic event, although I no longer look at it that way, was when I was seven. I was not too happy in water, but happy enough to allow my older cousin to piggy back me across the pool. She slipped, and quite naturally I think, clung to the nearest stable thing. Unfortunately, this was my legs. We both went under and down. I can remember fighting, frantically trying to free myself from her grip – without success. I was running out of air. With one final panic filled struggle I pulled free and hit my head hard on the bottom of the pool. I stopped struggling, I stopped fighting for air, it wouldn't be needed where I was going. I relaxed, bodily and mentally. I was flooded with a sense of utter peace. I didn't have to stay. I was going back. Pink, gold, unconditional, absolute impeccability and love. At last.

Oh crude, harsh world. Here you are again, as my head broke surface, bursting lungs, coughing, spluttering, being thumped on the back, with faces, huge faces peering into mine. I couldn't get away with it that easily evidently.

Life progressed as it does and must and I became more and more grounded into my new home planet. Events would always arise that constantly kept open my knowledge that things weren't as they always appeared. It was the invention of colour television that brought to notice my next unusual experience. Actually it was not exactly the invention of colour TV, but its appearance in our own home. What excitement this twelve inch colour magic box brought to our lives. Even then advertisements were part of TV life.

'How clever,' said my sister, 'how do they do that?' She was referring to the warm orange glow that surrounded the children who drank a hot cup of hearty Bovril. For once I could answer with confidence as I was quite familiar with the different colours that surrounded all the people that I knew.

'Easy' came forth my reply■ 'Everyone has a glow, except they are different colours. They've just changed the colours so they are all orange.'

Oh dear, dear Daddy – whose fear of psychic or spiritually abnormal matters was great, could not allow this.

'Don't ever talk such nonsense. If anyone hears you say such silly things they will lock you in a mental hospital.'

The result was obvious. I learnt not to see auras from that time on. Perhaps even more importantly, I learnt not to tell others of things that happened, just in case. After all, if others didn't see or experience the things I did then here was added proof of my misplacement and that must never be disclosed.

My spiritual life was always with me, although I didn't see auras any more I could feel and sense them along with fairies, I would often tell imaginative stories about the fairies in our open fire. What everyone thought was a vivid imagination was totally real to me.

I was baptised, attended church with my sisters and then, with a group of thirteen to fourteen year olds was confirmed at Bradford Cathedral. I was truly entranced (literally self hypnotised) during this ceremony and ritual, believing every word that was spoken during the entire proceedings.

I was so disappointed. There had been no doves, no bolts of lightening. I felt just the same as I always did. I had not metamorphosed into a 'good' person. Had Jesus forsaken me, wasn't I good enough, had I neglected to be fully present during the ceremony? I slowly learnt to live with my 'failure.' It was the story of my life it seemed.

I attended Bradford Girls Grammar School following in Jillian's footsteps. To my eyes Jillian was so much older, a perfect daughter, student, everything, whereas I did not come up to scratch. The headmistress would send for me at the end of each term after the reports were written. Miss Hook, a tiny, wrinkled, bird like creature, highly respected in her field, but in my childhood memory she was mean spirited and she wheedled,

'Could do better, couldn't we? You are going to have to try harder, we only allowed you to attend the school because your sister works so hard.' Would I tell my parents? Absolutely not – how could I admit another chastisement and proof of my inadequacy? Constructive criticism is what Daddy called it. Criticism is never constructive. It is, has been and always will be destructive. Explanation, encouragement and help with difficulties is the only way to overcome problems. Attacking self-worth, belittling or pointing out what is wrong only exacerbates the situation.

At around the age of ten I had a friend Margaret, her father was the local Reverend at the Baptist Church. The snow arrived. We hadn't had snow for years. Mummy

columnists, interviews with fund managers and exclusive reader offers and competitions.

You can also access all the features and benefits of *Trust* in an easy-to-use online format at **www.bgtrustonline.com**. The site is regularly updated with investment news, topical articles and webcasts.

I hope you enjoy this issue of the magazine.

Yours sincerely,

LMGreig

Lindsey Greig
Director

We may record your call.

Baillie Gifford Savings Management Ltd.

...rs *Investment Trust ISAs and Share Plans.*

...d *in Scotland:* No 135636

Authorised and regulated
by the Financial Services
Authority

gave us permission to go down the lane and sledge down the hill in the farmer's field. Our deadline was to be home by 6.00 pm. We only had one sledge so we took it in turns. A young man appeared; he said he had come to watch the fun. As I climbed back up the hill after my turn Margaret was gone and so was the young man. I called her feeling pretty desperate, where was she? The church clock struck six – O help, I was late now.

My sister came walking towards me in the field – she looked an adult, five years older than me, and as I ran towards her shouting, the young man appeared and promptly ran away. Margaret came towards us, a little disheveled and frightened. He had sat astride her and threatened to kill her if she screamed. Her father in his religious position refused to prosecute even though the boy was caught. He said it would reflect on his daughter's reputation. Some months later the young man reoffended raping the poor girl involved – this was less than a mile from where the Yorkshire Ripper would be found to live twenty or so years later.

I would have reached the age of eleven when we went to live at the house known as Grove House. What a name to have – so grand. It was a terrace house, but then again as Daddy said, it was at the top of the hill and had gardens on three sides.

The day we removed was so exciting, this new house had attics and my elder sister was to have one of her very own as a bedroom, completely away from us all up there. My younger sister and I were still to be together but there was still room for us to have a room each when we grew older if we wished, which was quite something to dream about.

The house opposite was a big detached, with a large garden and concrete play area, which in actual fact was the roof of a double garage. There was a swing and a Wendy house in the garden and we had already assessed one girl of about nine years old and a boy of about seven years old. We could surely become friends and make up a little for leaving behind all our well tried and tested friends of the previous home.

After the van arrived with the furniture it began to rain but nothing could dampen our children's enthusiasm. By this time the little girl from the house opposite had brought out a child's wicker chair and table together with a glass of orange juice and biscuits. Away she went once more when the rain began to fall and promptly came back with an umbrella. Here she sat, for two hours, in the miserable grey drizzle, watching every piece of furniture and household utensil that went in through our newly acquired door.

Being the ages my sister and I were we could not resist taking turns at peeping every few minutes to see what she was doing. Surely she must be cold by now? On each and every occasion she was surveyed out would come her tongue – long and pink and quite, quite offensive!

This strange beginning was, as it happens, the start of a long and close relationship. We slept, ate, breathed and talked our friendship for the following eight years, when of course the inevitable boyfriends became a possible challenge to each others egos.

One day my period started. Not a subject Mummy found easy to discuss (we had to hide our sanitary towels in the bathroom airing cupboard in case Daddy saw them) so Jillian was given the job of asking if I knew what was to come. Of course I did. I went to a Grammar School, didn't I? I'd learnt all about the rabbits. I even knew that a man produced sperm and put his member (whatever that was) into the woman to make a baby.

I went to matron's office and was given an aspirin, a yard of thick, hairy string and a sanitary pad. The pad didn't have loops or a sticky back, it just had loose netting hanging off the ends of the pad. I gazed at these items in horror. What was I supposed to do? Eventually I tied the netting into a knot and poked a hole in it through which I threaded the hairy string and tied it around my waist. The initiation was complete. I was now a woman.

Health was always lurking somewhere, waiting to raise its head. As I now know health problems are our greatest teachers. So much of our literature is devoted to this subject. Deepak Chopra, Louise Hay, Leslie Kenton and many others.

At about the age of fifteen, symptoms of over active thyroid developed. I felt dreadful, convinced I had spinal cancer. I would lie on my bed with my legs hanging over the base board, trying to alleviate the gnawing ache that spread from my back to my toes. I was unable to tell Mummy as she was already worried about my sister. A rather misguided Doctor had told her Janet's illness was either some rare and incurable form of cancer or glandular fever. Fortunately it turned out to be the latter.

Occasionally we would drive out to a small Yorkshire village for Sunday tea, ham and eggs. A treat for someone's birthday, anniversary or whatever might present itself. We parked the car and walked through the fields and down towards the stream where we often went on these outings. Janet had brought along a ball and a game of catch soon followed. My now familiar feeling of sickness and lethargy was with me. I was taking pep pills, prescribed by a doctor who thought my looming GCE's were causing my problems and I just needed a little kick up the pants to get me going again.

I sat alone as the family played.

'Get over here and don't be so lazy.' shouted Daddy. This would normally have worked. It must have been obvious to him as he watched me that something was really wrong. The game was brought to a halt and we returned to the car. I sat on the back seat and my neck began to swell. I think Mummy and Daddy were more amazed and frightened than I was as it threatened to obstruct my breathing. My neck was swollen from my chin down, I didn't have a chin it just became my swollen neck. A complete stranger, a woman, at this point appeared from nowhere and peering into the car announced,

'Her's got a goitre, my sister 'ad one. It's serious and she'll need it cut out!' Just what we did not need at that moment was her melodramatic intervention.

Tea was off. Everyone bundled into the car and away home we went.

A visit to the doctor the next day and subsequently a specialist within four hours, confirmed an over-active thyroid gland. Hospital visits and tests involving drinking radio active iodine, dispensed by a nurse in special shielding clothing and large leather gauntlets followed, with pills that caused weird and bizarre symptoms.

Despite these strange happenings I continued with my education, left school, went to Technical College for one year to train as a Secretary and on to work for a subsidiary company of the Arndale Property Trust. Most people will have shopped in one of their, at the time, very modern developments.

My first boss was a charming man with an eye for the ladies, and on the wall of his office he had a calendar that reflected his appreciation of the naked female form. Before I was allowed to enter to take dictation, however, he would pin clothes on the monthly attraction. For his benefit or mine, I'm not really sure, but he proved to have a heart of gold when my various hospital visits and test results resulted in an operation and determined that I should not work for six months.

My job was kept open and there I was at home, eighteen years old with nothing to do or think about. A distraction was needed.

Then I heard that the Young Conservatives needed a secretary, nothing too demanding, just a few hours a week on a voluntary basis. I could manage that. I applied and was accepted, glad of the opportunity to attend meetings and make new friends. I quickly discovered the organization was as much a dating agency as a serious political organization, though I have to say that a lot of work was undertaken very effectively on behalf of the Party.

The Young Conservatives became a source of much friendship and by this time I had involved my long-time friend Jennifer and sister Janet as support. It was election time for local Councillors and it was all hands on deck to bring in the voters. On Election Day, Jennifer and I were assigned to the school hall in Allerton. Jennifer's father drove us there and we walked in, side by side, chattering happily.

At the far end of the hall was a group of people, among them stood a young man in his early twenties – tall, broad shouldered and blonde. His voice echoed down the hall.

'I need a babysitter, so that number 29 Greenway can come to vote.'

Well, Jennifer was blonde, attractive and not at all shy. She had a brother who had cheerfully knocked the corners off her. I, on the other hand, was mousey brown, shy and unworldly. I was a girl from an all-girl, patriarchal family, who had attended an all-girl school.

For the first time in my life I made a snap decision. I strode forward, unabashed. This was where I was to prove that I was not a sheep waiting to follow. The young man just stood there grinning –

'Which one of you then?' he said.

Whether it was precognition, destiny, or something else altogether I don't know, but Jennifer was left standing. A neat flick of the wrist to distract her and I was striding down the hall at full pelt.

'I'll go. That's what I'm here for.' I heard myself say. Our sons now joke that Dad never stood a chance.

Chapter Three

Richard – A Life After Life Partner

This was what I needed to fire my potential determination, my decision making, and my assertiveness. A tall, hunky incentive! An unknown young man, from a distance of thirty yards, had opened up my future. For he was my future – no question about that. I just had to persuade him this was so.

Some years later, I learned from Richard's cousin Ben that Richard had two-timed me for almost three months. He got female friendship and affection from me while getting his kisses from someone else! Richard says I emanated a china doll quality that required care and respect. I fear that after nearly fifty years he now knows differently.

On my first visit to Richard's home I met his parents and his older sister, June. Richard's mother was a very organized and disciplined lady, hard to get close to, and it was many years before our relationship came into a happy balance of respect and affection. I am, even now, amazed that a quite strict, very tidy and organised person can mother an enormous, passionately alive and untidy son. Perhaps the mother's instinct to encourage male prowess has something to do with this. Little did I know at this time my maternal instincts were to be tried and tested three fold in triplicate personalities of the boy mentioned above!

His father was the classic gentleman, a diabetic from the age of twenty six, just one year after the discovery of insulin to which he owed his life. He was tireless. Not content with running a woollen mill and a farm, a home and family, he also worked in local politics, it would exhaust most people even to think of it. He achieved Councillor in our well fought campaign.

Sister June was, and is, a very strong character. I realize now that she was extremely protective of her little brother.

'You know he's been going out with someone for two years,' she greeted me, 'he's bound to go back to her.'

My mousy reply was a timid little,

'Oh.' but deep in my heart a voice was saying 'I think you are mistaken on that, my dear.' Again, as the years rolled by, June and I developed a deep understanding and affection for one another. I guess due to our mutual love for her brother.

I chased Richard unashamedly, with my role as secretary to the Young Conservative's as an excuse.

'There's a dance, an outing, a fund-raising event,' I would say. 'I need to know the numbers. Can I put you down?'

A trip to the Blue John Caves in Derbyshire was to be the highlight of the year. My sister Janet already had her name down. She was fifteen going on eighteen and signed her boyfriend up as well. Apparently, Richard spent the entire journey trying to figure out where I fit in, and if he should make a move, or whether it would be considered cradle snatching.

My lucky star was shining that day and it just so happened there was an empty seat next to mine on the boat through the caves while Richard was looking for a seat. Fancy that. We went into the caves as casual acquaintances and came out friends, with Richard's arm firmly around my shoulders – to keep out the damp and the cold, of course.

Mummy and Daddy took Granny Andy, my maternal grandmother, to the Isle of Orkney to see her elderly cousin, Uncle Willie Lesley. Janet and I accompanied them and Jillian now an Air Stewardess with BEA flew up to meet us all. Janet and I didn't meet Uncle Willie as he was old, unwell and any noise was not appropriate. We pottered about amusing ourselves until Jillian arrived.

One morning probably our second day we all walked to the coast, where it turned out the cemetery was situated. The west coast of Orkney is beautiful, powerful seas traveling from the far Atlantic, its rugged coastline giving way to a rocky shore line with the land slowly and levelly entering the sea beyond the walled cemetery.

I became ill – to the point of fainting. I don't know how they did it but Jillian and Janet crossed their clasped hands and made a seat for me to sit with my arms around their necks as they carried me back to the Hotel some three quarters of a mile.

For a couple of years different pills with different side effects were being tried to alleviate the thyroid problems. That night as we went to dinner I was covered from head to foot in a brilliant red rash. The dining room emptied very quickly. At bed time, the itching was unbearable every orifice tickling beyond belief. I sat on the bed, the three of us talking and laughing, me scratching. Jillian passed me a glass of water to take the prescribed sleeping tablet. They told me the day after that I had been sitting up talking and then suddenly I flopped back, out cold. Eventually the doctors decided that an operation was necessary.

Many, many years later, on our 25th Wedding Anniversary Richard took me back to Orkney.

I had been having a recurring dream. I dreamt of an old man sitting in an armchair, his knees covered in a tartan rug, his hair shining silver, his ice blue eyes glowering at me. It was not frightening but disconcerting. I plied Mummy with questions, who was he, what did he want? For many months she didn't know until one day she suggested it might be Uncle Willie. He had trench feet from his time as a soldier in WWI and sat in the cellar of his terrace home – and yes he would be wrapped in a tartan rug. I still have the newspaper reports that Mummy gave me with his obituary, proclaiming him to be a pillar of the community. I needed desperately to go there – what for, I didn't know, perhaps to honour his memory.

The day after our arrival on the island Richard and I climbed the hill with terrace houses on either side, looking for Uncle Willie's home.

We came to a house that was vibrant and colourful, emanating cheerful music through the open door. It was some sort of Arts Centre for children – puppets, artwork, music, and theater – a joyful place. I began to tell the girl in charge that we were looking for Willie Lesley's house. It had been a Chandler's shop that sold everything. She just stared and after a minute said,

'This is it! You're here.' and of course we were then all related, in the island sense of heredity. She continued,

'You need to meet Old Peter, they would be contemporaries.' Old Peter, in his eighties duly arrived. Introductions brought forth his question,

'Of course you know why you're here don't you?' Well, no actually I didn't. He kept insisting I did, so I told him about the Newspapers and how I just wanted to follow it up. No, no – apparently that was not why. The dream was a clue. What came next was mind blowing.

Here is the story. The newspapers were wrong Peter said, Willie was a mean bastard! He didn't like women or children. He treated his wife Elizabeth very badly, like a slave and children who came into the shop were treated like mini criminals. His shop was a cold, miserly place, he would be turning in his grave to see it so full of happiness. Old Peter offered to take us to the grave, having given me this devastating news, as he thought Willie was asking me for forgiveness. Why me I wanted to know? Old Peter enlightened me – because I was female and I had seen Willie's plight and responded.

Next day we went to the cemetery to retread my steps of all those years before. As Rheumatoid Arthritis had now taken hold walking was painful and difficult. I sat on the wall for much of the time as Richard and Peter walked round and round and round, squaring the circle so to speak.

To no avail – Willie was not there!

Old Peter then sent us to Marie's house. She had been Willie's housekeeper, she was at the funeral, she would know where to find the grave.

After explaining who we were Marie said she would be happy to show us the location of the grave, so off we went again. She knew where it was. No, same again. Round and round we went, but it was no good, Willie just wasn't there. Marie was flummoxed.

Peter was intrigued. Although it was now after five o'clock on a Saturday, he rang his friend – the equivalent of the Town Clerk – as we were now all related – and he immediately turned out and produced the local records. We found the notice of Willie's death, but no record of his burial. According to the records Uncle Willie had never been buried.

The Town Clerk unearthed the information that Willie had bought a burial plot. We made a note of the plan design and the plot number and the next day, back to the cemetery we went. We found the grave as it was marked on the plan, clearly and boldly engraved 'Elizabeth Rob' (women in Scotland retained their maiden name).

Richard dug down with his hands into the base of this headstone, pulling away soil and grass. There, in small and insignificant lettering were the words William Lesley. We were taken aback. We went back to Peter and the Town Clerk and arranged for the records to be amended. Uncle Willie's burial was now a matter of public record. Quite a holiday, not what we had planned or expected.

Some weeks later the dream came again. Only this time as I looked at those glowering ice blue eyes they softened, Uncle Willie took off his rug, walked towards me with arms outstretched, and gave me a hug.

Chapter Four

Trauma and the Gift of Life

My health problems persisted and when I was eighteen years old it was decided that the time had come for an operation to remove part of the thyroid. This was a major operation, at that time rarely performed on one so young. The date was set for September 18th two days after Jillian's upcoming wedding. In many ways this was a blessing, as the bustle, preparation and excitement around the wedding succeeded in keeping thoughts of the impending surgery at bay.

Jillian and John's wedding was a great success, and Jillian, of course, was a dream. A sister to be proud of.

We were six bridesmaids, in satin dresses of rainbow colours, mine was sky blue, Janet's pink. Mummy always dressed us in our special colours, and the wedding was to be no exception. Whether we grew into these colours or whether Mummy intuitively knew them I don't know.

My only disappointment was that Richard would not be able to attend, as his cousin Ben was to be married on the same day and he was to attend his cousin as a groomsman.

The groomsman allocated to me was a shy young man with few social skills. His sole topic of conversation revolved around my impending surgery and he plied me with questions such as,

'Aren't you afraid? Will they actually cut your throat?' and 'What time is the surgery?'

I was happy to see Richard when he came to the evening party. Mummy had arranged a buffet supper. Foods of every description were served, including Sylvio's special cream cakes, with their very special, very large meringues. Richard would have a meringue, or so he thought – I'm afraid I couldn't resist it – squash – as he raised it to his mouth. I swear my hand worked on its own volition as it pushed this huge confection into his face. Hysterical laughter followed as we scraped up the mess and fed it back to him.

'I certainly didn't enjoy that as I should have.' he proclaimed, 'I better have another one to taste it properly.' and so he did.

I remember very little of the pre-op period, apart from the obvious nervous tension. I only remember waking up in what appeared to be a cot. I felt as though metal wires had been placed in all my veins and arteries. I hurt from head to toe and felt frightened as to the meaning of these unpleasant and painful sensations. I couldn't cough, after all the slash across my neck might not hold, apart from the pain, but I felt I was filling up with mucous and my breathing was so loud and rattly it drowned out all other sounds.

I pressed my bell for the nurse, perhaps a drink would help. A young nurse came and offered me a drink from a cup with a spout, like a little teapot. It did nothing to alleviate my difficulties and she promptly disappeared into the dark, leaving me alone. I seemed to feel less fear. I was becoming very peaceful and detached, it no longer seemed to hurt as much and I was quite happy now, floating in this soft cloud of peace.

Suddenly it was all hell let loose. Four young doctors appeared at my bedside and proceeded to carry out the procedures necessary to save my life. I don't even know who it was who stayed at my bedside through to the next morning but someone did.

My memory erased this period, I did not know how close to death I had been until some thirty years later when I was diagnosed with Sjogrens Syndrome. This is an autoimmune disease where the mucous membranes of eyes, mouth, throat, vagina and rectum do not produce moisture. Other symptoms include chronic fatigue, nodules developing on internal organs, general malaise, rheumatic type pains, and difficulty swallowing due to the lack of moisture along with the peristaltic action of swallowing causing the actions of the throat to go out of synch, this results in choking problems. I experienced these effects alongside rheumatoid arthritis, which can be a precursor to this illness.

It was thirty years before I learned what had happened. During those thirty years I would have flashbacks and nightmares. Men holding me down; me screaming, screaming, but no sound coming forth. Strangling, struggling, fighting, and terrible fear. Deep, deep fear. I felt I had been gang raped, but as Richard has been my one and only sexual partner, how could that be?

As I sat with the Consultant he asked me when I had had the tracheotomy.

Tracheotomy? That was news to me. I denied all knowledge of such a thing. Eventually, he pointed to one of the scars on my neck and proceeded to read my medical notes out loud. I could now piece together my nightmares.

On confirming this revelation with my sister Janet, I found she was amazed that I did not know. A nurse had told her the morning after the operation,

'We nearly lost your sister last night. You're lucky she's here to visit.' Janet also told me that the hospital had rung Mummy and Daddy at 2.00 am to put them on standby ready to come in if they were needed.

In my deep memory, however, at eighteen years old, I had undergone the equivalent of gang rape. Three doctors held down my head, my arms and my legs and a fourth doctor, basically, straddled my struggling, hysterical form so that he could break into my windpipe to allow me to breathe to survive.

I was oblivious to all of this. My brain just blanked it out and as with things like the subject of death these matters were not discussed by my parents. My only concern was a letter from Richard, saying that he would not be able to visit me on Saturday. Was this the end? A 'Dear John' letter? I should have known better of course and when he did come, it was with eighteen beautiful red roses.

I do remember that when I was allowed up I was given the job of serving patients their afternoon cup of tea. I was without a voice for some weeks after the operation so it was all down to sign language. One lady requested three sugars. Only as the sugar took effect did it come to light that she was diabetic and entering a coma. I was learning, not only from my own traumas, that hospitals can be dangerous places.

The operation, followed by the tracheotomy, was an experience that needed deep healing. Over the years of my search for spiritual understanding I have learnt how to reconstruct past events and change the present by changing the attitudes of the past. Instead of death and rape I knew I must find life and love and replace my new understanding of that traumatic event with the truth.

I had received the gift of life from four young men I never knew or ever had the opportunity to thank.

Chapter Five

Marriage and Young Love

Richard was the Leader of the local Youth Club and they put on a Pantomime each year. The night of the Dress Rehearsal the leading lady went down with measles. I was co-opted with twenty four hours to learn the lines. I was so euphoric at my engagement that my nerves were not a severe problem – with the help of Aladdin's Sultan prompting me and everyone in the cast cheerfully responding to my ad-libbing all went well, apart from standing on a drawing pin during the dance of the seven veils or more accurately dance of the three scarves.

My Mother's Mother, Granny Andy (Anderson) we called her, came to live with us after Grandpa Andy's death. We lived in a three storey end terrace house and she was in a room on the top floor. She spent her time in bed but the room was equipped with commode, TV and chairs for visitors. She had a view from the bed down the street across a bank of lovely trees. This must have been hard work for Mummy as she could be quite demanding but then who wouldn't be confined to one room.

It was Christmas and Mummy and Daddy had brought Granny down to enjoy the meal. Richard was present and towards the end of the meal, Granny was unwell and wanted to go back to bed. She was sitting in a carver dining room chair, the kind with arms. No-one knew how we would get her back to bed. Richard stood behind her, picked up the chair by its arms and carried her two flights of stairs to her room, where Mummy put her to bed. Granny talked of nothing else, her lovely Christmas party and her ride back to bed. Richard gained many brownie points from this heroic act. Sadly she died shortly after.

Richard and I had known each other only a couple of years when we got married. Our engagement was celebrated with an exclusive, romantic dinner for two. Neither of us were very worldly, particularly with regard to alcohol and of course drink driving was not even talked about back then.

Richard ordered a shandy for himself and a Babycham for me – as today drinks were advertised as though they were fruit juice and did not convey the potent kick that they actually carry. He also ordered a bottle of wine to drink with the meal. We giggled our way through the meal, feeling adult, suave and very sophisticated. As we drove home Richard declared himself sleepy and we stopped in a lay by. I cuddled into his shoulder and – we both promptly fell asleep!

Daddy was very strict with his three daughters, 10.00 pm was the normal curfew, but we had a half hour extension for this special occasion. He was not at all happy with my engagement at eighteen, such a young age to know my mind he thought. When we awoke and saw the time we shot out of our reverie and sped home. Daddy had obviously been pacing the floor for over an hour and was furious (obviously as parents do, fearing the worst). The cross examination started, Richard was highly embarrassed and all I could say was,

'There was this long delay as a herd of pink elephants were crossing the road. All traffic was suspended for a long time.' It didn't come out quite like that as I giggled and hiccupped my way through it. Richard was in double trouble, bringing me home not only late, but drunk.

Before our marriage, Richard's grandfather offered us a plot of land that he owned next to his own house where he lived with his daughter, Richard's Auntie Mollie. The price was one hundred and fifty pounds. Of course we accepted, and for an additional fifteen pounds we found a student architect who drew up plans for a three bedroom detached house, three storeys high. This would lift the house to the level of the road in front allowing a view of the pretty local park and allow a garage area in the basement. As a last minute thought we added a downstairs toilet, located under the main stairs, this was very modern thinking.

As I was working for the Arndale Property Trust – one of the first mall-type shopping precinct developers – I proudly took the plans of our house to show my new boss, the Chief Architect. His round, happy face split into a wide grin as he examined the plans. Looking up with a twinkle in his eye, he asked,

'How tall is your fiancé?'

I was puzzled.

'Six foot one. Why?'

'Mm. Is he used to crawling on all fours?' Then, taking pity on my confusion, said,

'Well, my dear, the headroom to upstairs is two foot six.'

Back to the drawing board and revisions that would allow the ability to walk upright yet still have a toilet downstairs.

Richard's wage was at that time below the national average wage. It was obvious that a mortgage would be needed and in trepidation we went to see the Bank Manager. In 1962 he was a force to be reckoned with and held your life in his hands. After long discussions and much attempted dissuasion on his part, he agreed to lend us the necessary £2,000 with the dire warning that this would be a millstone around our necks that we would be paying off the day we retired!

Richard has often been asked,

'How do you build your own house when you have no experience?' Richards reply was that,

'You pick up a spade and stick it in the ground.' In fact he had built has parents a double garage in their garden the year before so had a little experience with that. After work we dug foundations, concreted them in, took delivery of bricks, timber, roof tiles, stacking and preparing them for the Bricky, erecting scaffolding and ordering and estimating.

I had moved from Bradford to Wakefield the year before as my parents were building their own house in a village just outside Wakefield. My father was a Roofing Contractor so we at least knew we wouldn't have a leaking roof with his expertise to hand. I travelled back and forth by train – using the journey to knit Richard a rather splendid sweater and then at weekends stayed with Richard's parents to be available to work on the house.

It wasn't unknown for Richard to ask me to pass him a bag of cement, which I did – all seven stone two pounds of me. The house was completed and decorated ready to move into in fifteen weeks. At one point we needed to break into the water main – this was situated in the road – a busy main road, two old pence electric trolley bus ride into the centre of Bradford. The buses ran every four minutes. Without more ado Richard jack hammered the road up and poked about down there until he found the connection, promptly filling the hole in again. Can you imagine that with today's 'police state' red tape policies?

We employed two school boys to help – one in particular, Stuart, was a real clown, swinging from the scaffolding three storeys up. One day, after we had in-filled the front garden, he fell two storeys, head first into the gravel. What a fright we had until he bounced up, laughing and grinning with hardly a bruise.

Richard and I were married on the 22nd June, 1963 in Wakefield Cathedral. Our wedding was a grand affair. Whilst my parents were building their house we lived in a small flat above a shoe shop in the Bull Ring, Wakefield, which placed us fairly and squarely in the Cathedral parish. The Bull Ring was a large roundabout surrounded by shops, Wakefield Cathedral being just fifty yards down one of the main roads off the Bull Ring. My youngest sister was my Maid of Honour and two young nieces the Bridesmaids. My dress was a fairy tale and cost the equivalent of three weeks wages.

My father and I left the new house in the wedding car only to have to return as my bouquet had been left behind. I enjoyed every moment as we rode round the Bull Ring and all the shops emptied of shoppers and assistants and they all came out cheering and waving as though I was royalty. The whole day was a dream of happiness.

The lead up had its moments of humour and less humourous events that even now I find difficult to understand. Just before we got engaged we went to Glasgow for a short holiday, to stay with friends of my parents since WWII. Mummy told me that the only reason Richard was allowed to come with us on this short holiday was because Janet, my fourteen year old sister, had given her permission.

We were out shopping. A tantalizing aroma wafted from the roast chicken that Janet was carrying for lunch. She kept pushing it at Richard's nose and teasing him until he snapped and told her to grow up. The atmosphere of judgement lasted all day until Mummy took me on one side to tell me that Richard was not the sort of person we wanted in our family and I was to end the relationship immediately on returning home.

Richard and I spent the evening in his car as I cried and sobbed and considered the future without my love and hero. He listened and allowed, as I realised I had been set a choice. The loss of Richard and my family's approval or my family's disapproval and remain with Richard. With great distress over the consequences – there was no choice. If Richard had approved I would have run away that night. He didn't and we didn't. Was this a first in such a dramatic stand against my parent's wishes? There was no confrontation, my actions made clear that I would not give Richard up despite the disapproval and this over a fourteen year old and a roast chicken! Thankful to say Richard and Janet have a good relationship despite a rocky start.

After our marriage we were blissfully unaware of our young ages that had so concerned our parents, and only when something happened did a query arise in my mind. Like the day I bleached Richard's underpants and turned them all pink, or turned the chip pan on and went away and left it to fill the house with smoke. I was twenty-one within six months of our marriage and arranged a family gathering. Sixty guests and I did the catering, Mummy and Daddy providing the cake. I felt so proud.

The plot of land we had bought off Richard's grandfather to build the house included a section at the back that sloped gently uphill to a road along the top edge of our land. This road fed a row of large stone built terrace houses with not enough room for them to have their own garage. Richard applied for Planning Permission to build twenty one lock up garages on this land. There was no access from this road through the stone boundary wall on to the proposed building land so planning for these garages would be refused. Six am one morning Mike (one of the young men who helped build the house) and Richard went out with what Richard called a silent hammer and crow bar. Quietly enough not to disturb the occupants of the houses the wall was breached by unknown forces!

Planning permission was granted, as access was already available and the work commenced. Richard had bought an old petrol driven cement mixer for £1. The reason it was so cheap was that the interior was solid with old cement needing to be chipped out. It built a double garage for his parents, a three storey house, twenty-one garages, a porch and downstairs toilet for his parents, a large extension to a house, built a long drive and many smaller jobs, at which point he sold it on fifteen years later – for £1. At eight months old James sat in his pram watching the building work and keeping Richard company.

We shared a Mini car with Richard's Mother so timing and booking access for the use of the car could pose a problem. This day when I had the car and was visiting Mummy, we were shopping in Wakefield; I turned right to go down a side street.

'Oh, you can't go through here any more, they've put bollards in the road.' Mummy said,

'Too late, I'm already here. Anyway I can get between those, it's only a Mini.' The scrape of metal is a horrid noise isn't it? Oh my goodness not only how was I going to tell Richard but how was I going to tell his Mother? We went back to Mummy's house, all the way she insisted,

'Don't worry I can deal with it so long as it isn't dinted.' It wasn't and I was right, I had got through – just – pretty poor judgment though. Out came the brasso and a soft cloth, gently and methodically she polished off the paint made by the scrape from the bollard and amazingly dissolved the car paint work to cover any minor scratches left behind. It was pristine, the only way you could tell anything had happened was that that area was cleaner and shinier than the rest, so I spent the next hour bringing it all up to the cleanliness of this small area.

I did tell Richard but he couldn't see what I was talking about – nothing to see. Even better there was nothing to confess to Mother-in-Law.

We were happy in the house we had worked so hard to build, close to Richard's Grandfather and his Aunty Mollie. Indeed Aunty Mollie and I became firm friends. She had never married. A gruff, Yorkshire lady with a heart of gold, she would flap her hands and declare,

'Don't kiss me. Don't kiss me.' whenever she was introduced to someone new. I remember clearly her dining room table being covered with cyclamen plants of every hue, flowering non-stop throughout the year.

After our marriage I worked part-time, and it was not too long before we agreed it would be nice to have a dog. We chose a sleek black Labrador and, if we'd had any sense, we would have realized what a handful she would turn out to be on the day we went to purchase her. Let loose in the garden, she chased around like a black tornado, biting the heads off all the flowers and swallowing them whole.

A couple of weeks after obtaining our puppy we came home from work to find our beautiful new linoleum ripped up and a square silver-coated board on the kitchen floor. Whatever could it be? All too soon it became apparent.

45

The middle layer of our wedding cake had been stored, wrapped in plastic, in a tall cupboard in the kitchen. How on earth a ten week old puppy could have got into the cupboard and pulled out the cake, we had no idea. But she had. She had eaten every last currant, every scrap of icing and now her tummy was so extended that her legs scrabbled to reach the floor.

We rushed her to the vet and I cried all the way, convinced we would lose her. The vet administered a child's aspirin and warned us to be ready for the evacuation that was sure to be dramatic. It was.

Richard had attended a Public School with strict rules and conventions and had a very tidy Mother as I have already said. His wardrobe was labeled and everything had its proper place, so when we were married I think he rebelled, he came in at night from work, nudged all the pictures hanging on the walls so they were cockeyed and scattered his newspaper in different piles around the room.

'That's better, we look lived in now.' I was trying my best to be the 'perfect' wife and like to live in a reasonably tidy environment – what is within is reflected by what is without and vice versa – it was not to be and I have never caught on to this idea of living in relative disorder, although if you saw my office you would wonder how I dare say this.

We were married two years before our first child was born. My midwife was away on holiday, so I was attended by another young midwife who, it turned out, had no experience or qualification to be in charge of a birth without supervision.

Arriving at 6.30 in the morning, this young lady announced that all was well and the baby would be born that afternoon. As the day wore on and afternoon turned to evening, she decided she would break my waters to speed things up.

The pain got worse. She administered Pethadyn, which can cause hallucinations, and I became very agitated, convinced they were plotting to take the baby away, or even that it was dead. Eventually, my mother intervened, threatening to dial 999 if the midwife did not. The ambulance arrived and I was taken to the hospital, where I was left on a hospital trolley in a dark corridor in what seemed to be a lonely, living nightmare. The drugs caused me to phase in and out of consciousness, and the next I knew I was in the operating theatre, surrounded by masked doctors and nurses.

James was delivered face up (face to pubes), with the cord around his neck. Panic ensued as the doctor forced the baby's head back in enough to release the cord. I was told afterwards he was delivered by a high forceps delivery, the highest position possible when a Caesarean is too late. He was born facing me and the nurse raised my shoulders to see the head and one arm of my baby, red faced and screaming as he grabbed my thumb and hung on as the rest of him was born. I can still feel that feeling of elation and ecstasy even today. Eye to eye and physical contact before he was even born. He was alive, he was well and that was all that mattered.

Then my baby was whisked away and I was left with a dreadful feeling of abandonment as they stitched me up and took me back to a small ward. Twenty four hours later a kindly nurse found me crying.

'Why don't they just tell me he's dead or ill? Anything would be easier than not knowing!' I said to her query of concern. Her response was caring and genuine,

'Oh, my love,' she replied, 'he's perfectly fine. He just had a very traumatic and strenuous birth so he's being cot-nursed for forty eight hours.' At which point she put me in a wheelchair and took me to look at him through the nursery window.

When my baby was finally brought to me, we were moved to a large, long ward. The lady beside me had thirteen children, six of them physically and/or mentally disabled, and all of them by different fathers she proudly told me. I was dumbstruck. What a sheltered life I'd led! One day she saw me stroking the hair on the top of James's head and shouted at me,

'Don't touch him there! You'll cause brain damage.' I couldn't help but feel pity for her sad experiences.

Each day in the hospital, because my blood group is rhesus negative, and Richard's is rhesus positive, they would take blood from James to test. This was achieved by picking him up by his feet and stabbing his heels to procure the blood. Now – not only had I been sent to and born on the wrong planet but I had given birth to another soul who surely too could not have chosen to come here and experience this start to his life.

I was to discover that it can be extremely dangerous to have a baby when the parents are a mix of rhesus positive and rhesus negative blood type, as we were. Fifteen per cent of the population lack the Rhesus factor D in their blood and are rhesus-negative. In pregnancy a rhesus-negative woman carrying a child with rhesus-positive blood inherited from the father, may pick up some of the baby's blood cells and produce anti-bodies against the rhesus-positive factor. The antibodies then enter the blood stream of the unborn child and destroy its blood cells. Modern treatment can prevent the antibodies forming, but until the 1940's it was not uncommon for these babies to be born dead. We were lucky, and blessed beyond measure, to eventually have three healthy young sons.

When we were first married, Richard and his cousin Ben worked in the family business at the woollen mill, but it soon became evident that the woollen industry in Bradford was in decline. Richard was working days some weeks and nights others, with his cousin working the opposite shifts. There were times, however, when Richard would ring to say he was working through the night after working all day, as Ben's ulcer was playing up again. They did everything they could to keep the business alive.

Eventually the mill had to close and Richard helped his father set up a small spinning mill where he could work until he retired. Richard got a job at Nelroyd and later moved to Burnleys, working with special machines using sapphires which were strong enough not to break the thread as it passed through the spindle at such high speeds (6 – 10,000 revs per second). The filament they produced was Crimplene – it became a best seller and all the rage – and Richard played a large part in turning this into a million pound business for his employers.

Richard was travelling abroad one week in four, often in Italy with manufacturers and he brought home lengths of the most beautiful fabric, silk, gold lamé and fine wool fabric.

'For your lovely wife.' The Italians would say.

A local shop took in alterations and dress making so I began to design my own clothes.

One design was for a length of gold lamé, full length A-line, with a small polo collar and sleeveless, very elegant and demure until you saw the back. This had the polo, invisibly fastened with a hook and eye, and then the back was completely cut away to the waist line. I wore this to the Lord Mayor's Ball, meeting up with ex bosses who couldn't believe that mousey Miss Smithies had matured into something so daring. I had a wonderful evening, feted and danced with more than any other time in my life. Richard's Mother was quite perturbed and queried how I knew all these people, after all she and Father were the honoured guests and Richard and I just the add ons!

Richard was offered the opportunity to go to America for three months, researching and training. James was three months old when Richard left and he was sitting up, attempting to crawl when his daddy returned. We wrote to each other every day and I sent a recording of James laughing and laughing as he bounced in his baby bouncer, which Richard received during a lull in his hectic schedule whilst staying with his Canadian cousin and family over Thanksgiving.

I had spent weeks planning James and my outfits for his arrival home so we looked our best. I had designed a suit of dark turquoise and blue woollen material and had knitted James a suit of leggings, jacket and pixie style hat in pale turquoise.

Richard arrived home and came through customs and baggage check talking to another man who he had sat next to on the long flight. He introduced me and gave me a peck on the cheek and greeted James with a smile. He then set off and made his way to the exit continuing his conversation with his flight colleague, James and I following three paces behind. I felt confused, my bubble had certainly burst. He had written to me everyday of the three months, long, informative, passionate letters. What a strange disillusion.

When we got home he started to organize his briefcase, he was going straight into work! Fortunately his boss told him he must take a couple of days to unwind before attempting to return to work. He found it hard to adapt with all the emotional trauma of returning home and relearning to be a husband and father.

When James was nine months old I took to bed with very severe pain and gastro enteritis. James had to stay on the floor as his movement on the bed was unbearable. After two or three hours I rang Richard at work and asked him to come home. He rang me back ten minutes later to tell me his boss wouldn't give permission. He arrived home at 6.30 pm and called the doctor. I was an emergency admittance with suspected burst appendix. Twenty four hours later I was still having rectal examinations clenching a face flannel between my teeth. The doctors thought it <u>might</u> be an abscess on an ovary. The exploratory operation did indeed prove it was an emergency appendix with difficulties of getting it out without it bursting.

I was in hospital and my nine month old baby was not allowed to visit. I was in a ward with a young woman with cancer. She was being given horrendously painful dry injections. Her voice was like a man's and she was developing a beard that any testosterone filled male would be proud of. Poor girl – what did I have to worry about? Except perhaps the next visit from a particular nurse. She was a loud, obese (by anybody's standards) girl. She would enter the room and leer at us both – fortunately she left the other girl alone – but she came to my bed and wound up the base (the old fashioned one that had to be manually wound up) until it was six inches above the ground – she then pulled the pin and dropped it with a bang to hit the floor. This within two to three days of an appendectomy.

I didn't complain, what was wrong with me? but then nobody had time to listen if I had and it was in the times of Matron when Matron was the archetypal battleaxe. She would come into a ward and if a patient's bedclothes weren't crisp and straight, as though nobody was in the bed she would create havoc.

I was told not to lift or strain so we went to stay with Mummy and Daddy for a week to give me help with James for this short period at least.

Richard had missed me he said and just ten days after an emergency appendectomy made love to me. I reasoned that this was his way, perhaps a male way, of showing his love, although I also knew we hadn't made love, it had been an act of sex, a lay back and think of England moment.

Only as I look back in hindsight can I see a pattern of, in a way, being frightened of denying Richard. Somehow I had developed this notion that a good wife happily and willingly devoted her time and energy to her husband and subsequently their children.

This is not a human behaviour, as we look at it in the twenty first century, but a left over from animal behaviour, the subservience by the female to the male as the act of survival of the species. It is very rare in the animal kingdom for males to take over the role of producing, or even nurturing, the offspring. Seahorses are the only one I can think of where the male becomes pregnant and rears the young.

Subservience then can be defined as 1. to surrender, to submit, to give in to a stronger force, or to be subservient or eager to follow the wishes of another, or 2. surrender and acceptance, as surrendering to God's will, not through giving in but through agreeing to work with and combine one mission with another.

I chose the latter liberating both of us. Not despite, but because of this decision I fostered a life of my own outside the home and yet never neglecting or short changing the home. It was the food which fed the fire of my determination to find my path, alongside the most important job of all, being a wife and mother.

Chapter Six

Search for Spiritual Understanding

Whenever I could, I would catch up on my reading. I had always been interested in the weird and the wonderful. I also had a great need to communicate, and to understand the complexities of relationships. I read and read any book I could lay my hands on that helped expand my knowledge base.

When Edward was a baby we went on a cruise without the children – my reading matter for that holiday was a three inch thick book 'ESP (Extra Sensory Perception) behind the Iron Curtain' so I have always had a penchant for researching and learning and understanding the less usual trains of thought for a young wife and mother who had led a pretty sheltered existence. I learnt a lot through the Yoga and the reading and began to put that knowledge into practice in my daily life. Until that knowledge became experience it really was only words – and somebody else's words at that.

I was always seeking, thinking, reading, learning, attending courses, whatever I felt might help me understand the meaning, not only of life but the times/spaces surrounding life. Whilst living at Greaves Farm I studied with the Jehovah's Witnesses, they came to our home each week for eight weeks. They were lovely, genuine people, who believed totally in their concepts and beliefs in the bible. They did not question – they just accepted, so alien to my way so far. I think this is probably the only time I frightened Richard that I had taken a route that he felt was so alienating to so much of our world and family. He need not have feared, there was no danger on any score.

I, as always, needed to know what others thought and believed in order to understand the diversity of human nature and behaviour. What stands out is the revelation that this particular group scoured the newspapers, they told me, for bereaved people or women who had recently given birth. These vulnerable people would then be targeted. For the rest of our time living in this area I would meet up with these kind, but in my opinion misguided people and they would fling their arms around my neck begging me to join them as I was destined for purgatory if I did not.

I pursued my quest for understanding and continued to read anything and everything, and over the years studied teachings that spanned in range from Jehovas Witnesses to Krishnamurti, to an Ancient School of Wisdom, from the wisdom of Sophia to quantum physics. There is nothing more exciting to me than to learn and grow and to acquire new knowledge.

At about this time, Richard put up as a candidate for Councillor for Calderdale, following in his father's footsteps. This was how we had met and was, therefore, familiar territory. A lot of hard work, now the children had to be taken into account, and everything fitted in. One day whilst canvassing I was given the address of a farm.

I arrived to find a small red faced individual, obviously the farmer with his ruddy, outdoor complexion. He was more than happy to be entertained by a young lady, and yes he would definitely vote for my husband. We needed a sensible family man with a bit of Yorkshire 'nouse' he said.

The farmer then invited me to see a new born calf in a small pen in the barn. Big blue eyes and huge curled eyelashes, like a Jersey, so beautiful. I petted and stroked it and it sucked my fingers looking for milk.

'Seven days old tomorrow – big day!' I was so innocent and ignorant. 'Yep, tomorrow morning, bullet between the eyes. He'll make the finest veal.' I must have fled faster than the wind. I was a borderline vegetarian to this point. Upon leaving that farm I was a fully committed vegetarian.

Thankfully, Richard did not win this election – he was never a committee man. He is too free spirited, too dedicated to getting things done, rather than talking about them and too practical and down to earth to listen to some of the pie in the sky discussions that take place at these levels. Want proof? Look at the ridiculous laws and regulations government brings out from people behind desks – lack of equipment for soldiers in any war being an extreme example. But that's another book. Who is it that spends their time discussing and preparing this legislation?

Here's a small example that is not widespread in the media. The Government has created 3,600 new offences in the ten years between 1997 and 2007. Here's a couple of examples to make sure a safe world is what is your priority – the sarcasm is deliberate – It is a criminal offence to allow an unlicensed concert in a church hall or community centre; it is a criminal offence to offer a game bird for sale that was killed on a Sunday or Christmas Day; by the way don't forget the offence of 'bin police' having the right to enter your home, to seize the contents of your bin and to take photographs – if you refuse them entry you can be fined up to £5,000. Feel better? Nor me.

My first real spiritual teacher was Krishnamurti. Krishnamurti was born in southern India of Brahmin parents. In 1911, at the age of fifteen, he was brought to England by Mrs Annie Besant. He was educated privately and groomed for the role of World Teacher (Messiah, even), but in 1929 he disbanded the organization which had proclaimed him and of which he was the head, and declared that he did not want disciples. He then travelled ceaselessly around the world giving public talks and private interviews.

The essence of Krishnamurti's teaching is that only through a complete change of heart in the individual can there come about a change in society, and thereby peace in the world. It was his sincere belief that this radical change can take place in every individual. He helps us to see ourselves as we really are, for it is in this seeing with complete clarity that the inner revolution takes place. These were my sentiments entirely.

I also studied Yoga. The Yoga teacher was a French lady and her life partner (it was quite something forty odd years ago to live together without being married) had been a Tibetan monk. She taught Hatha Yoga and I think I was in awe of her knowledge and wisdom. I continued to do this for many years, meeting people who were Gurus, Teachers, Masters where I would feel in awe and bow to their wisdom, not feeling inferior as such but wanting to know what they knew and how had they learnt it so that I could progress my spiritual path.

The disappointment was great upon discovering that so many of them had clay feet, and all of them were human – even great channeled entities were channeled through less than perfect beings. I remember being told that when we meet someone who we appoint as angels, or teachers or gurus and then discover their limitations we have then to reverse the appointment and dis-appoint them, hence the term disappointment – it works if you think about it even for situations and things. Yoga was an unusual hobby – probably about the time the Beatles were emerging with drug experiments and gurus. I know my parents particularly, thought I had started on the road to drugs and hell – if by association only.

I am going to jump to the late seventies, early eighties, when we were living in our new house at the Garth Caravan Park. We had a family staying in the cottage throughout the winter, and John worked with Richard to help towards their rent. John had very long hair and I wasn't sure what my Mother (Mummy and Daddy were staying with us for a week) would make of his 'hippie' appearance. Nothing was said until one day she was looking out of the window and she said,

'He's a nice man isn't he, he even looks like Jesus.' Well, our 'Jesus' introduced me to a Dr Pillau who had come to England to offer Ayurvedic massage and medicine, to be held at Gurton College, Cambridge. The course was run by Dr Padmanabha Pillai, a director of the Institute of Yogic Culture in Kerala, India. Dr Pillai was known simply as Guruji, a term of endearment meaning little teacher, and he was a practitioner of Siddha medicine, a natural system of medicine derived from the wisdom of the ancient sages.

John and his partner Jenny were, and still are following a deeply spiritual path. Through John's information I decided it was my kind of therapy and booked for the three weeks.

At the initial meeting Guruji gave a talk and explained what it was that we were all going to experience. He sat beside Richard and took Richard's hand and held it between his, as if he was warming it, and stroked it. After a good five minutes he turned Richard's hand over,

'Oh, a lot of money coming in – a lot of money.' he said. Paused for a minute and then said 'Oh dear, a lot of money going out too.' We laughed so much, as yes the money had started to come in but it was nearly all allocated to bringing the business into the twentieth century and bringing in adequate electricity, water and new sewage systems and septic tanks, the money was certainly going out not least through the sewerage system.

It was a wonderful three weeks of quiet, rest, treatment and meditation. The ayurvedic massage consisted of the therapist holding a suitably positioned rope above her head and massaging the recipient lying on the floor, with one foot, whilst balancing on the other and being stabilised by the rope. It was amazing how the foot fit the contours of the body so perfectly. It was years later that I discovered that the pain coming from my neck, down my arms and shooting out of my middle fingers was actually, in Chinese medicine, a major meridian line. I used to hide under the bed clothes in the dark because I was convinced I would see fire, or at least a bright light shooting out of these fingers.

As usual Richard and I wrote to each other every day. I also wrote to my Mother and Father to tell them – I wanted them to know (how often do we tell people?) how much I loved them. Within two days I had a reply, with most of the letter written by my Father. I had never received a letter from my Father before, nor have since but I do know that after all those years we had made a breakthrough and each forgiven, at an unconscious level at least, our unfortunate and delayed start due to the war.

After a couple of weeks Guruji took my hand, as he had with Richard. At last, I thought, I am about to find out my destiny. At last I will know where I am heading. He turned over my hand and studied it carefully, closed it by turning my fingers in as best as they would go. He then stood up and walked away without saying a word. I lay awake all night pondering, what had he seen? Was it too awful to say? Was I dying? Was my future too awful to be told? I was not to know. In retrospect I like to think he knew that, although my path would be difficult, I would go on to explore and experience my spiritual calling.

He had told us, yes karma exists, but it is not insurmountable, we need not carry it to our grave and into the next lifetime, but can transmute and work through it. It is said that a true initiate can handle the biggest and the baddest! Where do we start? Sickness and pain can be our means to face up to the challenge and learn through it, it can be a ticket to freedom in the sense that one cannot get caught up in the distractions and illusions of life if one is constantly held in check by immobility or pain, by hobbies, shopping, TV, sport, going out, soap operas, and living a life that is based on 'pretend' and not your own. This struck me forcefully one day when a friend said,

'Isn't it tragic about so and so's baby dying?'

'Oh, how awful' I replied. 'Do I know her personally, is she a friend of yours?'

'No, no,' was the response and then she told me it was someone in her favourite soap opera. These characters are real, more real than real, to so many people. Whilst you are engrossed in this or football or any other sport or distraction you do not query the world, the government, your own lot in life.

While I was attending this ayurvedic medicine and massage retreat at Girton College I met a lady I shall call Lisa. She was a little younger than me, a yoga teacher who had gone to India to be taught the ayurvedic massage technique by Indira, Guruji's wife. Richard and I struck up a friendship with Lisa and her partner Eric and they told us they were building a Spiritual Centre in Spain in a valley called Val de Paz, Valley of Peace, but unfortunately they were running out of money and struggling to complete it.

This was my dream, to have, or be a part of, a spiritually based Healing Centre. We went to view, as a short holiday, their beautiful bungalow with small self-contained annex and swimming pool. Richard and I talked far into the night. Aunty Ida had died and left us some money. Should we invest in the project? We had never had such a large amount of money before and we sank our inheritance into the Centre with great enthusiasm. As my physical condition worsened, winters in Wales had become difficult for me, and the doctors recommended spending time where the weather was warmer and drier.

We wanted to spend approximately twelve weeks a year, in short bursts of three to four weeks in the annex, in return for our financial input.

Eric and Lisa's relationship was far from stable. The aggression and volatile behaviour we only discovered through living with them for a few weeks. Lisa had brought crockery, bedding and even Marks & Spencer roses to plant in the garden trying to live as she would have done in London. Although she spoke Spanish well she seemed not to be adapting to her new life of Spanish customs. Suddenly we were receiving bills for 50 per cent outlay on TV's, video recorders etc, when our input was for less than ten per cent

This Centre never did manifest, our decision to pull out was based mainly on the fact that Lisa and Eric had not told us that they did not own the property they had only paid a deposit. We think they thought we might provide more to bail them out especially after Guruji's palm reading of 'a lot of money'!

They split up rather acrimoniously I was later told. How very sad with such potential. I was disappointed, disillusioned and troubled – was I to go on finding so called spiritual people who were so lacking in morals and integrity? Indeed I was, but that comes later.

This was not what we had signed up for and we needed to extricate ourselves from this situation before our nerves and finances were in tatters.

We found a small villa with views over almond and orange trees. It was perfect. We managed to finance the purchase and enjoyed many happy times in Spain for the next ten years, sometimes alone and sometimes with family or friends. I loved to pick and press the beautiful flowers that grew all around and started a new hobby creating flower pictures. I pressed a lot of mimosa from the garden – handling it was an exotic experience, like handling live baby chicks. It is soft and warm and alive, with a most exquisite perfume. We also enjoyed oranges, lemons and grapefruit from the garden. What a treat it was to pick a basket of fruit to take home with us to Wales.

In order to encourage our family to bring their children to use the villa we looked at putting a plunge pool in the front garden – it wasn't big enough for anything larger – permission had to be granted and this was refused. Some time later on a subsequent holiday we had a visit from a man who asked,

'You want a pool? Well the mayor is tending his grapes in the field down the road. If you take a plain envelope with 'x' amount of pesetas in it, you will get your permit.' Thank you – but no thank you. We were not prepared to become part of and thereby encourage and perpetuate this corruption.

When the day came to sell our villa the price was stated on the Deeds, an amount for the sale and a second amount of cash – a set percentage in fact. This was clearly stated on the Deeds, signed by both parties and the legal people and yet was totally illegal! Corruption was rife but not hidden – tax evasion, buying favours etc were considered normal.

Another anomaly was when we came to sell the villa, the Estate Agent said they could not sell our property, which had been on the market for six months and she wanted us to reduce the sale price by £10,000 this would have left us out of pocket again. For whatever reason I intervened and said,

'No, we'll put it up by £10,000.' She had no option but to take this crazy woman's word for it. The villa sold within three weeks. We had been top of the bottom price range, now we were bottom of the middle price range. The purchaser had money left over to effect changes and alterations to their taste. A win win situation, thanks to intuition.

During our ten years visiting the villa there were many changes and events. We both studied Reiki, taking both Stage I and Stage II courses. We have found this tremendously helpful throughout our lives but yet again I did discover the dangers in the spiritual hierarchy.

A Reiki Master – what is that exactly? In Japanese the word means teacher. I have a couple of very dear friends who live by the principle that they are teachers and are still in the process of 'Mastering' but have also met other Masters who truly think they are.

Spiritual arrogance should be one of the deadly sins. Spiritual arrogance is when we as individuals have a hidden agenda, when what we believe to be 'our thing' over-rides others, when our spirituality has the effect of subduing, rather than empowering others. To be so wrapped up in our own beliefs, channellings, visions, that we impose these on others to the degree that we cannot see the beauty that they have to offer, and then we need to beware of spiritual arrogance. These gifts can be used to draw attention to ourselves, to claim power as we seek recognition and love that maybe we feel has been denied, or even that we don't feel truly worthy of.

When we embark upon a spiritual path we can sometimes encounter in our meditations, lights, shapes, voices, visions; the gifts of clairvoyance, clairaudience, seeing of auras, devas and other dimensions and realities. Remember these are gifts, share them, use them with integrity and compassion, but also remember they can be a trap for the unwary. They can become the destination instead of the journey. Journey on accepting these gifts, but do not allow the gifts to slow the progress by becoming so enamoured by them that the true destination is abandoned.

Spiritual arrogance is like a cut glass goblet, banged down hard on a table it will crack and not ring true. Spiritual wisdom is when it is delicately placed with grace; then, when it is struck, it will be forever clear and true.

Self discipline is another difficult expression, without it there can be no spiritual progress. Use self discipline to meditate, to pray, to carry out necessary disciplines. Use self discipline to give choice, not to be hypnotised by TV, stuck in survival mode; but use self discipline to say,

'What do I want beyond the limitations of everyday life?' We need self discipline to release those limitations. A good parent teaches a child from birth the art of self discipline. To live in society a child learns socially acceptable behaviour, the self discipline to belong to a loving functioning community, self discipline to listen to others views without imposing their own, self discipline to recognise their own hidden agendas and act to remove them and to be open to the one and only agenda of truth.

The crystal goblet cannot ring its clear note of truth unless someone has the self discipline to pick up the striker.

I was taught,

'Look to each other for wisdom, we are great teachers. Remember, something is true to everyone, but there is only one truth. Accept and recognise that truth through self discipline and spiritual wisdom. Nurture your recognition of that truth and accept the results brought about by that recognition; for we are co-creators and gods in the making.'

You hear people say after a serious accident or illness,

'God saved/healed me. I must have something to do and that is why I have been saved.' Well, didn't all the others who didn't survive have something to do? I don't know how their 'God' makes his choices. Why would he heal or save one person and not another? I cannot come to terms with this, what appears to be, arbitrary saving and healing. If there are criteria I would dearly love to know of them. But then when you think of the old saying 'the good die young' the two don't quite tally.

I don't believe it has got anything to do with God, it is something to do with either the choice we make in our life and whether the time has come for us to complete this life and leave, or something to do with social consciousness and social choice. Just look at the third world countries where babies die within hours of being born or are raped because some morally misguided voodoo doctor says it will cure Aids. I have a friend who believes it is the persons karma – my belief is, if it is karma then it is social karma and not individual karma. Humans allow the spread of disease, famine, war and lack of clean water not God. He provides all that we require but we choose how to use it. The bible says God feeds the birds but nowhere does it say it arrives on a silver platter. We have to work at it and choose whether we spend billions on weaponry or feed the world. Nature will provide our needs but not our greeds. It takes 8lbs of grain to produce 1lb of protein, yet 80 per cent of America's grain is fed to livestock to produce meat. One tasty beef burger feeds one person, but left as grain it would feed so many more.

How often have I been confronted with the attitude – if you were as spiritual as me you would be healed. Let me heal you! When I had the PEG feeding tube fitted I was inundated with people visiting who came specifically to heal me. It was not always accepted graciously by them when I asked that they not heal me as such, but send energy for my higher good. What if by healing someone you remove their path of learning and then they have to learn some other, maybe harsher way or even need another life time to learn that teaching?

The two years previous to having the feeding tube fitted was the period that the Seed of Life Foundation was starting and I did a number of talks in Spain to groups about the plans, explaining the part Tom played (he lived permanently in Alcalali) and how the Seed of Life symbol presented through Gregg Braden's books and videos had been chosen.

I had a friend in America who ran a TV talk show, interviewing the leading edge thinkers on all matters of spirituality, health, earth energies, the reversal of the sun and the earths magnetic poles – the sun reverses poles every eleven years, so every twenty-two years it reverts back, north becomes south, south becomes north. The earth's magnetic reversal again is the process by which the north pole is transferred into the south pole and the south pole becomes the north pole. Earth's reversals are not predictable but evidence for these reversals is found in volcanic rock and ice core samples, particularly Norway and Australia: also the beginning of and reasons behind global warming – long before we laid the entire blame at humanity's feet; quantum mechanics; other dimensions – which are now being proven; the meaning of life, and the power and workings of the brain. I am sure I have not covered the full repertoire. This absolutely fascinated me. I wanted to know more and more.

The pulse or heart beat, the Schumann resonance, of the earth has been 7.8 cycles per second for perhaps thousands of years and this pulse has been used as a very reliable reference by global military communications. However since the 1980's we are told that this resonance has been slowly rising, it is now over 12 cycles per second. The data for this comes from Norwegian and Russian research although the scientists do not know what to interpret from these findings. Whilst the earth's pulse is rising her magnetic field strength is declining. It is believed by some scientists that the data indicates that the earth's magnetic field is approximately 38 per cent lower than 2000 years ago. Greg Braden claims that the human heart and brain resonate to earth's beat and all matter including human cells strive to maintain a constant resonance or tuning with the pulsed heartbeat of the earth.

As the heart beat of the earth increases this means that what we knew as twenty four hours per day now feels to be two thirds as long or a perception period of sixteen hours in every twenty four. Our clocks still measure in hours, minutes and seconds and our day is still measured as twenty four hours but we perceive time as speeding up.

'Where does time go? The years fly faster as you get older,' we say. Maybe they do, certainly in our perception if the scientists are correct.

I brought back my friend's videos from America and started a video group, for some reason this was always better attended in Spain than in the UK. Much of my interest was being fired and expanded upon by my attendance at an Ancient School of Wisdom. None of this fazed or frightened me as I have always had a 'what if?' approach and attitude. We don't need 'set in stone' answers, we need more 'what if', what would that mean, how would that feel, what difference can it make? and if it can for the better why not try it?

One of the people we met and became friends with in Spain was Tom, an enormous bear of a man who described himself as a professional treasure hunter. Tom was a dowser – someone who can tap into unseen energies in order to obtain information on people, places and objects. He would become instrumental in the planning of a large gathering at Dolguog, but unfortunately our relationship took a turn for the worse as I will explain later. What was it about Spain that led us to meet people who had such opposite sides to their natures?

Chapter Seven

What is Death?

The great Sufi Master Rumi, said,

'The mind sees things inside out, what it takes to be life is really death, and what it takes to be death is really life.'

An ancient writer of Greek tragedy, Euripedes, also said,

'Who knows but life be that which men call death and death what men call life.'

When a baby is born we celebrate its birth into our known life and when someone dies we grieve their passing and celebrate their life and its ending. Birth = Life: Death = No life. Suppose we interchange the definition and meaning and say Birth = Death and Death = Life! as the two great men above believed.

If the baby in the womb were to be told,

'Now shortly you are going to die. The life you have known so far is going to come to an end. You will feel squeezed and pummeled and pushed, ahead of you is a tunnel, as you pass down this tunnel you will see a bright light, head for that light. Don't be distracted by the pain and discomfort at being pushed and pummeled. It will be painful.

As your head emerges from this tight tunnel you will experience bright light and noise. You will be picked up by your feet, probably smacked, to force you to suck air into your new lungs and take a breath and then they will sever your life support cord.

You will be on your own, don't worry, your new breathing system will take over, all will be provided and all will be well. Death will commence but we can't tell you what your death will entail as no one has ever experienced your death before.

Now you try. As what we term death approaches you are told,

'Now you are about to live. The process may be painful and this will mean departing from and leaving behind your body, your life support system. But don't worry you won't need it any longer. You will be on your own and live in this new environment quite happily without a body or the need to breathe, eat or drink. Life will commence but we cannot tell you what this life will be as no-one has come back to tell us.'

What's in a word? Something to ponder I think. The unknown to one is the known to another.

Fear of death is not what is required; respect for life is the overarching principle. Respect for life can encompass the ultimate respect for death. Death without fear. Life and death are a balance, each one needing the other.

We humans have the audacity to question whether there is life elsewhere but would we in fact recognise it if we found it. In our arrogance would we assume it needed the same elements of say oxygen and water or could we accept that it took some other form, perhaps no form at all. My experiences tell me that we humans still exist bodiless, totally independent of outer form.

How do you live when the thing that you live for is taken away? How do normally active individuals live when they suffer loss of limbs, pain or paralysis. How do 'beautiful people' live when they age or are disfigured? How do people survive when they cannot see or cannot hear? Or in my case cannot eat?

There is only one answer. They discover something beyond themselves, their bodies. They discover who they really are. The person, the image or façade that we each present to the world is imaginary. We decide what we want to present to the world and create it, like an artist or actor portrays the world in their art form, it is a picture behind which the true 'I' hides.

Humans are usually slaves to the body. The body rules. It seeks its pleasure, what it considers are its needs and dominates, not only the personality, but the spirit, the soul. The body gets hungry and it feeds and is satiated. The body gets thirsty or tired and drinks or rests.

This is still not 'I'. The body is the vehicle, the instrument. Each instrument will choose a different tune, will make a different sound, each vehicle will take a different route, use different fuel, but within is the soul, accepting the challenges as the personality deals with them on a daily basis. In the acceptance of who we are we become empowered. This acknowledgement and acceptance from the soul demands absolute independence of thought. It is not helpful to want to apply other peoples thoughts in your life; you don't need an intermediary,

'Don't expect help from outside until you have sought help from within.' We are told this by many spiritual teachers and traditions.

You will meet Gurus, Masters, religions, individuals, who claim they know the answers and yet are not in harmony with themselves. Masters who tell you they are such advanced souls this is their last incarnation – why then the need to tell others? True advanced souls will be found not bragging or even realising their role but in humble people living life to its full potential and realizing the manifestation of God/Love that is within them is what is advanced.

This is where our powers of discrimination come into play this is where we can practice on ourselves and on others. Can we accept that spiritual advancement is not something that belongs to us or is a right of birth but is achieved and given through the understanding and meaning of life beyond life, beyond the physical, the actual true identity of who we are.

No words can explain this, even actions cannot fully present the true picture, experience is what is learnt or rejected. Participating in something is not the same as watching it on TV or even reading about it. Experience through participation is the key that opens the doors to learning and to our evolution.

The Egyptians spent 3,000 years studying what lay beyond this life. They came to the conclusion that that altered state of consciousness, death, takes us on a bodiless journey. A journey into a new life, affected by our past physical life. What we do in this life is of supreme importance to us as individuals and to humanity as a whole.

How can we, who have not studied it to any high degree, dispute their findings? We can choose how we use our consciousness. One of the few things we can choose is how to live our life deciding who we are or who we want to be with the many challenges. Ultimately how we act or react is who we are.

Christmas can be a difficult time for families, do we spend it with the wife's family or the husband's family? We overcame this as Richard's mother always had a 'Christmas Day' a week before Christmas Day and then we could all go to her. She had a delightful custom, which I adopted, of not having Christmas crackers but a central table piece with small wrapped gifts for each member of the family.

We were all seated around the beautifully presented Christmas table when she said,

'I think the visitor should open her present first.' We all looked around searching for the visitor and when we couldn't find one, back to her. Her eyes were fixed firmly on me.

'Mother, after seventeen years of marriage and giving you three grandsons, she is no longer a visitor,' said my sister-in-law. I must have a warped sense of humour as I thought it was hilarious and on reflection it put a lot of things into perspective for me.

On another occasion she told me,

'You see June's (her daughter's) children are truly my grandchildren, as June has my blood and her children have her blood. But your children have your blood and are not truly my real grandchildren.' I know I didn't trust myself to say anything but I definitely thought 'she's a crazy old bat!'.

Science had not at that time known about the role that the male and female DNA played in the ancestral genetic history of humans.

DNA studies indicate that all modern humans – male and female – share a common female ancestor who lived in Africa about 140,000 years ago and all men share a common male ancestor who lived in Africa about 60,000 years ago.

When DNA is passed from one generation to the next most of it is mixed by the processes that make each person unique from his or her parents. Some special pieces of DNA however remain virtually unaltered as they pass from parent to child. One of these pieces is the Y chromosome. This makes a man male (males have an X and a Y chromosome, females have two X's).This Y chromosome is passed from father to son only.

Another piece, mitochondrial DNA, mtDNA, is passed from mother to child – of either sex. Everyone male and female will have received their mtDNA from their mothers and in turn those mothers received their mtDNA copies from their mothers too. In this way, the path of the mtDNA has traveled down the generations through the direct maternal line.

The kingly succession of the Pharaohs was modelled specifically for leadership. Aspects of knowledge, culture, awareness, wisdom and intuition made them highly advanced compared to their contemporaries or subjects.

In order to keep their bloodline as pure as possible they always married within a close kinship, even fathers with daughters, sons with sisters or mother, what we now consider to be incest.

This was because they fully recognized that the prominent gene of the succession was carried within the blood of the mother, what we now call mitochondrial DNA. How did my mother-in-law know? – it was me that was the 'silly young bat' for not trusting that unusual wisdom.

Many religious beliefs give instruction in karma. Karma is a very popular word – often thought of as a punishment for wrong deeds which need to be rectified next time round.

No, karma is not a punishment it is a merciful education and evolutionary process to offer, through free will, the opportunity to make restitution or learn from experiences we have not understood. Our testing is, in fact, largely determined by our behaviour.

Our journey ends for the body but the soul endures through the cycle of birth and death, giving us this choice, this opportunity to evolve spiritually.

Children have been my great teachers throughout my life.

When the grandchildren travelled in the car I kept some mint imperials in the cubby hole on the dash board for emergency tummy aches. In they climbed and before they even sat down Taionee asked for a mint. I said,

'No, of course you can't have a mint. How can you be feeling sick we haven't even started the engine. Anyway I'll tell you what my Granny would have told me. She would have said –

'You can't have one for asking and if you didn't ask you couldn't have one because I wouldn't know you wanted one. You've got to wait two minutes now for asking and then I'll let you have one.' Well, of course, he didn't wait the full two minutes and asked again.

'No, you didn't wait so you have to wait again.' Well, this time I forgot and Richard caught my attention and let me know.

'Your two minutes is up now so you can have one'. And I passed them the mints.

After a few minutes Taionee said,

'Grandma, which Aunty was it?'

'What Aunty dear?'

'The one that said you couldn't have something for asking?'

'Oh she was my Granny.'

'Well where is she now?'

'She died.'

'Why did she die?'

'Well she was really sick.' Whoops, so am I. I didn't want to frighten them. So I added,

'She was very old.' Whoops again, to them I was very old wasn't I? I would be about the same age as Kiera when Granny died. So I reassured them by saying,

'Don't worry I'm not planning on going anywhere just yet.' There was silence for a full two minutes, then Taionee's voice came floating out of the back,

'Grandma when are you thinking of dying?' I just love this honesty that children display. They see things as they are without preconceptions.

Kiera has made greetings cards with me since she was very young but I didn't think Taionee would take to it, however he did and he's really good at it. He was with me on his own when he told me,

'Grandma I am so sad in the night and I cry because I don't know what to do.'

I was shocked thinking perhaps he was being bullied or something at school. 'Do you sweetheart? What makes you cry? What makes you so sad and makes you cry?' He answered with,

'I just get so sad. It's you, I'm afraid you're going to die.' Whoa, that took me aback. I had been pretty ill in hospital earlier in the year and he had either been told how ill I was or figured it out for himself. I told him,

'Everyone's going to die, we all live and we all die.

Death is part of living. Even a tree, a flower, animals die. Just some people die younger than others. That's just the way it is. Anyway, you're not to be sad about it because if and when I die – I don't know when I'm going to die, but when I do, you needn't be sad because if ever you want to talk to me just go somewhere quiet and talk to me in your head. You won't be able to hear me with your ears, but you'll hear me in your head. It won't be a noise, just a feeling that I talk back to you.' Oh that was great and he was much comforted.

After a couple of years Kiera was talking to me,

'You know the angel sculpture on the Hotel lawn that we put there?' I didn't interrupt because evidently something profound was about to happen. 'Well, we put it there to remind us of you.' She also had taken on board that when Grandma had been ill recently she may not come home again.

'Taionee says that when you die we can go to that angel and if we talk to you, you will answer us back, but we won't be able to hear you with our ears, we'll only be able to hear you in our head.' The two of them had clearly talked about this situation and reassured each other and still remembered and used it two full years later. How profound and enlightening.

What is death? I attended a local lady who became a friend, who practised Shiatsu (acupressure). She lived in a small Welsh cottage. The kitchen had a breakfast bar across the centre of the room, the other half being a dining area and entrance. My little finger had dislocated, which it did frequently for no reason, it was pretty painful until it was relocated and it had just happened. As we were in her vicinity we called. Back it went with her expertise and all was well.

Her husband John was a big chap in his early sixties and lived for fishing, duck hunting and the like. He was rarely seen without a cigarette in one hand and preferably a glass of wine in the other. Before we left he impressed upon us his excitement at the following days planned duck hunting expedition.

Eight o'clock the following morning the phone rang. I was still in bed awaiting Richard's help to get me dressed and help me downstairs. He came to tell me that John had died from a massive heart attack in the night. Pamela's relatives were in the Midlands and he thought we should go to see if she needed help, but not to rush, I was to relax for another half hour in bed as he had a couple of things to do.

I closed my eyes and my irreverence rose again.

'What the dickens have you been doing, John?' In a flash he appeared, although my eyes were closed, I knew if I opened them he would still be there, fully physical, fully vibrant. He looked at me, puffed the inevitable cigarette, raised his glass, which was a spectacular, enormous, engraved goblet, winked and said,

'I've gone fishing.'

'No you haven't you were meant to be duck hunting, and now you've missed it.' I responded. He raised his glass again, winked again and repeated,

'I've gone fishing'. He disappeared as quickly as he had appeared.

When Richard came to dress me I told him of my strange encounter. Whatever I did I couldn't possibly tell Pamela, his wife. We drove to her cottage and she welcomed us and offered a cup of tea. As we sat drinking the tea my mouth started to move of its own volition. I couldn't stop it however hard I tried. The story came out, I was mortified at my own lack of control in such uncaring sensationalism. As the story finished someone came to the door offering condolences. I was surprised at the speed she dispatched them but put it down to her grief and trauma.

She came and sat back at the small table, looked at me with great seriousness and said,

'Repeat, word perfect, and I mean word perfect.'

What on earth had I got myself into? I repeated, as requested, at which point she went to the closed-in wooden spiral staircase, opened the cupboard underneath it and began to bring out various objects, a box, a vase, an ornament, a goblet – a spectacular, enormous, engraved goblet.

'This it?' she asked. All I could do was nod, dumbstruck.

'He only ever used it on very special occasions, Christmas, his birthday. It was his favourite possession. She came back to sit with us.

'You couldn't possibly know, but John and I had a pact. Whichever of us died first would get a message to the other if life continued. We had a secret code. The secret code was,

'I've gone fishing!'

When I recovered I asked her, why me? Not for the first time I received the reply that many people are called on the telephone and often they are engaged. John had found someone who wasn't engaged and who would not only listen but pass on his message of inspiration.

Chapter Eight

Moving On

When James was a year and a half, our second son, Anthony, was born. I had been having mild contractions for a couple of weeks and James was left with Granny Rhodes while Mummy took me to the hospital for a check-up.

I told the Doctor about the contractions, who dismissed the idea abruptly but decided to give me what he called a membrane sweep (running his finger round the neck of the cervix) and impatiently told me to come back in eight weeks.

Mummy and I headed back to collect James and enjoy a welcome cup of tea. Before the tea was even finished I insisted,

'We need to get back to the hospital,' and off we went again.

Three hours later, Anthony arrived in the world. As James had been such a difficult birth the bossy, unpleasant midwife decided firm action needed to be taken, so she strung up my legs, produced a scalpel and cut the opening.

'So the baby won't tear you.' she said. Ha!

It was so unexpected and painful, I called her a bitch. Not the best thing to do when you're strung up like a chicken about to be gutted, and would need stitching back. The midwife got her revenge with the stitching.

'No anaesthesia needed, won't take long.' she said. My only consolation was that Anthony was a normal, 7 lb bouncing boy and labour lasted less than five hours.

When the doctor made his round, he stopped at the end of my bed and frowned.

'What are you doing here? I told you to come back in eight weeks and not to waste our time.'

'Perhaps I should introduce you to my son, we plan on calling him Anthony, he didn't seem to want to wait the eight weeks.'

About a year later I had a miscarriage. It was one of the most traumatic things I have ever experienced.

I was losing blood and rang the doctor. He came immediately, and instructed me to ring my mother-in-law to ask her to look after the boys. She was busy, she said, and I would need to take them to her house, I put my hand over the phone and told the young doctor who promptly grabbed the phone and told her that not only was the baby's life at stake but so was mine as I could haemorrhage before they got me to hospital.

My mother-in-law duly arrived and I was whisked away in an ambulance. When Richard finished work he hurried to my side and he called a nurse as the contractions were getting stronger and closer together – it was obvious what was happening but he was told to leave by a young nurse who claimed I was getting over-excited.

Shortly after he left the nurse brought me the requested bedpan and when she returned some ten minutes later I told her that it contained my thirteen week old baby. I had carried it for thirteen weeks resigning myself and even looking forward to dedicating myself to nappies, bottles and motherhood for however long it took.

One of the hardest things to cope with was that I was placed in an abortion ward, with women who had chosen to terminate their pregnancies. And my baby, they told me, would have been a little girl. How we would have loved the addition of a daughter to our family, even if it would have been tough, with two young boys already.

The doctors kept referring to my plight as an abortion, while I insisted it was a miscarriage. That's when I learnt that the coil did not prevent pregnancy but aborted the foetus in its early stages. I had been unlucky to carry it for so long they said.

I didn't understand at the time that the tremendous guilt I felt was grief; I would only understand that much later, when Richard and I were on a visit to Japan.

Rosemary and John, Richard's cousin and her husband, were living and working in Japan. They encouraged us to visit as they were sure we would never otherwise holiday in Japan. Their daughter was receiving treatment from one of the top acupuncture doctors in Tokyo, a fairly young man, in his mid-thirties, and it was suggested while we were staying that I should have a couple of treatments with him.

'That would be lovely,' I said. 'Perhaps he can help with the arthritis.'

So it was arranged. I sat down with him and we talked, and he got me to lie on the floor, at which point he looked at me and said,

'Rheumatoid Arthritis. You do realise that you have to make forgiveness between you and your father?'

Rheumatoid Arthritis, he said, was directly related to a person's relationship with their father. I didn't understand. I had always known our relationship was different than the one my father had with my two sisters, but I wouldn't have called it bad, even though I challenged him a lot.

Then the young man looked at me and said,

'And the scar around your neck,' – meaning the thyroidectomy scar and the tracheotomy scar below it – 'this is from a past life. In a past life you were either beheaded or garroted, and you lived through that spiritually. This lifetime you have to live through it physically.'

Well! That was a lot to take in, but his next question floored me.

'When did you have an abortion?'

My eyes shot up.

'I haven't had an abortion!' Even then, I was still in denial. 'I've had a miscarriage.'

'You've had an abortion.' he insisted. 'When did you have an abortion?' So I told him when, and he said 'You need to ask that soul's forgiveness for denying it entry into this world and that soul has to ask your forgiveness for its not coming, and so leaving you with the grief and trauma in your life.'

His next instruction was that I should go to every shrine and temple I could find and do this the whole time I was in Japan. What he didn't tell me was that every street corner has a shrine to aborted or dead babies. Little stone models with knitted hats and socks, surrounded by little gifts and flowers, and even statues of the Buddha.

Well, even in my state of not being very physically mobile, I climbed every shrine on every street corner and begged forgiveness and had a weep and, I must admit, at the end of our three week visit I felt much better. My long-held feelings, which I had believed to be guilt, were in fact grief, and now this grief had been purged from my soul.

People in Japan work for the good of the whole and not for the individual and when I asked why so many people on the streets of the city of Tokyo wore masks I was told that if they have a cold or an illness it is better that they are uncomfortable rather than risk infecting others.

When we went to get on the train to travel to Hiroshima we had a small lady guide carrying a flag to help us with understanding and interpreting. She took us to a painted line on the platform and told us to get onto the train when it stopped and get off after so many stops. We were not sure if she was joking, but she certainly was not. The high speed Shinkansen train stopped within half an inch of the mark and people entered and exited simultaneously in seconds and yet in a calm and orderly manner. As we had awaited our guide in the station we looked down on the lower concourse. The noise was deafening as it was packed with hundreds of school children, different coloured uniforms denoting their different schools. They were excited, noisy and full of energy. I put my hands over my ears it was so loud. As the teachers wanted to catch the children's attention one of them stood up above the children and raised his hand in the air. It was like turning a switch, the response was immediate. Total silence. I know many teachers who would like to know how to make that technique work.

Land in Japan is at a premium and is sold by the tatami. The tatami is a measurement, a mat of 6ft by 3ft. Accommodation is sold or rented by the tatami, two, three, four or whatever measurement is appropriate. Families live together and sleep together in very small spaces. Hotel rooms can be rented by the hour to give couples privacy, which otherwise would be non existent.

Richard's cousin and husband were living in high luxury due to John's position with the Shell company. Our bedroom gave us an uninterrupted view of Mount Fuji, one of Japans holy mountains, just a small pyramid in the distance which belied its true size.

It was approaching Christmas and John and Rosemary hosted a Christmas luncheon for all the ladies of the Anglo-Japanese club The Elisabeth Kai group. Mrs Tattori, mother-in-law to Prince Takamodo, cousin of the Crown Prince sat next to Richard, along with Embassy wives and important Japanese ladies. The dining area seated at least fifty people for a full sit down meal and Richard was invited to take John's role of carving the turkeys. There were servants but servants in Japan, although the best in attending to your needs, are never subservient, they are your equal. It is a highly effective and pleasing way of working. None of the ladies would sit down, until Rosemary whispered in Richard's ear that until he sat down the ladies would remain standing. After the wonderful Christmas dinner was over, Richard entertained the ladies, a group of Japanese ladies took me up to the bedroom to dress me in a beautiful kimono. They decided it was essential that I knew how to put on a kimono correctly.

This took a very long time and they adjusted my attire with great enthusiasm, giggling and joking and joining me into their humour, despite the language restrictions. I have always had an affinity with Japan and I think this just accentuated it. Perhaps I had lived there in a previous life.

Our three week stay gave us a chance to visit, Mt Fuji, Kyoto, Nara, Hiroshima and the Peace Park. We attended functions with John and Rosemary and when asked where we lived we almost always had the reply,

'Oh, I know Machynlleth well.'

Part of our holiday included going to Hayama to John and Rosemary's weekend house. It was cold and snowy and the house was a typical beautiful Japanese design, wood built with 'pagoda' style roof. At bedtime the Houseman/Gardener stoked up the wood burning fire to heat the hot tub. Westerners are dirty! They get into the bath and soak for half an hour in their dirty water. The Japanese thoroughly wash or shower before getting into a bath or hot tub keeping the water clean. The hot tub was like a large copper pot, the kind cannibals cook explorers in! It was really hot and you climbed in and squatted down to cook, and that's really what it felt like. I was first and Richard banged on the wall to tell the man it was hot enough. It turned out we had the wrong signal so he kept on adding more wood and blazing it up hotter and hotter. When we came out we glowed, we were literally glowing red. The snow and frost could do its worst outside, we were generating our own central heating.

The bed was a futon rolled out on the living room floor, Japanese style. As I sat up in the cosy bedding, glowing with self generated heat it was like a fantasy world. The paper walls, small rectangles in wooden frames allowed the moonlight to penetrate and as Richard opened one of them it framed the ellipse of the moon against a solid black background. I gazed around the room at the Japanese furniture and the ikebana flower arrangement and sighed. It was almost as if I had returned home. The moon's light bathing everything in a tranquil, soul enveloping soft glow. This was one of the most profound experiences of my life. I slept long and deep, any pain subdued by the wonderful warmth that stayed with me through til morning.

What a great gift to be able to visit and stay with wonderful friends in a country that would normally have been inaccessible to us. Everything was written in Japanese, not like today where the English alphabet is used, and was totally indecipherable to non-Japanese speakers.

Down to earth and back to the children, Edward's birth was again unconventional. I saw the gynaecology doctor at the hospital; I was six months pregnant – being sick most of the time. After examination the doctor told me I was <u>three</u> months pregnant – the shock was tremendous. He said the first foetus had died and then I had become pregnant again without realizing it.

Well – three months later I was taken by ambulance to the hospital on a night when the snow was so bad that only emergencies were being attended. My notes would obviously say I was only six months – however two hours in hospital and the contractions stopped – home next day. One week later it all started again. On admission the midwife asked why was I so scared?

'I'm scared of it all stopping again.' Silly me – on came the enema. Edward was born thirteen hours later – again Richard was sent home an hour before his birth. The ward was so busy that two ladies had given birth in their beds. I eventually persuaded them that I would be the third if they didn't take notice and I at least made the delivery room just in time. He weighed 6lb 8oz.

After Anthony was born we had moved from the house we had built to a larger house in Wyke, a modern, detached house onto which Richard built a wonderful playroom for the boys. The house was one of several built in the grounds of a very large house occupied by a lovely Irish family with eleven children – ten boys and one girl. It was when we were living at this new house that Edward was born.

This was when I knew for certain that the Universe, 'the Management upstairs' a friend calls it, has a sense of humour. Why else would my all girl family and upbringing and schooling lead up to my being provided with three sons? In my experience the only way to cope is to acknowledge and return that sense of humour.

We had a large garden, which always seemed to be filled with children. Several of them owned large, shiny toy tractors, but these were often left standing in the drive at our front door neglected, as their owners joined our boys trailing large cardboard boxes hitched together with string behind a couple of less than perfect trikes.

One day, when Edward was a little under two years old, there must have been six or seven children playing in our garden. I was busy baking – a frequent occupation with so many hungry mouths to feed – when I noticed a constant traffic of children coming through the narrow kitchen to use the downstairs toilet. What was going on? I peered around the door and saw Anthony creeping upstairs. I followed.

The front door to the house had a flat roof area between the living room and the garage, with a support pole inset from the roof. To my horror, I watched as James, aged four, climbed out of the bedroom window on to the flat roof, leant over and grabbed the support pole and shimmied down the pole and Anthony, three, on the roof, pushed Edward, eighteen months, to be caught by James when he reached the ground. Then it was Anthony's turn to shimmy down the pole, fireman style and back to climb the five foot gate into the garden and start again. I put an immediate stop to this little game, while sending out a silent prayer thanking the family's guardian angels.

Chapter Nine

Greaves Farm – The Good Life

When Edward was two we moved house again. I had been looking in the newspaper and found an advert for a small-holding and converted farmhouse. When Richard came in from work I told him I had found our house. The one we had talked about and dreamed of before we were even married. An ideal home in which to bring up our family.

We went to view. It was a stone built, four square house with a barn attached. It comprised a family kitchen with Aga, boot room, dining/family room and lounge or 'Sunday' room. There were four bedrooms, three of which were only large enough for a single bed with fitted wardrobes between, not enough space to get untidy. A spacious bathroom completed an ideal family home.

The present farming owners were moving just a mile to a larger farm. We sold our modern detached house in Wyke at a good profit as the large family/playroom Richard had built on made it a very desirable property.

Outside, Greaves Farm had seven acres of sloping land with a stream running through. And just over the

__1__

hill, completely out of sight, the new M62 motorway was to be built, with the exit just a couple of miles away, so convenient for Richard to get to work in a much shorter time. We fell in love with it instantly, despite the fact that the view from the front of the house was obscured by several large, black wooden huts containing thousands of hens.

All we had to do was tell our parents. Richard and I both had parents who thought we were far too young to get married, let alone have children and make big decisions like this. So we had developed the habit of acting first and telling them later. It seemed to work.

We couldn't be happier. At last our dream was coming true. Our children would know what it's like to run with the wind in their hair and grass under their feet. They would learn how to nurture and love others in their care. Ponies; cats; dogs; chickens; ducks and hamsters and an aquarium of brightly coloured fish. Even week-old calves that we taught to suckle from buckets of prepared milk formula. The day the cow calved James came running in,

'Come quick the cow's had her baby and it's still in a plastic bag. She's trying to get it out.' My education as a 'townie' had not fully prepared me for such remarks.

I don't know how we found the time to do all the wonderful things that we did, but we did. That first year, with not a clue about gardening, we renovated a huge dilapidated old greenhouse.

As a family we cleaned it out, dug fresh soil and generally prepared it for its first crop of tomatoes in many years.

In our naiveté, we set off to purchase our tomato plants. The folks at the Garden Centre never said a word, but they must have wondered if we were about to go into competition with the big boys. Fifty plants we bought that day, then dutifully took them home and planted them. Disease? Pests? Special food and watering? We didn't have a clue, and ignorance is bliss.

How many people smiled and sniggered I wonder as I look back in retrospect? Our joy and the expectation of enough organically grown tomatoes to feed our family was all we knew.

Our crop flourished. Eat your heart out Jack and your puny beanstalk! However, as the weeks went by we realized how big our misjudgment had been. I ran out of people to give them to. Tomatoes filled the freezer. Bottled jars abounded and tomato soup became a thing of dread. Each week I would take buckets, filled to overflowing, to my Yoga teacher and classmates.

Alongside the overflowing greenhouse we grew potatoes, carrots, onions, cabbage, lettuce, radish, beetroot and more. Richard in his wisdom had laid out the rows with just enough space to rotovate between. Brilliant. Hardly any backbreaking weeding to do, just a quick run through with the old rotovator.

It was one of those times in life when the summers seem long, hot and sunny, filled with laughter and happiness. Picnic teas in the paddock field, days in the greenhouse composing poetry for a college project whilst gathering and tending those humungous tomatoes. Days surrounded by wildflowers while carving a plaster sculpture, discovering a piece of Ash when carved and chiseled with care, held an owl waiting to be released. This owl was one of my favourite works and I still stroke him and handle him and wonder how I came to release him from his imprisonment. I was lost in creativity until the boys came home from school, rushing through the gate laughing and clamouring for food and attention.

As I said when we moved in the view from the front of the house was blocked by large black hen houses, which had housed hundreds if not thousands of hens. These we demolished, we laid a circular drive around the old farm house and tidied a garden area. This consisted of lawn area and a small garden border. Neither of us were gardeners in the formal sense and wouldn't have had the time anyway as we were always extending, renovating, rebuilding, enhancing our home and surroundings.

Richard decided we needed a second vehicle, a run-about for dirty jobs and carrying building materials. At this time he was Production Director of a Jersey Fabric Production company and was provided with a car. A bright, canary yellow Triumph pi, top of the range car. A real male conversation piece. We found our second car, which of course would be 'mine', when it wasn't a work horse. It was a canvas backed, Mark I, double declutch, no heater Land Rover. It was the summer school holidays when Richard took the boys and me to pick it up. He left us and went on to work.

I had arranged to take the boys to Kilnsey Crag, North Yorkshire, a drive of approximately sixty miles, two hours drive on a hot, blue skied, sunny day to meet with a friend who was camping with her three sons. After the odd 'kangaroo petrol' jump start and the occasional crunching of gears, we arrived. We had an idyllic day – the six boys were in paradise, running, climbing, splashing in water and Megan and I sat, providing cold drinks and food and generally putting the world to rights. It was Megan's youngest who would count his fingers, 'one, two, free, pork pie' and to this day the family use it as a family joke. He came running in on one of their visits –

'James has …..' James always seemed to be singled out for trouble, and was developing quite a reputation. and as I began to chastise James, this little chap shouted,

'No, no, not that James, that James.' and he pointed at Anthony. I often wondered how often James had taken the blame before or even since. That day in the sun, was one of those lovely memories of carefree children, sun and laughter.

When it came to driving home I didn't change, I stayed in my bikini top and shorts and flicked my long hair behind my back.

After the first half hour of driving I realised what was happening was not a one off. Not just lorry drivers, but cars were stopping on roundabouts and road junctions to let me in. Mouth agape the drivers stared. Was it my young age, my bikini top, or a woman driving a Mark I Land Rover? I didn't care it was great fun. We sang all the way home, the boys buoyed up by their day and still full of fun and energy. Only in the colder, winter months did I come to hate its cold, rattly interior and its double declutch gears and the energy required to manoeuvre this heavy work horse. It really came to a head when I asked Richard what I might get him for Christmas.

'I've been thinking about that,' he said 'I'd like some sheepskin rugs for the front seats of my car. They'd look plush and really cool.' I'll tell you the polite version! I told him he could have his sheepskin rugs when the boys and I got a heater.

When Richard took on the milk round we changed the Land Rover for a VW campervan, bright orange, but a bargain is a bargain and colour choice didn't come into it. It meant that on the one day Richard wasn't up working at 4.00 am, we could set off and have a family day out, able to stop for a home cooked bacon and egg brunch and drinks and snacks on hand, keeping our costs to a minimum. We would visit Richard's Aunty Ida in Masham, North Yorkshire. She thought it was wonderful, to trip off for a picnic in our little home on wheels.

I remember living at Greaves Farm as a good time. Jillian and John and their three children were staying when the three children came running into the kitchen to say,

'Aunty Diana, come and look at James, he's like a monkey.' Jillian and I went out to see what the fun was all about. In the yard was a twenty foot tall scaffolding pole, it must have carried a phone line at some time, with a cross bar approximately eight inches long and six inches from the top. James was sitting astride this bar dangling his legs. He was around six at the time. I looked up,

'Oh, yes, I'll go and make a drink and a biscuit for everyone if you'd all like that.' I turned on my heels and went indoors, Jillian following.

'How do you keep so calm?' she asked.

'I don't,' and I held out my shaking hands. 'Put the kettle on, Jillian.' And I promptly sat down.

I knew if I had reacted any other way there was a chance he would fall, I had no option but to pretend it was normal and I was unfazed or what would he do next to get a reaction? A few minutes later the children all came in for their drinks and the episode was not repeated – that weekend Richard sawed the pole off at its base.

Jillian's Labrador had lost a front leg and coped remarkably well on the three he had left. One morning a neighbour was found banging on the back door.

'There's a dead dog in your field, a beautiful golden Labrador.' As she spoke our black Labrador came to the door. He was wearing a large vet's head collar, to stop him chewing his tail. The 'dead' Labrador then walked up behind her. I thought she would faint, but she listened patiently, even a little confusedly, as Jillian explained that when he was tired he just collapsed until he recovered enough energy to continue home. Poor lady, but then again what a lovely story to tell and retell her neighbours.

It wasn't long after this that some other 'friends' came to visit. Their boys were older and were using the home made go-kart faster than it was designed to go. Down the hill they would race from the back of the barn, round the ninety degree bend, and on down the drive to the closed gate at the end. Unfortunately one of the boys crashed into James as he walked back up the hill. He somehow struggled back home. He was a sickly shade of green. I laid him on the sofa and tried to put a blanket over him, but he was hysterical at the thought. My 'friend' and her husband responded to my suggestion of hospital with,

'Oh my God, stop fussing. Anyone can tell he is just after attention. Leave him be, he'll soon be up and playing when he realises we aren't fooled.' Richard dispatched them politely but quickly, saying we had had a good day so far and it was a good time to end. When they had gone we got James into the car and off to the hospital, where they encased his leg in plaster for a nasty fracture.

I loved the school holidays; my friends moaned about when could they get their kids back to school. Why have children if you can't spare the time and attention to enjoy them? We had rolls of scrap wallpaper, drew round their bodies and painted clothes, added hair, buttons, shoe laces. We painted a huge tree and stuck on autumn leaves and seeds, made papier mache hedgehogs with cut off straws for spikes and I left them to climb and swing on a rope ladder, chase chickens and catch tiddlers in the small stream.

Pony riding was more time consuming and took a little more fitting into an already full programme, but grooming and brushing were still a pleasurable occupation.

We spent many of our weekends preparing our two Blue Cross ponies for shows – washing, grooming, and loading on and off – and we were successful, winning many prizes. Naiveté again! It was our greatest weapon.

Our animals included a Jack Russell terrier, docile and no trouble at all. Until one day I read about a dog with ingrown eyelashes and decided that our dog had this problem, too. Off we went to the vet, who groaned and complained,

'Not another one! Those James Herriot books should be banned.' However, on closer examination he declared our Jack Russell to have the worst case of ingrown eyelashes he had ever seen.

The vet operated and we took the dog home. He took one look down the field across the stream to the opposite field and shot off like a rocket. Before anyone could stop him he had killed six of our neighbour's hens. Needless to say we had to find a new home for him straight away. It was him or ostrasization from our neighbours. We could not risk having to replace hens, ours or others, every time he went outside.

Richard left for work at 7.30 am and didn't return until somewhere between 7.00 pm and 9.00 pm so weekends were precious.

Aunty Ida was a great encouragement and one visit the boys went ready for a fancy dress competition. Edward was Liberace, wearing a black riding jacket, white shirt and jodhpurs, paper doilies tucked into his cuffs and at his neckline, finishing his ensemble. His piano was made out of a cardboard box with a string around his neck. Anthony had sprained his ankle so he had to think again, with a crutch, a 'peg leg' and a spotted kerchief and eye patch he made a perfect pirate, his elaborately drawn parrot on his shoulder was a masterpiece. James was dressed up again in black jacket and jodhpurs, bow tie and white shirt. He had drawn and coloured an 18 inch tall bulldog taped to a stick so that it 'walked' alongside him. He was the British Bulldog, the Winston Churchill. I can't remember if they won anything, it was the fun of making their entries and the taking part that was so important.

For a time while we were at Greaves Farm and before I attended college we fostered children. Just short-term, whilst their mother produced yet another often unwanted child or faced short, sharp shock therapy with two weeks in jail.

I remember our first foster child, Joanna, blonde, blue-eyed and angelic looking. Joanna arrived with the Social Services worker, she was dressed in a smart wool duffle coat and wellingtons – provided by Social Services I soon realized. Upon removing the coat and wellingtons I found a five-year-old dressed in a shabby skirt and blouse two sizes too big. One man's grey, woollen sock and one white sock possibly meant for a three-year-old. The vest and pants so small, so grimy, that it looked as if they had been growing along with her for the past two years. She smiled up at me and revealed a row of decayed milk teeth.

Joanna stayed with us for six weeks. Social Services had assured us that children's foster homes were kept strictly confidential and yet she was forcibly removed by mother and boyfriend at 11 o'clock one cold and rainy night. Richard was out and I was alone with the children when an abusive, drunken man stormed through our home looking for his girlfriend's child. After more than thirty years, I still send this child love and blessings and hope she came through those difficult beginnings.

She didn't understand that when we went shopping, we all went shopping. One day she wouldn't put her coat on and when I asked her why her reply left me aching inside,

'Me?' was her reply, 'but I don't go shoppin. I 'ave to stay 'ome and look after't baby. I din't think I could come.'

My Mother-in-Law, was a lady of definite circumstances, and was insisting that Joanna should do a particular thing in a particular way. Joanna could see no sense. Mother-in-Law persisted.

'F... off' replied Joanna succinctly. I did attempt to explain that the child had no idea that this was anything other than normal language and had not meant to offend. To no avail I fear, and dear Mother-in-Law was more than happy when my energies were directed into the much more acceptable profession of teaching.

Chapter Ten

Disaster! – Enforced Lifestyle Change

So here we are, living in our dream home. A smallholding to compete with the television series The Good Life popular at that time, with three happy, healthy young boys. I was thoroughly enjoying my time at College and there wasn't a cloud on the horizon. That is unless you counted the problems facing the textile industry in West Yorkshire.

Richard would come home with news of more redundancies, unhappy because he, as the Production Director, had to tell the unfortunate employees they no longer had a job.

'I feel like leaving myself!' he said, angry at the way the whole thing was being handled. I persuaded him to stay until he had an alternative and he gritted his teeth, and hung on.

I was doing well at College. I had just taken the first of two A levels and was scheduled to take the second the next day. Richard was going to be home early to be with the boys, a special event. The two A levels were needed to qualify to continue the Certificate of Education for teaching which I was engaged in, for those students commencing the course the following year these A levels would be needed to turn it into a degree qualification. I was happy to be in the final year that Teaching qualifications would be allowed without the extra year to incorporate the degree.

After taking the first exam I drove home, up the long drive flanked on one side by a row of Yorkshire stone terraced houses and on the other side by one of our fields. Our smallest pony, in the guise of a female Thelwell, and her foal, were grazing. I could see Richard with a scythe slashing the long grass for haymaking in the far field. There was something about the way he held himself, something, a distinct aura around him that made my heart miss a beat, I felt something dreadful had happened. My first thought was for parents. I could see the children clearly playing and unperturbed by events as yet unknown.

I jumped out of the car and we ran to each other – in slow motion as in a film – and stood hugging each other. I'll never forget the look in his proud but uncomprehending eyes.

'I've been home since lunch-time. I don't have a job anymore. I'm redundant.'

The textile industry was in general decline and we knew in our hearts that many companies were living on borrowed time but it's never going to happen to you is it?

We ate supper, bathed the children and put them to bed maintaining as normal an atmosphere as possible whilst our minds raced with unanswered questions. What will we do? How will we cope? What about bills? A new career? The children? Our wonderful life and home? Most people live to their income level and above, and we were no exception.

The following morning, I left for my second exam, leaving Richard with at least something to occupy his mind – three very active youngsters to get to school. I sat in the exam room gazing at my question paper. Some question about the life of Picasso and how I could prove the points I was supposed to be about to make.

I looked around at my colleagues. My friend Rona was two ahead and to my right. I smiled. 'Laurel and Hardy'. She was tall, taller than me at my five feet six inches and must have weighed seventeen stone to my seven. Yet we forged an immediate friendship and were always to be seen together – the short and the tall, the large and the small. Head down, scribbling, scribbling. What could she find to write about? Where was I? Oh yes, Picasso. Picasso? Picasso? My husband's redundant! Where is our next pay packet coming from? Picasso? Where will Picasso be tomorrow? Where will we be tomorrow? Picasso – arms and legs, eyes and noses, all in the wrong places. That's how I felt. How would we maintain our home, the mortgage, the electric bill, the food bills? How could we afford to re-shoe the boys for goodness sake?

I looked down at my answer paper – five lines of writing. Rubbish! What would my ideas on Picasso matter tomorrow? My husband was at home and he needed me.

My chair screeched, that ear-splitting screech that chairs make when they are supposed to be still and silent. I rose, picked up my paper and walked to the front of the room. My colleagues' eyes seemed to burn into my back as I deposited my paper on the adjudicator's desk. I opened the door and left. Richard was waiting for me, expecting me. Our communication channel was open as usual.

Ten days of hell followed. I was affected by getting up every morning, putting on my best clothes, fixing my hair and makeup and striding, head tall out into the world.

No-one was going to feel sorry for <u>me</u>. No-one was going to see the hurt, and panic and insecurity that gnawed at my solar plexus. Richard was affected differently. He was lethargic, he wouldn't or couldn't wash or shave. He sat dejected, desperately hurt. His pride, his ambition, the whole meaning of his life shattered, no longer able to provide for his life's work – his family.

Ten days it took. Ten long days. I stood over Richard and shouted at him. Told him he was a dirty, disgusting shell of his former self. He had hidden long enough and it was time to come out and be counted again. He shouted back. How could I float about like Lady Muck, as though nothing was amiss? Didn't I realise the significance, the seriousness and consequences of what had happened?

We collapsed into each others arms and grieved. Grieved for what had been. Our decision was made. Maintain our home – a basis of stability for the family. Our priority had to be the boys, stability and continuity of home would help alleviate any other problems.

Six weeks later Richard bought a milkround, using the small redundancy payment that just covered the purchase. In the north the goodwill and address book of a milkround could be purchased as a business. No dole money was forthcoming as he had found a job too quickly.

The vehicle used for milk delivery was a two-ton Bedford flat back. He started work at 4.00 am and from 6.30 am on he was joined by three teenage boys, who helped deliver the rest of the milk.

He enjoyed these times. Each day they would have a new word to see how many times they could use it throughout the morning. Redundant was never one of Richard's favourites, but abundance was! Occasionally, however a major problem would arise. Richard would reach to turn his cab light on and bang, his back would go. He would experience excruciating pain and an inability to do anything physical for two or three days. If it was during the week we had a problem, weekend less so. Children would be farmed out and I would take over the driving – Richard sat huddled in the corner of the cab popping distalgesic. Sometimes James and Anthony would come along to collect money or help deliver but Edward was always left behind with Granny, too young to be allowed this 'treat'. Even now he tells the story of his jealousy and sense of unfairness. The other two had to be awoken, whilst he was sitting on the staircase, wide eyed, eager and rejected!

One evening in deep snow, we were trying to finish the Christmas morning delivery on Christmas Eve so we could have a real uninterrupted Christmas morning, I was out there, wrapped up like an Eskimo. I ran down a hillside between two blocks of flats. Unbeknown to me a low, knee high, wire fence crossed this area hidden beneath the snow. Woof, two hand held, ten-bottle milk carriers went up in the air and over as my legs tried to follow. I clung on to my cargo regardless and snowballed down the hill. I lay, exhausted but hysterical with laughter until Richard tried to pick me up. My kneecaps must have been the height of the wire and now I knew what it meant to be 'cut off at the knees'.

Richard's mother was forever sending us newspaper advertisements for 'tea boys' in the woollen industry, when he was, of course, still looking for a corporate position. One day he came across an advertisement for a job in Lima, Peru. Now didn't that sound wonderful! What an adventure and what a great opportunity for the children to learn and grow. Not that he stood a chance of getting, it, of course, but he applied, nonetheless.

The job on offer was with the Office of Overseas Development, working with the government of Peru. A two year contract liaising between Technical Colleges and Universities on the one hand, and factories and businesses on the other, to make sure the teaching and requirements of each were fully accessible to both parties.

We were amazed and excited when a letter arrived inviting Richard to attend for an interview, with a three day trip to London, all expenses paid. Such a treat for us both and we enjoyed that special time together very much. Richard was applicant number 303 so we didn't expect anything to come of it and went home to await the letter informing us that he was not the chosen one. How wrong we were.

Richard got a second interview, but even so, when the letter came offering him the position, we were stunned. Our plans were quickly set in motion. I had a Spanish 'O' level which obviously needed to be brushed up and Richard was to attend a three week intensive crammer course so that he would be fluent enough to cope with the language demands of the job.

It was arranged that I could return to college to complete my Teacher Training course when we returned from Peru, and in the meantime I was assured I could easily get a job teaching English as a foreign language.

The advisors said we should let our home rather than sell it. We found a tenant and Richard found a buyer for his milk round. Toys, books, ornaments etc were all boxed up waiting to go into storage. Four weeks to go – three of these Richard's language course.

Then – our plans were shattered. A letter came in the post to inform Richard that the position was no longer available. The heading for the letter was 'Position for the Indonesian Government and Industry'. It seemed most peculiar, so Richard rang to find out what it meant. Apparently, it was so rare for a Government to retract that they only had one other record of its happening. The typist had picked up this letter – retyped and sent it out forgetting to change the heading to Government of Peru. This threw us completely – another sweet carrot whipped away. What would we do now?

We picked ourselves up, put on our thinking caps. We would run a Caravan Park. No more producing what the Salesmen couldn't sell, no more making money for someone else, just a quiet life in the country dealing with happy people on holiday. I would teach and Richard would drive the school bus and run the Caravan Park. Silly dreams. Pie in the sky. How could we afford even to think this way?

Some eighteen months later we entered into negotiations to buy a Caravan Park on the South West coastline of Wales.

The owner selling the Caravan Park had a minor disability – his tongue was split at the tip into a distinct fork. We actually joked, saying we hoped he didn't really 'speak with forked tongue'. Unfortunately, he did.

On a sunny blue skied morning, the children at school, and a morning when I was not required to attend lectures at the Teacher Training course for mature students, and Richard was home from delivering his one hundred and fifty gallons of milk, we were lying together in our bed. The bliss of lovemaking enveloped us. The 'phone rang. Richard said,

'This is to confirm the signed contracts have been exchanged and received.' No – yet again a hiccup in our dreams. It was our 'forked tongue' friend, suggesting he had another buyer and if we still wished to purchase the price had gone up by a quarter. To this day we have never found anything, not even the proverbial bucket of cold water, so immediate as to cool the desires of the flesh.

We walked around in a daze for a few days, wondering why we should have come so close, only to have it snatched away when we thought our plans and ambitions were coming to fruition. This had happened two many times in the last few years and was no longer something to laugh at, forget and move on. We were depressed. What did the future hold for us? Richard couldn't go on for the rest of his life getting up at 4.00 am to deliver one hundred and fifty gallons of milk. It had been a stop gap, a gathering of funds, ideas, energies. This would give time for me to qualify as a teacher in order to have another string to our bow.

Relax – we said, go with it – we said. Richard's dear Aunty Ida said,

'God must have something else in mind for you, dears.' No doubt, but did he have to keep dangling these carrots in front of our noses and snatching them away as we were about to bite?

We had thought that going from a senior management position in textiles to the income of a lowly milkman, would curtail our lifestyle – not that it was ever extravagant, we had and still have the knack of getting value for money – but found very quickly our thoughts had been misconception. We had not taken a dramatic drop in income, only a dramatic change in the way the income was earned.

Richard had been a rather shy person, in the sense that communication with strangers made him nervous so that he developed what my mother had called, when she first met him, 'a slight speech impediment', to my mind a slight, rather endearing, nervous lisp. Meeting people in many different states of attire, some more flimsy and revealing than I might have wished, when he called for payment, soon educated him into his now normal, relaxed and easy charm and manner that take him anywhere.

A holiday, that's what we needed. The boys also needed a break. Children are very sensitive, they knew some great happening, some great upheaval had taken place in their parents lives just two years earlier. James was nine years old, Anthony eight and Edward just six.

This brings us to St Ives. It was wonderful weather but a long drive from Yorkshire with three young children and all the packing. Eight hours confined to a car is not always an auspicious start. We all, however, seemed to understand what this holiday was about. Sun, fun and the old adage the family that plays together stays together.

One morning, the boys dashing around, in, out, up and down the small holiday cabin, we decided exercise was obviously on the agenda. First a swim and then off to the town we would go to collect fresh bread and milk. The swim was more than we had bargained for. I had always had a fear of water having nearly drowned and experienced a near death experience when I was seven. This meant that I was always to be found where my feet could touch the bottom. The boys had worked out that if they shouted,

'Mum, you're out of your depth.' I would respond with much flapping and spluttering.

Richard and the boys were racing and splashing, my priority had been to teach them to swim without fear at a very early age. I was being ladylike and subdued at the shallow end. It was an outdoor pool and very busy. I looked down. What was that on the bottom? A piece of clothing? A burst ball? Oh, my God – a child, lying on the bottom of a pool 3 feet 6 inches deep. Where would I get the courage to go down there? I ducked and grabbed. Nothing. I screamed at Richard as he approached and ducked and grabbed again. I shouted and screamed at Richard again above the noise and clamour and he swam over as he realised what my frantic gesticulations were conveying. Down he went and with one hand had the strength to haul the child out and onto the side of the pool.

He lay on his stomach, a child of about ten, coughing and spluttering water. As he recovered we sat him up and I sat with a towel and my arm around him. His parents needed to know and Richard was making enquiries. A man came dashing across and we quickly explained what had happened and that perhaps a hospital check would be in order. The man reached down to the child, for a hug I thought. As he reached the child he slapped him around his shoulders and dragged him to his feet.

'You stupid little b….., thick as two short planks. What do you go an' do that for? Get home to your mother quick, she'll have a slap for you too.' It doesn't sound humourous but our faces must have been a picture.

It took a few minutes to gather our wits and realise what had happened. We laughed more in relief than amusement.

St Ives is a pretty place, we wandered down the street licking ice-creams and feeling the sun dry our hair. We walked passed an Estate Agents. We were always interested in house prices, house designs and other areas, so we stopped to look. Lots of places for sale. What was this though? Caravan park – mid-Wales, potential for new owner. We looked at each other – not many Caravan Parks came in a price range we could consider. This we could at least consider.

A Welsh cottage, ten acres, a river, and thirty nine caravans? We couldn't get through the Agent's door fast enough. Suitably equipped with our precious information we returned to our holiday cabin.

In my usual debate with myself I thought it would be awful, No it wouldn't. It would be dilapidated. No, it wouldn't. We wouldn't be able to get a mortgage. Well, not without trying anyway. It would be sold. Why was it being advertised, then? The questions kept coming into the small hours. What was I doing, torturing myself this way? Something was going on here. Yorkshire folks on holiday visiting Cornwall and finding property in Wales. It all seemed a bit strange. All we could do was go to visit when our holiday was over.

Our holiday was soon over. Richard back to his 4.00 am starts and me back to college, the boys back to the routine of school. Our social life was non existent, 8.30 pm found Richard nodding and snoring somewhere in a quiet or even a noisy corner come to think of it.

Chapter Eleven

The Garth – A New Beginning in Wales

Richard continued to be a Milkman until I qualified in 1977 when we had discovered the Garth Caravan Park in Wales. We set off to visit – with all our camping equipment, three sons aged eleven, nine and seven, a niece Kathryn aged about twelve and a Labrador dog called Sandy, all packed into an old Peugeot estate. I had the flu and the curse.

Richard set off with the children for a walk, having first boiled a kettle on the primus to make me a hot water bottle, and then visited the local pub to bring me back a double brandy! Cloud nine. I slept all night, despite the boisterous, excitable kids who were over the moon with such an adventure.

'Mummy, I'm so full of laughter I don't know what to do with myself!' said Edward at one point.

We went to view the Garth next morning. Bear in mind how hard we had worked at Greaves Farm, moving the hen huts, creating the garden, the vegetable garden and paddock, turning the upstairs area of the barn into a fabulous 24ft x 14 ft playroom, complete with rope swing and billiard table. Now that was a game of skill as the slate bed was warped and it balanced on a single bed!

We arrived at The Garth in radiant sunshine, brilliant blue skies and not a cloud in sight. It was paradise. Like fairyland, in fact. The owner was infatuated with Italy and had built several miniature buildings, none more than 8 feet tall. There was a church, a Rapunzel tower complete with internal staircase and castellated top, and many more smaller structures all on an Italian theme.

The cottage that went with the Park had once been two separate dwellings, one for each of the two water bailiffs working for the Londonderry Estate. They had been turned into one by breaking through the 3 foot adjoining wall. Staircases in both cottages had been left in situ, so there were four staircases in total in the three storey home. The bathroom was a lean to on the back of the house with a huge electric boiler to heat the water for the large bath. The bath was positioned on the 'outside' wall, which was bright pink, gloss painted and sloped at a steep angle from the roof (can't call it a ceiling!) The answer regarding this pink wall was that this was the bedrock of the hillside. We must never leave the plug in the bath as when it rained it came pouring through the bedrock wall! The living room was packed with ornaments and bits and pieces, glass, silver and all this immaculate. Not a speck of dust in sight. Muriel kept this amazing house like a show piece, they obviously both loved it and cherished it. Oh, I forgot to mention, the toilet was another lean to on the bathroom, this with a leaking roof, but it did have the advantage that if you left the door open you could sit in a state of contemplation with the most fantastic view. Mark, the owner was a fantastic character, it turned out he with his wife Muriel, had moved from the south twenty-five years earlier when he was diagnosed with tuberculosis and one year to live. They came to Garth, kept chickens and built up a small museum – including a special building made of chicken wire and cement with an incredible relief map of Wales on the floor – some 15 x 30 feet in size.

After a full inspection and many queries we found there were thirty-nine caravans, only one of which was connected to water, none of which were connected to the septic tank. The toilet block was built of home made concrete blocks with six toilets, six wash basins and a separate shower for the ladies, four toilets, four urinals and a separate shower for the men. The cleaning of these was to become my full time job during the holiday season, using up to twenty-four toilet rolls in one day and necessitating cleaning three times a day. It was quite a social whirl in the morning between 9.00 and 10.00 am as everyone met up for a gossip.

We left our inspection visit and drove to the coast to give the children some time on the beach. All the way there I kept saying to Richard,

'You can't expect me to leave my beautiful home to come to something so basic – but it was beautiful – it wasn't real – all it needed was Alice in Wonderland or the seven dwarfs and we'd have fallen down the rabbit hole. But it was beautiful! Yes, but what about in the rain it'll be awful. But then I suppose if we took out two of the staircases and redid the bathroom. No, I can't live there when I think of my beautiful home.' This verbal assault of mine went on for some time. Richard allowed my one sided tirade.

We went for another look and decided I needed to see it in the rain. It wouldn't look so paradisiacal then, I was sure. Some few days to think, talk pros and cons, check out the finances and make some very profound decisions for our future and the future of our children.

Several days later we went back in the torrential rain. It was abysmal and I was wrong, the Park was just as enchanting in the rain.

We checked out schools, the local hospital, A & E being an essential requisite. The Garth was one and a quarter miles from all the amenities and yet in a hidden valley accessed by a single track lane.

We were hooked. If truth be told, we had fallen in love by our very first glimpse of the property. Now it was time to see if we could make this work financially.

Of course it was a wrench to leave Greaves Farm. We had been so very happy there, and we had turned our home into a wonderful home compared to what we would be moving into. But the decision was made and Richard sold his milkround and I completed my Certificate of Education. On signing the purchase documents, we left the solicitors with only a couple of pounds, literally, in our pockets and a very large debt.

One of my sisters is married to a solicitor and Richard's sister is married to an accountant. We couldn't go wrong could we? We also had a friendly Bank Manager, who perused the necessary documents and said,

'Let's give it a whirl.' It took a moment or two before Richard and I realized that he meant,

'You've got your loan.'

We sold Greaves Farm at auction as we couldn't risk waiting for the normal selling route, or risk the need for a bridging loan.

Mark and Muriel allowed us to have the keys almost immediately before full completion – what a way to do business – as they had found another home and wanted to move out before the winter fully took hold.

When we arrived in Wales the local Bank Manager disputed our loan as the place wasn't worth a fig in his opinion and he knocked off a tenth of the original loan. That left us really tight and certainly nothing to do up the cottage with.

My cousin ran a business supplying to Bradford market, some of our land was covered in Christmas trees Mark had planted years before. So when Richard got the idea to harvest the trees before Christmas and before we owned the place (but with Mark's permission) it was a lifesaver. A wagon was hired and Richard cut and shipped the trees back to Bradford. One thousand of them at £1 a piece. What a windfall. Without this we would have been in real trouble.

We moved on January 1st 1978 in sleet and hail – using a rental lorry. The ponies we left at home awaiting our return and the new owners of Greaves Farm kept the chickens to avoid having to move them. It was hard work driving four hours, offloading and four hours back only to find someone had opened the gate to the field letting the ponies out. So the next two hours were spent catching and returning the ponies. The next day we took the ponies to Wales and prepared the caravan ready to live.

We had decided that we would give the house a coat of emulsion throughout, as once the house was empty it really did need some attention. The old horsehair and lathe plasterwork left it looking in need of a face lift. How Muriel had kept it looking so pristine I will never know.

All was now in Wales – we settled into the static caravan, Richard plumbed it in and we at least had running water and electric. Five of us, a dog, a cat and three hamsters. It was an exercise in time and motion study getting everyone up, washed, fed and off to school. Looking back it was only to be expected that our health would be affected. We were all suffering from various strengths of bronchitis. Each week I turned the mattresses on the beds – this week when I turned them they were sitting in four inches of water. The condensation was pouring off the windows and doors and living in a tin box in the depths of winter was not a sensible idea. Using bottled gas aggravated the situation as each blue bottle contains approx eight pints of water which evaporates into the air as the gas is burned.

We gave the top storey bedroom in the cottage a coat of white emulsion. As the cottage had no heating the condensation was slightly less, so to avoid any problem we pushed the beds together in the middle of the room, climbing over each other to get to our own sleeping quarters like a large raft adrift in the sea.

We fitted some Economy 7 night storage heaters (to be paid for in installments on the electric bill) and things seemed a little brighter. The fireplace in the living room, although we had plenty of wood, was a tiny affair and the logs had to be cut and prepared accordingly. Burning wood warms you three times they say – once when you cut it, once when you split and once when you burn it. After a time we did fit a fantastic wood burning stove as finances were side tracked into what was most important.

Now to the kitchen – on the wall was a water heater – (the only supply of water to the main house area was one cold water tap situated in the kitchen) the kind you find in an office holding approximately six pints and used for making tea or coffee instead of the smaller normal kettle. The spout or arm from this was too long to fit into the sink and any water from this was left to be caught in mid air. The sink was the original stone sink and measured approx 8in x 12in. The only washing up bowl that would fit, which Muriel had kindly left behind, was a child's potty.

You had to manoeuvre the potty into position, turn on the tap, catch the hot water and turn off the tap, putting the potty in the sink – all without spilling a drop – if you could have done that you were a better man than I.

As half term came our friends Carrie and John and their three children came to stay. John's electrical knowledge was going to help us with extra plugs etc. Six children, four adults and all the pets – in very basic surroundings to say the least. The children were running about giggling, the taps were tickly. We adults could not feel anything and thought it was just a joke. Until I made a fruit jelly for tea that is. I bent down to put the jelly in the fridge and spilt some onto the slate floor – as I mopped it up with the floor cloth I ran my hand close to and under the fridge to soak up the liquid. Bam, like a mini lightening strike, I received an electric shock. John immediately rang the Electricity Board – on a Sunday – they came straight out.

When we knew we were moving and would have no income for three months we had bought in bulk the essential necessities, a 56 lb sack of wholemeal flour and of potatoes; a catering box – 25 lbs of cornflakes; 15 lbs of porridge oats, sugar, tea, coffee; items for cooking, cornflour, gravy browning, dried onions, beans, anything that would keep our expenditure down in those first months of having no income.

A thirteen cubic metre freezer was packed with home grown fruit and vegis. Our only income was the family allowance – at that time £4 per week – this purchased a pound of sausage, a pound of mince and a large 'free' marrow bone for soups and stocks and to keep the dog happy.

The Manweb electrician made his inspection – we had no earth and the electricity was running reverse polarity around the house. He had no option but to cut off our supply. I burst into tears – how was I to feed my family if he cut off the supply to the freezer? He reluctantly relented on the condition that no electric appliances were used, including the vacuum! as he looked at me over his glasses, or the freezer opened until they came to rectify the life threatening situation. It was agreed that yet again this rewiring of the whole house could go on to the electric bill as we could not possibly have afforded it otherwise. They came a couple of restless days later – fortunately the cooker was run on bottled gas.

As we returned to life with electricity we could relax a little. By this time Richard had a job. He drove the minibus to collect the children from outlying villages and farms and then returned them home after school. Five days a week – the wage for which was £3, in fact not paid in cash but in fuel. We could now save up our fuel supply and go off shopping or even back to parents in Yorkshire, if we saved enough. During these settling in months we had visits from both our parents, who came bearing gifts of food, perhaps a chicken or joint of meat, what luxury.

Richard's Aunty Ida wrote frequently and would occasionally include a £5 note (a fortune, our only income being the Family Allowance) always coinciding with a time when things were really tight. It was when she was staying that I attended an interview for a part time job at the local High School, teaching typing and Business Studies. She coached me and encouraged me and off I went.

There were eight applicants for the position and my Welsh, although more than when I arrived, was very basic. I only went for the interview experience and the fact that I could not get a job in Infant/Junior without being fluent in Welsh. To my astonishment I was offered the post. Apparently it was almost unheard of to find someone with Secretarial and Teaching qualifications.

This was embarrassing as I hadn't told them I would be away for three weeks in November. They sent me away to wait and I truly thought I had blown it. However they called me back in and said they would allow the three week absence and the job was mine. I was ecstatic, part time, teaching and less than two miles away. This would make such a difference to our income.

Richard had also acquired another job, as a Retained Firemen. He had to undergo strenuous training and be available on call twenty four hours a day, seven days a week. We decided straight away that my income would cover the housekeeping and Richard's would cover unexpected bills and now even holidays. The early spring and summer had seen the sale of caravans take off. We had worked tremendously hard and our financial situation was much more stable. Originally we had worked out that we would never make our fortunes but nor would we go bankrupt, if we ran the business sensibly.

The land where we had cut the trees came under the original planning permission for the Caravan Park and therefore could be used for extra caravans to enlarge the site. However the planners disagreed about these extra caravan pitches and would not allow them. Only after a big struggle and Martyn's intervention in his role as Solicitor did they succumb and admit their error.

In fact we did have permission, we only needed to tell them of the change of use from agriculture to caravans. Thanks to Martyn's intervention we gained fourteen caravan pitches. As we sold them our bank balance began to look healthier. We had a choice Richard said, we could either build a new shower/bathroom or have a holiday. The choice goes without saying – what's life if it's not an adventure – we chose the holiday.

When the electric had been disconnected, the only thing that we were not allowed to reconnect was the large boiler that heated the water for the bath. Once a week we brought an old tin bath into the living room, filled from boiling pans of water which took a long time, and took it in turns, youngest first. Friday night was bath night!

There was no television reception at the cottage, so when the TV licence van arrived we could cheerfully show him our old TV wrapped in a blanket on top of the wardrobe, facing the wall. Entertainment therefore was all up to us. Each evening before bedtime we would gather round the log fire (you needed to be close to feel the heat from such a small fireplace) and take it in turns to read from 'The Borrowers'. We talked as a family, what had happened for each of us during our day, about the past, present and future. It was great family therapy. One week Granny and Grandpa Smithies were staying, which made the circle round the fire even tighter. The Borrowers was put to one side until the boys mentioned it. Granny and Grandpa were keen to join in and the story could continue its way. Other pastimes included jigsaws, games and knitting, all to keep idle fingers busy in the cold wet winter. Knitting produced scarves, pompom hats and some rather strange shapes.

Often there would be a Dawnsio Werin or Twmpath arranged by a good friend. An evening of Welsh country dancing, good company, energetic excercise and good food.

I was vegetarian and usually cooked for Richard and the boys with me using the same vegetables but a vegetarian home made alternative to their meat. Once a week, however we all ate vegetarian. A delicious five bean casserole with mushrooms creating a thick, rich gravy was a favourite. The boys would come home from school,

'What's for tea?' they would enquire.

'Bean stew.' I would answer.

'We know it's been stew, but what is it now?' came the cheeky reply.

When we first arrived at the Garth I wanted to continue to keep hens. They are a good supplement to the income and always clucking happily, they make you smile. A farmer was advertising hens due to his closing down. We went along to purchase – not his biggest order – just twelve. The boys were let loose in the barn where the hens had been released from their cages, as these too were to be sold. The hens were quite bald, not a feather in sight. These poor pathetic creatures were herded up and dropped into cardboard boxes as the farmer sealed them and kept a tally.

'Pay my wife at the office.' The farmer said. This was the embarrassing bit. We didn't have any income as previously stated but we did have the float bag from Richard's milk round. Half pence, one pence, two pence and the highest denomination, five pence.

I proceeded to count these coins out until we had acquired the correct amount. The farmer's wife did not see the funny side of it and was quite grumpy about the transaction. We all piled into the old Peugeot estate, happy and cheerful with our acquisitions. Richard started the car ready to leave when the farmer's wife appeared at the passenger window.

'You overpaid.' She said sarcastically and pressed a half pence into my hand and turned on her heels.

We laughed all the way home. The hens new home was the old pigsty, cleaned and made ready for their arrival. As we counted them out we found we had thirteen! We kept the hens inside for a week which is normal practice, for them to become accustomed to their new home. However even then they did not return home as they usually would when it got dark, I think they were too thrilled with the great outdoors. There was nothing for it, to catch them or leave them for the fox.

I ran down a banking to catch one, only to find I had sunk up to my knees. Although grassed over, this area had been where Mark had tipped the hen manure over the last twenty five years.

I don't know how they got me out, most of their effort went into being bent double with side-splitting laughter. My wellingtons fared less well. Thirty years later they remain buried in a twenty foot pile of hen manure. Perhaps they will appear on a Time Watch programme in years to come. The hens, with our tender loving care grew back their feathers and became great layers.

Once we had sorted the Planners with regard to the extra area for caravans, we had to site them. Our old Peugeot estate had a tow bar on the back and on the front. Richard tied a rope to the front tow bar and attached this to the caravan. He manoeuvered the caravan by hand as I gently and slowly drove the car forwards with great trepidation and fears for Richard's safety, lowering the caravan into position. The caravans had a habit of 'crabbing', moving sideways, making it extremely difficult and hard physical work to move them across the hillside into position ready to be fitted to water, electric and sewage.

For many years Richard's main topic of conversation was septic tanks. When James' and Mandy's son, our grandson, Arron came to stay at the age of about ten, he would continuously talk about taking over the Caravan Park when Grandpa retired, and as his Dad was the eldest son he didn't see why it shouldn't miss a generation. That is until one bright sunny day. A man-hole lid was sitting on a two foot pillar of human excrement – why was it always just before Sunday lunch was served that this happened. There was a blockage, the pump wasn't working, Grandpa and Arron were dispatched to sort out the problem. The lid of the septic tank was removed and Grandpa went down to find the fault. He found it alright and as he did the pump began to work. He came out of there covered, just his eyeballs showing. Not surprisingly Arron was less keen on his future employment than he had been.

When the boys were young and I wanted them to return for meals or homework I had an old fashioned school bell that I would ring. James, who would be thirteen, responded and came trundling up the track with a fishing hook embedded in his forehead and a large fat worm dangling down in front of his glasses. A trip to the local hospital followed where the Doctor on duty removed the offending item and gave him a good dressing down for having the worm threaded wrong. He promptly showed him the correct way to thread a worm onto a hook, just for future reference.

Around this time we had relatives visiting from London and Richard was showing off our new Yotul wood burning stove. It was a fantastic heat producing machine using no more wood than the old tiny fireplace had done with 200 per cent more heat.

It was the noise that alerted us. Richard went outside to find our chimney like a giant Bunsen burner.

'Call the fire brigade – I'm off.' He jumped into the car, horn blaring and sped to the Fire Station. When I spoke to the 999 emergency services operator she asked if they would find us easily.

'Very easily, one of them lives here.' I assured her. They arrived, lights flashing, sirens blaring and quickly restored peace and harmony.

Six burly firemen, our visitors on holiday and the family, sitting in our kitchen where the old walls, slatework painted over, each little ledge of each little slate stone balancing sticky black soot. Laughter and home made brew made this quite a memorable evening.

Eventually what we had nicknamed our 'shower room holiday' arrived. We had reserved a Winnebago motor home and seven of us, including Mummy and Daddy, set off to tour America and Canada. This was why I needed three weeks off school. We went to Niagara Falls and to Toronto, where Richard's cousin lived. We also visited New England, Detroit, Philadelphia, New York and Washington DC. What better way to learn than through our own, real life experiences.

We were in New York Times Square booking a ticket for a boat trip round The Statue of Liberty. The Booking Office and café area was crowded and James was desperate to spend a penny. At the age of thirteen he set off on his own. As I watched, his head disappeared as he descended the staircase. A cold chill swept over me. I got up and followed him. It was a long, wide, steep staircase. There was a man stepping off the bottom step and James was disappearing into one of the toilets. I watched with utter horror as this man opened that same door, went in and shut the door behind him. I went down that staircase like the proverbial bat out of hell, yelling and shouting at the top of my voice. No hope of any help from upstairs with the racket and din of raised voices and loud raucous music. I hammered on the door and screamed,

'What the hell are you doing? Get out of there.' The man unlocked and opened the door and banged into me as he shot past, up the stairs and away. The toilet was at the far end of a fifteen foot narrow room and James had not locked the door. I grabbed him and ran back up the stairs shouting,

'Stop that man. Stop that man.' Too late, he had disappeared into the crowd. Not that anyone was paying any attention to this deranged woman with an English accent. I think I shook all day with visions of what might have happened, but then it's not a good idea to get wrapped up in what might have happened. It didn't – learn from it – move on and be thankful.

During this holiday we stayed over in Chessapeake Bay. Duck hunting was due to come into operation the following morning, Monday. You couldn't move for ducks and geese. Hundreds and hundreds of them. All our hunting neighbours said,

'Wait until eight o'clock tomorrow morning there won't be a duck or goose in sight. They know to the hour when the season starts.' We laughed thinking it was a joke.

The men were all practicing their hunting calls with little wooden instruments. James, able to entice a tune out of a hose pipe or watering can, could easily mimic a duck. He was adopted, fed and watered or so we thought, until we fetched him home. We had the dubious pleasure of bringing home a rather inebriated thirteen year old.

Monday morning saw us awaken to a glorious day, blue sky and sunshine. Not a duck or goose in sight!

Chapter Twelve

More Health Problems

Menstruation always caused me a problem with excessive bleeding and pain. I was only given a respite when I was pregnant. At the age of thirty six things had got out of hand, the week before feeling low and in pain, the full week of blood loss often putting me to bed, and the week after recovering, leaving one week a month when I could feel normal and live accordingly. It was discovered I had endometriosis where the wall of the womb grows through into the stomach cavity.

A hysterectomy was required with the removal of the womb and one ovary. The night after the operation in the early hours of the morning, I had what have since been described as 'the rigors' sometimes preceding death, where the body goes into an uncontrollable seizure of all muscles.

The Consultant/Surgeon came to see me first thing next morning.

'Well, Mrs Rhodes, what <u>have</u> you been doing?' I opened one eye and replied,

'I haven't been doing anything, I'm alright from the neck down, but I think my brain has melted and if I move my head it might run out of my ears. So what the hell have <u>you</u> been doing?' The curtains were whipped round my bed for privacy, more his than mine I am sure, and examination, my blood count was way down and I needed a transfusion.

I had had a massive haematoma (internal haemorrhage), as it turned out they had missed tying off a main vein. Eventually it had sealed itself and the bleeding had stopped. This male doctor with his large hands attempted to burst this internal 'bag of blood' up to five times a day. The nurse would pass me my face flannel to bite on as he, quite cheerfully forced his hand into my sore and stitched vagina trying to release the pressure.

One day a lady doctor came – she used a catheter to empty the bladder before she attempted the procedure. When I asked her why she explained that if she didn't I would be incontinent later in life.

The surgeon eventually decided that the wound was not internal – it must be behind the wound. He reopened the wound (on the ward, after many days of healing) and withdrew the now congealed blood, what he jovially described as 2lbs of blackcurrant jelly. As I am a rare blood group I was on a drip for many days and as the blood wasn't always available I was left on plasma between times. Even thirty years ago – no matron to answer to, the hygiene and cleanliness left a lot to be desired.

When I finally returned home and after I had recovered fully from the operation (which took about three months) I felt better than I had in years. I put on weight, and returned to teaching.

The hysterectomy and stay in hospital should not have caused a problem as Anthony was to be the chef. From a very young age Anthony had made the lightest pastry and scones and the fluffiest Yorkshire puddings to be had. All was in hand, no-one would go hungry.

As I sat attached to a drip I was surprised to find I had a visitor. In the morning? As Richard walked towards me he stepped sideways to reveal Anthony – a plaster caste enveloping his right arm. Oh, well, Richard was a dab hand at bacon and egg, beans on toast and boiled eggs.

A more impressive menu was restored on my return home, when Jillian came to stay for the week.

Within eighteen months of being so much better in health I was to find myself struck down with RA. Various hypotheses have been put forward, one that it follows from thyroid and hysterectomy and one that it was in the blood of the blood transfusion and was probably viral in origin. They cannot test for Rheumatoid Arthritis but I was lucky because at that time they did not test for AIDS either.

My first visit to the Rheumatology Hospital was to see a specialist who had what they called an aggressive attitude towards tackling RA. He calmly told me that no illness or disease could be cured, not even the common cold. He said,

'We can cut it out, burn it out, or mask the symptoms. We can not cure, not even the common cold.'

The Consultant informed me that,

'If we don't replace your ankles within the next three months I cannot be responsible for you walking again.'

'I want to start with your ankles and then your knees – your hips are alright.' He went through my body, 'Then your shoulders, your elbows, your wrists and most of your fingers.' He was going to replace them all and it would take years to do it and get through it all and then, a bit like the Forth Bridge have to start at the beginning again. Once this process started I would be committed to a life in hospital recovering from one or other of these operations. Then came the argument, whether they would replace my knees and ankles first or my shoulders first. The shoulder man didn't want crutches for knees messing up his work and the knee and ankle men didn't want my shoulders to interfere with their part of my body.

In the end in sheer desperation having shunned the idea of replacement joints I decided to go ahead with some of my finger joints being replaced. The surgeon arranged that I could have a block anaesthetic to block the whole arm with a local anaesthetic, as I was frightened of the consequences of a general with my throat problems.

'Don't send for me in March, I'll be away in America.' I said.

When I returned Anthony said,

'They rang up to see where you were. They had sent a letter to you last week to be in hospital for your operation and you never turned up.'

They had explained that my hand would be in a special splint for approximately six months and not useable. My only worry was, how on earth would I pull my knickers up? It all seemed too much to contemplate, if they couldn't follow a simple instruction over dates how could I trust them to carry out the operation without hitch. I decided to cancel the operation and try my own route. Painfully I went back to the computer – just one finger at a time, frustrating when I had not only been a fast typist but actually taught it as a subject. Its surprising how fast, in small sessions, two fingers can be! But don't tell my ex pupils.

I never had any replacement joints which seemed right for me. I met a lady who had arthritis in her feet and yet could walk the dog for up to an hour. She was going into hospital to have a toe removed and others fused. It was, she felt, the right path for her to undergo this surgery but not at any time did I feel this was right for me. It must be a decision taken with all information to hand and the full prognosis taken into account to make sure the benefits outweigh the difficulties of surgery.

The Consultant's approach included gold injections and strong drugs which he said would take fifteen years off my life.

'But you will still live to sixty, so that's alright, isn't it? I want you to relax and give your body to me and I will look after it, you have no more worries.' My reply was,

'I don't feel that is a very good idea, because if you think about it, you finish work at 5 o'clock, don't work weekends and have holidays. Who will be looking after it then?' I was surprised when he told me that no-one had ever said that to him before. I asked about the possibility of diet and other more natural approaches. He cruelly laughed me out of the office.

'Go away and try it, but in six months time you'll come crawling back to me on your hands and knees!'

Off I went to struggle on my own. I tried to avoid as many drugs as possible, adjusted my diet, took supplements and generally tried various different natural approaches to the problem. And while I would never suggest that anyone else should follow my example, I do believe that my minimal exposure to drugs in those early years has meant that my body is better able to cope now that constant medication is unavoidable.

Sadly the doctor in question died in his forties from an aneurysm. I often wonder how he would have felt about having his life cut short in such a manner.

Some years later on a scheduled visit to the Rheumatology hospital, the clinic nurse asked if I would mind seeing the new Consultant Rheumatologist.. The department didn't work on the prognosis theory she said but if they had I was probably the worst case the previous Consultant had seen in his career and she wanted the new man to see what could be done without such aggressive therapy. Here I was, still functioning without the aggressive therapy I had been told was necessary.

'Not at all.' I replied. 'All I want is a course of hydrotherapy.' Richard would put the passenger seat into a lying down position, wrap me in a sleeping bag and lie me on it with a pillow until we drove the one and a quarter hour's drive. That half hour in the pool was worth the journey because the warm water was the only time I was free of pain. I went in to see the doctor.

'Hello, Mrs Rhodes.' We shook hands. 'Now I want you to tell me what drugs you're taking.' (Note: Rheumatoid arthritis, often called RA is not arthritis but is a disease of the blood and is a chronic, progressive and disabling auto-immune disease. It is an incredibly painful condition which can cause severe disability. It is also systemic, meaning that it can affect the whole body including internal organs such as the heart and lungs).

'I don't take drugs, doctor, just soluble aspirin and I'm taking ten of those a day.'

'Hm. Let's start again. Will you tell me, Mrs Rhodes, what medications you're taking?'

'Just soluble aspirin.'

'Mrs Rhodes,' – he was making a great effort to be patient with me – 'please will you tell me what pills and medicines you are taking?'

I looked at him, said,

'Watch my lips, doctor.' and repeated that I took only aspirin.

Oh dear. I really didn't fit the mold.

'I'm terribly sorry, I didn't mean to be rude.' said the doctor. 'I'm going to have to look at your notes again.'

We sat quietly for several minutes as he read through the notes. He looked up at me, looked me straight in the eye, and said,

'You are a very sick woman. You shouldn't be walking about.'

What was I to say?

'Would you like me to keel over now, or later?' I asked. The good doctor was full of profuse apologies, and genuinely interested in what I was doing in order to keep going. I listed a few things – meditation, relaxation, diet, acupressure.

'Well, whatever it is, keep on doing it,' he advised, 'because I'm telling you now there's nothing I could do that would get you as well as you are.' And from that moment we became firm friends.

I went to see one doctor who was head of the Vegetarian Society at the time. He had six brothers and sisters who all became top doctors, obstetrics, paediatrics, orthopaedic and this one who was very much into diet. He showed me the uric acid crystals in my urine through a microscope – incredible – and said this was what was causing my disease and causing the tissue and bone to break down. I had been vegetarian for twenty years and was now vegan, I should stay at least vegetarian and once a week fast for 24 hours, after which I was to eat two slices of wholemeal bread to soak up the acid crystals. I was having trouble swallowing even then, so trying to get this bread down even with a bit of water was very difficult. I tried this regime for nine months, but the weight was falling off me, I had no energy and was in a very poor state. One day my sister Jillian asked,

'How long is this going on for, Diana?'

'I don't know.' I responded. The problem was that when I didn't eat or drink I could climb stairs, I could bend, I could walk, I could reach things – I could do anything, but the minute I had water or any kind of food, bam, the problems and pain were back.

I went for muscle testing. I couldn't raise my arm to be tested so I had to hold the practitioner's wife's hand and he tested her. We went through this procedure a number of times, with Richard and I taking numerous different foods and drinks to be tested each time. I was allergic, according to the practitioner, to more than a hundred and forty foods and drinks. The only two things that I could eat and drink with impunity were potatoes and whisky!

Enough is enough. I decided that I would just pay attention to what I was eating and drinking and move on from there, otherwise I could easily just become more and more sensitive.

Some years after the RA took hold I was having trouble with one of my legs. It wouldn't straighten and was causing great difficulty even standing to dress. It was arranged I would be admitted and given intensive physiotherapy. Because of the MRSA I was allocated a single room away from the other patients. I did have a toilet facility but no shower, just a three amp shower head in a small wash basin to use for the entire week. I was confined to bed and strapped up to a contraption called 'springs and strings'. The Head Physiotherapist came along,

'You mustn't get off this bed. If I see you off this bed you'll have me to answer to.'

Then the cleaners would come in. I was being barrier nursed so anything that went out of my room had to be bagged in the room and again at the door as it left. Orthopaedics definitely does not want MRSA. As the cleaner swept up she would open the door and sweep the dust and fluff down the corridor and out into the main ward. I told the Consultant when he asked if all was well,

'Apart from not being able to wash as the nurses are too busy to bring me the jug of hot water I was promised I'm fine but I am confused as to why my dirt and fluff are allowed to go walk about when I am not?' He was not best pleased and I think it caused a bit of a stir. The planned x-rays that were to take place to see what help they could give me, having been admitted on the Sunday, took place on the Thursday evening after everyone else had left, to prevent the transmission of infection. I was discharged on the Friday morning, what a waste of resources, these x-rays had no use whatever at this late stage. It was even more noticeable when I was discharged and the fact that I was in clothes rather than pyjamas was allowed to go to the café and mix with visitors and patients alike. Something is wrong with the organization of our medical services, infection control being such a haphazard affair and non-existent in many cases.

In the lead up to being diagnosed with Sjogrens syndrome I had spent many years unable to eat or drink without choking, eventually experiencing the 'you are going to die' episode. Before the PEG fitting the GP made an appointment for me to see a Professor at Guys Hospital in London. I had read about him in the Daily Mail, he was the expert in the field of salivary gland problems. On our way to London I had another appointment in Llanidloes with a lady who was supposedly the person in the area who dealt with such matters as Sjogrens syndrome. She carried out a number of tests and informed me,

'There is nothing much wrong with you, it is all in your mind.' I came out of their pretty distraught because the only explanation then was that I had a mental illness.

We continued our journey to London to see the Professor. After an hour's consultation he said to me,

'Mrs Rhodes. This is my specialist field. I am afraid,' here I thought was the mental diagnoses but no, he continued 'you are the worst case scenario. You have what's called a 'full house' of symptoms produced by Sjogrens syndrome. There is very little I can do but it might be an idea to have a barium swallow test just to make absolutely sure there is nothing else going on here.'

I came away so relieved that I did not have a mental illness but unhappy that there was little they could do to help me. What it did show, quite blatantly, was that there are people out there dabbling, who really shouldn't be dabbling. The difficulties are that like this lady in Llanidloes she had the titles to go along with her dabbling, pronouncing diagnoses that were totally wrong. As time went by it was explained to me that alongside the dryness of the mouth and throat from the Sjogrens syndrome and the peristaltic action of the throat muscles not working in sequence, this was causing the food or drink swallowed to cause choking fits, even occasionally entering the lungs and thus causing pneumonia. The choking fits were life threatening as they blocked the airways, making it impossible to breathe. Many an ambulance would arrive at our home with oxygen and paramedic, followed closely by our GP (who was our neighbour and knew where the ambulance was going) to find me in a state of collapse and Richard in a state of high stress and anxiety; there being very little he could do to help other than just be there.

This happens rarely now as I use a humidifier, which via a nasal cannula provides moist warm air for me to breathe. I use this all night and as much of the day as is practical. It keeps the passageways moist and clear of mucous build-up, and as I no longer eat I have no problems trying to swallow food or drink.

I did go for the barium swallow test. Upon arrival a young lady came into the waiting room where I and others sat waiting to be seen. She was carrying a clip board and pen. She knew nothing about me other than my name, address and the fact that I was there for a barium swallow test.

'Now, Mrs Rhodes, you have a swallowing problem. Well dear, I wonder if you could find a hobby or something to interest you that might take your mind off the swallowing problem so that it will alleviate itself.' I sat there open-mouthed. Richard was more vociferous.

'Do you realize who you are talking to? Have <u>you</u> spoken at the United Nations. Have <u>you</u> carried out peace work throughout the world. Have <u>you</u> had the Foreword to your book written by His Holiness the Dalai Lama? How dare you?'

She departed not even abashed it seemed and I was called into the x-ray room. The same young lady handed me a teaspoon piled high with tiny granules.

'I want you to swallow these and we are going to watch them on the x-ray machine as they pass through your gullet.' I burst out laughing,

'If I could swallow <u>one</u> of those granules I wouldn't be here. Just <u>one</u> granule would cause me to choke.'

'It's alright, dear' she said 'if you do choke we are all here to look after you.' I'm afraid my response by this time may have sounded sarcastic!

'Look, <u>my dear,</u> my husband has a powerful car out there and I think you should drive it into a solid brick wall at sixty miles an hour but don't worry it has an air bag and we'll all pull you out.' She was more than taken aback but took these stupid granules away and brought a liquid barium drink,

'OK take a large gulp of this and just swallow it.' I hadn't got through to her had I? Needless to say the tests proved nothing as they could not be carried out to even begin to give them the information they needed. The swallowing problem was just one of the life setbacks that I would have to live with.

Even today, not having eaten anything since 2000 I am asked by people, who obviously do not realize what they are saying,

'If you could eat what would be your choice, what was your favourite food when you could eat?' Would you ask a blind person what they would want to see, if they could see? A strange question or an inability to put yourself in someone else's shoes?

As the years went by I became very breathless and went to see a Consultant in Shrewsbury, in fact I didn't see him to begin with I saw his Registrar. When we had discussed my problem she asked,

'Do you mind if I call in my boss, you are a bit out of my league.' We had to wait a little while and eventually he came in and we went through the story again. I was expecting to be kept in as my GP had said,

'Take a suitcase because they will keep you in.' The Consultant talked with me and with his Registrar,

'What we really need is a CAT scan and the only way to have that is to be admitted as your GP rightly predicted, but I am not going to have you admitted, you are far too vulnerable. Do you realize this hospital is full of germs! Wait here a minute.' He went off but came back almost immediately.

'They are going to do a CAT scan now, but you have to be up there in the next two minutes so get your skates on.' We made it in our time slot and had the scan. We had to wait about half an hour before the Consultant could see me again, so within the hour of arriving he was reading that CAT scan and telling me the results. No three month waiting list and then weeks waiting for an appointment to get the results.

He brought the scan up on the computer screen and said,

'Come and look. Get a bit closer. Can you see these little things?'

'Yes', I said, wondering what he was showing me.

'Aren't they beautiful? Absolutely beautiful, just like little engagement rings.'

'Yes, they are beautiful.' I said, still not really knowing what I was looking at.

'Can you see little engagement rings with a little diamond in the middle there? Well, that's your disease!' He was truly in the right job with his excitement for his work and his compassion for his patients. He wanted to refer me to a Consultant in Aberystwyth which was nearer home. He took a copy of the DVD scan, gave it to me and said,

'Show him this.' In my understanding bronchiectasis comes under the term COPD (chronic obstructive pulmonary disease) Years ago it would have been called rheumatoid lung and is a side effect of RA where the lung calcifies and does not function properly depleting the ability of the lung to transfer oxygen into the blood stream. This is why I need to use oxygen as when the oxygen level in the blood becomes too low it has a severe detrimental effect on the major organs of the body, not to mention the tiredness and breathlessness.

I have pointed out the discrepancies, the attitudes, the faults and failures of the NHS and medical systems but it cannot be left unsaid that many of the individuals within the system are dedicated, committed, compassionate people, fully embracing 'Do no harm' and to these people I offer my heartfelt thanks.

Chapter Thirteen

Building the Business

All of our hard work at The Garth was beginning to show results, but as the Caravan Park took off we realized the position of the cottage did not lend itself to good business practice. Potential customers would come to the Park entrance but never venture far enough through the caravans to find the cottage, so we lost a lot of potential business. There had been a caravan with residential permission at the top of the Park, which had been occupied by someone helping Mark some many years before, so we had our permission already in place for a new house.

We designed a house to be built where the residential caravan had been, close to the entrance. We had to build to fit the contours of the hill and came up with an idea that featured bungalow style living accommodation with a double storey to accommodate the bedrooms. The house would be south facing with fantastic views, even though it overlooked some of the caravans.

Richard's skill with calculating and estimating again came to the fore. As usual, this was to be a self-build with the help of a good architect and builder. We approached the Bank Manager once again. Fortunately there had been a change since the over cautious one had cut our original loan.

As it turned out, the Bank Manager was to give some wise advice. The economic climate in 1981 was such, he said, that costs would escalate horrendously within the year. Our loan would therefore be arranged, but must take into account that he wanted us to purchase all materials, as appropriate, immediately to avoid this escalation. We took his advice of course, if we hadn't we would not have afforded to reach half way let alone complete the build. It was all hands on deck.

Edward was in a plaster caste from hip to toe as some weeks earlier I had heard a blood curdling scream. I thought he had fallen through the bedroom window of the cottage to the concrete path below it was so piercing and alarming.

He had in fact been to get Anthony a toilet roll and on his return he had opened the bathroom door with a high karate kick. His leg went straight through the frosted glass portion. We rushed to the hospital for emergency treatment, they couldn't operate immediately as he had just eaten and we had a long frightening night. I stayed in an upright chair all night beside his bed. What a terrible night, he was in pain and restless.

At home Mother-in-law had held the fort. On our return the washing line had three odd socks (I never did find out the significance) and a clean window to the main door. We were bottle feeding lambs and the boys thought it was extremely funny to flip milk at each other from the teat on the bottle, dodging round the front door in their weaving and amusement, pet lamb bleating in anticipation.

The house build began under Richard's expertise gained from years of doing it himself. The boys were of an age to be a great help.

James and Anthony were hail and hearty and ready for the challenge. James put on the slates to the two storey part of the roof, he was perfectly sensible and capable at the age of fifteen to do this task, even though he did get into trouble from the Headmaster for shinning a drain pipe to fetch a ball off a one storey, flat roofed building at school. The headmaster actually withdrew me from teaching a class to tell me of this heinous crime. Rules are made for a reason and are there to be taken notice of but how could I be cross when he had seen a job that needed doing and done it, bearing in mind what he had been trusted to do earlier that week at home on the new house.

Anthony was there usually at Richard's right hand, fetching, carrying, doing, the ultimate gofer. Anthony and I spent hours with teaspoons and a half inch paint brush getting out the small amount of fine gravel lodged in the fissures of the slate as it came to the surface, where the foundations were to be laid. Edward with his pot leg had to do things sitting down so he nailed the floor boards down in the living room – quite a job to ease frustration.

The Planning Inspector was a 'more than my jobs worth' type and didn't seem to have heard of building your house on a rock. The house, despite this, progressed and very quickly was ready for occupation, by our standards at least.

At this time the everyday work of running a business, siteing caravans, cleaning toilets, Fire Brigade and teaching ran alongside the house building. Nothing in our lives has been done instead of, it has always been as well as.

When we moved out of the cottage into the new house we let it as a holiday home. We only did that for one season as people have the strangest habits. We had laid a carpet over the slate floor in the living room and given the house a coat of paint throughout to start our first week of the season for visitors. The first couple had two Scottie dogs and by the end of the week the dogs had scratched off all the paintwork on all the window ledges. The next family with children left unusual lumps under the carpet which turned out to be where the children had hidden their unwanted meals and these were now in various stages of decomposition. Worse was to come. In the bedroom was a kidney shaped dressing table with six small drawers, each drawer was filled with human excrement.

The final straw was a couple who after arriving home wrote a letter of complaint with a list of faults. They wanted a percentage of their money back for the inconvenience. The list comprised of twenty faults in descending order of importance. There was a knot in the washing line – the whirligig type; when they came back at night there were slugs on the path, owls were keeping them awake. the faults then became more and more bizarre as the list descended.

We began to let the cottage on a long term basis but still continued to let a couple of caravans for holiday lets. One week to a doctor and his family, when they left the caravan was filthy. The shower base held four inches of slimy, green stagnant water, I never worked out how that could happen in a two week period. The next family in were a young couple with four very young children. They came bouncing over the Caravan Park entrance in an old jalopy and all tumbled out. My immediate reaction was,

'Oh my, if a doctor's family can leave it as they did, what now?'

The youngest in the family was a baby. He was sick and we were awoken by frantic banging on the door at 1.00 am The child's temperature had soared. I had had good training, because of my Mother's young brother Stewart and the risk of convulsion. Anthony had had a convulsion at age eight and later his son at age six, is there an hereditary factor?

Just before Anthony's eighth Christmas he came into our bedroom in the early morning. I reached out to touch the forehead of his red face as he climbed into bed between Richard and me. He was burning up and I thought I should do something. As I got out of bed he jerked and went into a full blown convulsion. Despite Mummy's insistence that we knew what to do with a convulsion, I was still terrified. I sent Richard scurrying for water and a flannel and began to sponge Anthony down to try to cool him and reduce his temperature as Richard phoned the doctor. He shook and jerked, his eyes rolling and I talked and talked to him in words of reassurance and explanation of what was happening as much for my own help as his. After fifteen minutes he went rigid and then relaxed totally. I thought we might lose him and even put a tissue under his nose to make sure he was breathing. At this point the doctor walked in and took over.

As it was Christmas Anthony was not admitted to hospital for observation but stayed at home with our close supervision. He was pretty poorly and looked like death warmed up for at least a week.

About nine months later, I was sitting having a coffee with a friend as the children played. Anthony sidled up and leaned against me and said to the friend,

'Did Mummy tell you I had a convulsion? It was not nice, but you talked to me all the time didn't you Mummy?' I was open mouthed as he repeated the words I had used describing healing colours and relaxing techniques in child oriented language.

'That meant I wasn't as frightened and now I'm all OK.' and he went back to play. I had thought he was unconscious to his environment, even comatose to whatever degree, but his hearing was as acute as ever, so much so that it was fully available for retrieval from his memory so many months later.

The young people staying in the caravan were distressed and provided me with what I needed to carefully sponge the baby down to reduce his temperature. Another child had wet the bed and needed dealing with. We were called upon a number of times during their two week stay. They seemed very young and we felt almost responsible. When it came to saying goodbye we had to go out and left them packing up. When we returned they were still there. Not only was the inside of the caravan pristine and spotless but the young father was cleaning the windows and the outside of the caravan. The whole caravan was immaculate. Yet again, never judge a book by its cover.

The new house was wonderful. So easy to manage compared to the cottage, although I missed the sound of the river and the feeling of living a century earlier. The low flying aircraft from RAF Valley which occasionally passed over were what reminded us we were living in the twentieth century.

Richard's Mother and Father came to stay and she complained that there was no lock on the bathroom door.

'You should be so lucky, there wasn't even a door until the day before you arrived.' Richard told her. A lock was fitted and she was saved the embarrassment of being disturbed by one of her grandsons.

Another bathroom story was when I was in the bath one day. Unable to get in or out on my own, Richard would put me in and leave me to soak in the hot water, when he would come and lift me out. My parents were staying and he got a fire call, a personal alarm that sounded and when this happened the firemen responded, their response was immediate and dramatic so you didn't stand in the way. After some time Mummy came to the landing and shouted to see if I was alright. My reply was,

'No, I can't get out.' Mummy had always had a hearing problem and she shouted back,

'Oh good.' And off she went. Fortunately, Richard wasn't away as long as usual and found me an hour later, having run off all the hot water trying to keep warm and as wrinkled as a prune! It became a standing joke that whichever firemen didn't get on the 'shout' as it was called, would pop up to see if Di needed lifting out of the bath.

One small difficulty arose in the new house as Manweb had lost our Application for electricity power supply. Nine more months we would have to wait they insisted. As it happens they connected us within two weeks as we were able to prove it was their negligence. For those weeks I ran a home with three teenage sons and all that entails with one thirteen amp plug on a long extension lead from the Cottage. The cooker was solid fuel, wood burning. I had no other form of cooking. As we had had a solid fuel Aga at Greaves Farm this did not prove a problem, and we soon learned which woods burnt hotter and longer. I still did all the baking and cooking, from home made bread – by hand not machine, to cakes and pies, to full meals, and filled the freezer for busier times.

Electrical appliances had to be used on a totting up basis. I could use the vacuum, electric kettle, iron, washing machine or fridge freezer. It all meant that everything not being used had to be turned off and a calculation had to be done to avoid overloading the thirteen amp plug because that meant a trip down the hill to the Cottage to replace the blown fuse.

As the main holiday season was over and the Park was quiet Richard and Edward went to Spain to give the villa a coat of paint. I stayed at home with the dog, a large German Shepherd. One evening I had had my tea on a tray on my lap, recovering from the fact that the dog had got into the field and eaten a rotting dead sheep. I took my tray into the kitchen and nearly tripped up. The lino covering the floor was like a roller coaster, with high ridges and low troughs making it almost impossible to walk on. The boiler of the wood fired cooker had burst, soaked into the floor and created this huge ripple effect. The dog, shut in the back entrance area had vomited back the dead sheep and I was alone with a mobility problem. I rang the plumber, who bless him, left his wife's dinner party and together with his guest came to sort out the water supply. I did bribe him with home-made chocolate cake!

I managed to scrape up the main mess from the dog and my friend arrived to mop and disinfect the floor like it had never been disinfected before.

When Richard and Edward returned from Spain the kitchen floor had to be taken up and the wood fired cooker taken out. As I had become less able to stoke it with logs we replaced it with an electric cooker.

My training in being sovereign and survival techniques came to the fore and all meals were cooked on the log burning stove in the living room which had been bought especially with a milled top. Huge pans of soup, casseroles with everything in one pan, the house filled with the aroma of food. We could eat healthily for the two weeks it took to replace the cooker and replace the floor and get back to normal.

Running your own business entails an enormous amount of paperwork and red tape and we seemed to attract VAT inspections with Inspectors with particularly unusual personalities. One was a large built lady of six feet tall in her stockinged feet. She confided she had never wanted to be a VAT inspector, she had always dreamed of being a ballerina.

The next was the archetype – aggressive, 'out to prove you guilty' type. Although we now knew why as our ballerina had confided something else. If the VAT man could find you owed money he/she received a commission. Quite an incentive.

This inspector was after his commission.

'Guard dog, guard dog? You're claiming food for a guard dog. What breed is this guard dog? How capable is he of guarding?'

Richard offered to show him the dog so he could judge his capabilities. The door to the Boot/Utility room had a window in the top half. Richard stood back and pointed at the window. This officious official stepped up to the window but as he did so the dog appeared at the other side. The dog stood up onto his hind legs, he was head and shoulders above the VAT man, a huge, barking German Shepherd.

I had never seen anyone take a six foot step backward in one go, never mind at that speed. Richard remarkably kept a straight face.

'Ugh, yes well, I suppose he fits the role.' Sadly for him, this gentleman left without his commission.

We continued to have pet lambs needing bottle feeding. Aunty Ida had given the boys a starter fund. Their remit was to make it grow. They each owned a sheep and Richard a few extra. These sheep lambed increasing the flock and the fleece was sold. The boys were entrepreneurial millionaires. The children from the caravans came to take turns feeding the lambs, they thought this was wonderful. During one feeding session a small dog appeared from the direction of the local housing estate, a small, waggy, terrier dog. He trotted up, being very friendly with the children. I was handing out the bottles of milk feed when the dog ran at one of the lambs, in an instant he ripped out its throat, dropped it, ran at the other lamb and repeated this horrific action.

Hysterical screaming ensued and parents came running. I, who abhor violence, walked up to this dog and kicked it in the ribs as I sobbed and shook in shock. This was true shock therapy, a lesson for dog owners living in or visiting the country.

My German Shepherd, as soft as a brush and as thick as two short planks would, on rare occasions, get out of the garden. He would then sit outside the front door waiting to be let in. This day was to be different. He must have met up with a couple of dogs and away he went. Richard was out looking for him when the doorbell rang, it was the farmer,

'Have you lost your dog?'

'Yes, yes, Richard's out looking for him now. He's been gone about twenty minutes.' I said. He turned towards his Landrover and said,

'I've got him.' I snatched up the dog's lead and followed him. He did have my dog. He was in the back of the farmer's Landrover lying in a pool of blood with a bullet hole in his head. I truly believe the farmer had no option but to protect his sheep. I had lived long enough in the country to know that dogs need only to chase sheep in the early stages of pregnancy to cause an abortion and in a pack become an even more deadly killing machine than the small terrier.

The shock of the way I found out was very difficult to come to terms with although I did forgive the farmer, he obviously didn't know how to tell me, but I will never forget standing with a lead in my hand and the dog I loved lying there with a bullet hole in his head. We replaced him with another German Shepherd, they are a loving loyal breed when treated correctly, and another farming friend shut him in a shed with a ram for a short period. That dog could walk through a flock of sheep without even glancing sideways. Richard and the farming friend had decided not to tell me until the deed was done. Perhaps the means warranted the end but I certainly would not have been happy to allow it if I had known.

Eventually my choice of dog had to accommodate my physical limitations and I had two apricot toy poodles. Poodles have the closest DNA to a wolf and are highly intelligent. They were great characters and full of fun, not to mention their ability to act as a hot water bottle.

My dog of the day is an Assistance dog provided by the charity Canine Partners. This charity trains dogs, who literally open doors to independence for their human partners. My first visit to the Centre after a preliminary interview was to work with some of the dogs. I worked with two big black Labradors, brothers in fact, and fell in love with them both, and then a female golden Labrador who would not work sensibly for me. The Charity trainers are well aware of the fact that a dog will work differently for different people and this is always taken into account. And then came Wallace, dogs are named as they are chosen as pups alphabetically. Well, with Wallace, what's the song? No two people have ever been so in love? He came towards me, turned his beautiful eyes up to mine and we were one. I was not to know which dog would be allocated to me until I attended 'boot camp'. Two weeks residential training – no not for him, for me, to train me how to handle and continue to train him at home.

Some of his abilities include: opening the washing machine door and pulling the washing into a basket; fetching his bedding to put in the washer; passing my purse to a high check out counter; picking up things I drop; opening and closing doors; fetching the phone; pressing the button to fetch a lift, and last but not least taking my socks off at bedtime.

The training included going into Chichester town shopping, putting him into a down – wait position in a busy shopping area and hiding for two minutes before going to release him (watched by trainers of course) and passing me his lead on my return.

On our first training trip out into Chichester he began to pull on the lead attached to the wheelchair, much to the trainers consternation. He returned to my knee and placed a white feather on my lap. There were dirty brown and grey pigeons in the area but not another white feather in sight. If you find or are given a white feather in unusual circumstances they say it is a message from the angels. Without doubt Wallace was my message from the angels and continues to amaze me with his abilities. There is no question that he thinks things through. If he is asked to carry out a task that is more difficult or presents a different than normal challenge he will attempt it and if it doesn't work he will stop and think again, head on one side, until he achieves his aim.

As I ride through other shoppers, people reach to stroke him, despite his wearing a jacket that says 'Do not distract me'. They say,

'Hello beautiful.' One day I will be quick enough to answer,

'Oh how nice of you to say so.' They stop with all the time in the world to talk to and about this beautiful dog and his lucky partner. The normal barrier of the wheelchair is removed by his presence.

Yes, the wheelchair is a barrier. One day approaching a flower stall in the entrance to a big supermarket I saw the assistant's face change into,

'Oh my God, it's one of those.' And I thought back,

'Oh my God, it's one of those.' She looked straight over my head at my son and said,

'Can I help you?' He replied, all 6 feet, 12 stone of him, as he pointed at my head,

'Me brawn, she brain.' This broke the ice and we all laughed and all was well. I know this would not have occurred if I had had Wallace at that time.

I was at a craft exhibition with a friend. I had a new wheelchair that lifts me up and down so I can talk with people eye to eye and reach things off shelves. By the time we got there I was so tired already, and I was going round with backpacks and coats banging in my face and I came out to the canteen area and said to Richard,

'It's no good I can't do it. I can't get near anything, I can't see anything, I'm totally invisible and I'm tired and fed up.' He looked at me and said,

'Raise yourself up.' I raised myself up to eye level and all of a sudden I became visible.

'Oh, my love, come here. Come to the front of the queue. You can't see anything back there. Come on everybody let this lady through.' The difference was incredible. That was one occasion when I realized that wheelchairs are not necessarily discriminated against, they are like pushchairs, they are literally not seen.

Another similar occasion, I cannot remember the exact reason why we needed to go to Birmingham but it was some legal matter that needed sorting, was when we arranged an appointment to carry out what needed to be done. All the caravan Owners are from the Midlands and when they heard I was going they all responded in the same way,

'Don't go Diana. The discrimination and abuse will be awful. You'll be mugged and your handbag stolen.' I could not believe in the late 1980's that this could be happening and set off totally oblivious to any potential danger.

As we walked through the centre of Birmingham, Richard went into a Travel Agent and we arranged to meet up in Marks & Spencers just across the road. As there was a zebra crossing I was sure there would be no danger. I sat at the road edge waiting for the lights to change to green. A very large man with Rastafarian hair down to his waist and a knitted hat on top, his skin the colour of deep mahogany, came to stand beside me, towering over me as I sat in the scooter. I could feel him looking at me and remembered the warnings I had been given,

'Whatever you do, do not look anyone in the eye if they approach you.' I could still feel him looking me up and down and thought,

'Oh well, just let the handbag go if it is grabbed and if you are lucky you won't get a black eye.' I kept my eyes on the traffic lights and when they turned green I set off. He outpaced me and got ahead, turned round, looked at me and announced,

'Ma'am ah dus lurv dat motah.' He disappeared, gently shaking his head from side to side.

This is probably the closest I have got to real abuse and shows me that we should not look for it when it is not present.

We do not need to look for the bad in life, as often we will be surprised by the good and realise that human nature truly has the potential for good.

Wallace likes nothing better than shopping in an M & S store. The racks of clothes are too close together to accommodate a wheelchair and a dog and he deliberately walks under the clothes and gets an extended stroke.

As I have said people cannot resist him and lurch at his head to stroke him, totally ignoring his jacket or any request not to distract him when he is working. Sometimes when somebody approaches you can see him flinch. We had had a morning of these 'attacks ', when yet another was striding at speed towards us. I turned to attempt to protect him as a gentle voice said,

'Excuse me, but your dog has something stuck to his jacket.' As I turned him to look, I saw something stuck to the small portion of Velcro left showing from the jacket fastening. It was the sexiest, laciest thong you could imagine. When this lady and I had stopped laughing we imagined the headlines,

'Disabled woman trains dog to steal sexy underwear.'

For all his training and impressive skills, he is still a normal, exuberant Labrador. Water is one area he will disobey, he can't help himself, he adores water. It doesn't have to be clean river or sea, any old water will do. His vice is smelly dead things that he rolls in and comes back proudly displaying his new coat of stink and muck!

He has changed our lives, on days when I am particularly low he comes and gently lays his head on my knee, gazing at me with his doleful, compassionate and understanding eyes. A precious relationship, a connection beyond most human contact.

A friend, Carolle wrote the following for the WI magazine and I couldn't resist adding it as it epitomises Wallace and shows how others see him.

Wallace the Labrador was lying in front of the fire beside Dee Dee, a Toy Poodle. Diana and Richard Rhodes have always kept pets but Wallace, although he is a dog, is not a pet, he is a canine partner.

We were discussing the upcoming Bluebell Walk to raise money for the charity Canine Partners when Diana, who has used a wheelchair for the past 30 years, moved out of the room to get the address book. Wallace jumped up, stretched, and followed Diana.

'He never leaves her side,' said Richard 'he sleeps beside her bed and if I am in the garden and Diana needs me, he comes to find me.'

Wallace has been Diana's canine partner ever since she was assessed and accepted by the charity.

Wallace can do an extraordinary number of everyday tasks. He is a 'Nana' dog like the Darling family's dog in Peter Pan for he will take off Diana's socks and open and unload the washing machine, pick up dropped items and bring Diana the phone.

But these are merely mechanical things and Wallace is no robot. On days when Diana is in pain he will sit beside her and place his head in her lap. Like all dogs, Wallace gives unconditional love for Diana says she is very aware that he is a dog and not a human in a dog costume and when he plays he is a 'typical Labrador idiot with a weakness for water.'

Every one of Canine Partners' dogs has undergone continuous training since puppyhood, so by the time Diana was chosen by Wallace he could perform over a hundred tasks. Going out and about on an intensive two week training course that the charity nicknamed 'Boot Camp', she learnt that in a big department store Wallace could not only press the button for the lift but hand over her purse to a sales assistant.

He has transformed Diana's life through his constant companionship and with Wallace at her side she has discovered a new found independence. Richard says that the greatest gift is that 'Wallace breaks down the barrier of the wheelchair.'

Many people, when confronted with someone in a wheelchair, shy away from contact. Both Canine Partners and Support Dogs, a charity which trains Disability Assistance Dogs for the same purpose, break down that barrier. They form a living, breathing bridge between their partner and the rest of the world and what people see is someone who is clever enough to own a very clever dog.

Chapter Fourteen

Teaching and Learning – Who Teaches Whom?

When we lived on the smallholding of Greaves Farm Richard and I became friends with Carrie and her husband John. They had two boys and Carrie had been a teacher. In the early seventies, Carrie and I were involved with the first multi-racial playgroup in the United Kingdom, based in Bradford as this was one of the first towns to be chosen by Pakistani and Indian immigrants. Edward went with me to the playgroup, James and Anthony were at school.

The Pakistani and Indian children were immaculately dressed, spotlessly clean and well cared for, their hair gleaming with oils and unguents traditionally used in their culture. This caused them to have a very distinctive, but to my nose, pleasant smell. Fathers would bring the children or women in twos or threes or accompanied by a male as the women generally did not speak English. The English children were pushed through the door by anyone – it was difficult to tell – generally they were dirty, unkempt, with runny noses, cigarette burns on their arms and tangled hair. Almost all smelt of urine, and a number of them with the distinctive smell of semen.

We were paid one shilling and sixpence per hour – about the cost of a bag of sugar. When I took travelling expenses into account, I'm sure I was actually out of pocket but through this attended many courses for preschool/ playgroup training.

I loved the work, I loved the children, I loved especially their honest communication. Nothing was held back. They communicated through facial expression, body language, and even what seemed like telepathy. The limitation of language and words were actually a barrier, not just to the foreign children, but to the English ones as well.

After a while Carrie and I decided to start a local playgroup where we lived. Carrie was a tireless organizer and a brilliant teacher. There was a closed-down infant school at Sowood, a village half-way between our two homes. What could be better?

Excited, we approached the local council and they agreed we could use the facility for our project. It was ideal. A large hall, toilets, wash basins, chairs and tables designed for tiny people. We couldn't wait to get started.

All we needed was equipment. John had access to a supply of Marks & Spencer seconds in towels, so off he went with Richard to buy as many as they could. Then we held a special sale and raised £90 – a phenomenal amount in those days. We bought all kinds of equipment from climbing frames to paper, paint, scissors and glue.

The big moment arrived and we were ready to open. We soon built up to four mornings a week with almost forty children attending and we continued to run the playgroup for about three years. Then Carrie announced that she was pregnant again and wanted to retire.

As a postscript, when Carrie and I left the playgroup we legally handed it over to the local community. Some thirty years later it was still running with the addition of several other community based projects, such as mother and baby classes, health support groups and more. It was very fulfilling to realize that we had planted the seed.

Carrie often told me I was a born teacher, and to soften the blow of her impending departure from the playgroup, she announced that she had discovered an outpost to Huddersfield Polytechnic for mature students, offering a Teacher Training Certificate of Education, just ten minutes from our home. My main subject was to be Art and age range infant/junior. It took Richard and Carrie some time to persuade me that this was to be my next big endeavour. The final persuasion was that its evaluation process worked on course assessment and not examinations.

There were twenty other students on the Teacher Training course ranging in age from early thirties to mid-fifties, and there was a very curious statistic concerning previous groups of students – each year for the past five years, one of the twenty one students had died before completing the course. In our intake, the unfortunate person was the only male in the group.

Having had a lecture where I asked,

'When will you teach us how to teach reading?' with the reply that,

'Children aren't taught reading, they catch it like measles.' I was already disillusioned.

This was soon followed by a half hour lecture from an outside Tutor on dyslexia. I sat mesmerized, for once I did not utter a word. When he had finished I approached him and told him he had just described a blue print of my youngest son. What could I do to ensure he received appropriate tuition? His reply was this,

"Well, we are now aware of this phenomenon, and we can diagnose it, but really we don't know how to teach it.' Here was yet another challenge.

Edward's future was in the balance. As I learnt more I discovered, Anthony, James and Richard were all afflicted to varying degrees manifesting various symptoms, not just in the art of reading. I had only one choice, I must learn to help Edward who was by far the worst affected, and by doing so would automatically help the older boys and even Richard. I started to research.

James was eighteen months old when Anthony was born, I invented games to play with him – I would write words in large letters onto cards – red on white. By the age of eighteen to twenty four months he could read twenty plus words. I would 'hide' them and whilst feeding Anthony send him to find a particular word. He thought this was a great game and the reward was his enjoyment and self esteem and my approval at his finding the correct card.

I am convinced this was part of why James' problem was less than it might have been. He could hold an adult conversation by the age of two. By the time Anthony was a similar age, life seemed to have speeded up and James could always outrun him to find any cards anyway. Anthony, however seemed to have less problem and he's always had a way with words both verbally and in the written form, although spellings could be a problem as with James. Edward, didn't speak until he was three, we always said it was because the other two spoke for him and he didn't need to or he couldn't get a word in edgeways. When he did speak it was immediately in sentences. When he first started to speak he called me to,

'Come quick Mummy, the washers 'weverberwating' against the cooker.'

As he got older his spellings weren't poor they were bizarre and often bore no resemblance to the word. I worked with him and had some not spectacular results. No help was offered by the Head of English, who thought dyslexia was a joke and didn't exist, just a middle class excuse for 'thick' children.

Edward was becoming frustrated with my efforts to help, it was either practicing his piano or his euphonium or working with Mum. His leisure time was becoming restricted. I asked the Headmaster if he would allow me to work with Edward in the lunch break or during Assembly but the answer was,

'No it would set a precedent!' I would need to find alternative help.

Whilst I was at College the psychology lectures were given by a gentleman who appeared to need his own services. He would pace a set route around the classroom, over and over, smoked incessantly and used definite and annoying repetitive phrases. He really exasperated me and I was always challenging his strange interpretations of human behaviour. One morning the girls ganged up on me and surrounded me. The spokesperson stepped forward,

'Diana we need you to keep quiet, don't challenge him! Here, chew this and keep your mouth occupied.' She handed me a packet of chewing gum and they all fell about laughing. Never throw a challenge unless you are ready for the consequences. The lecture was informing us of human behaviour and experiences and the impact on job choice.

'For instance,' he droned 'you will never, ever find a Milkman who went to public school.' The whole class swung to look at me as my hand slowly rose.

'Excuse me but my husband fulfils both those criteria.' There was pandemonium, but lets face it he asked for it.

We had to choose a particular subject to act as a Long Study or Dissertation, and my choice was to work with profoundly physically and mentally disabled children. My Tutor and the Head of the College both did their best to dissuade me, but I was adamant. This was what I wanted to do.

I spent a term working at a Residential Special School for these children and focused on the evaluation of one particular child whilst observing others. Every day for the first week I came home and cried myself to sleep, while giving thanks that Richard and I were blessed with three strong and healthy children of our own. But this would help no-one. I must either quit or pull myself together. I chose the latter.

Never have I learnt so much from so few. Society branded these children as handicapped, retarded and mentally deficient. Agreed, they were not normal by society's standards, but they were, nevertheless, extraordinary individuals.

The young girl I chose to study had no speech, but communicated by means of a Possum machine. She nudged a halter round her neck with her chin so a light would travel along a large board displaying the alphabet. As she reached the letter or number she required, she would double nudge to select it and the machine typed that letter or number on an old-fashioned typewriter. Bear in mind that she could not see what she had typed as the typewriter was not in her line of sight, so she had to memorise where she was in spelling a word while finding the next letter.

Our first session found this child very excited, wobbling around in her wheelchair and trying to contain her delight at being singled out by the new lady. I asked questions and she, with extreme concentration, typed the answer.

When we finished the session she became so animated with laughter that she nearly tipped her wheelchair over. I went over her answers, there had to be a joke in there somewhere, but I wasn't getting it. That caused even more hilarity and a teacher came over to find out what was going on. What had I asked?

Q. What's your name?

A. Nichola.

Q. How old are you?

A. Seven.

Q. Have you any brothers and sisters?

A. Yes. John, Alex, Susan, Jenny, e i e i o.

Of course! Old MacDonald had a farm ..... How could I have missed the joke?

Each visit, Nichola would fix me with her eyes, bouncing them from me to the ceiling.

'Not yet,' I said. 'work first, then upstairs, okay?' Work accomplished, we would take the lift to her bedroom and I would read to her from a favourite story book.

Another child had a concave skull and as she grew it pressed more and more on her brain. She was not expected to live more than a few years and at 6 years old had no means of communication, or so I was told.

On one of my teaching days I took this child to the patio window to see the birds feeding. I told her about the birds, and what kind they were. Some of the teachers thought she was totally uninterested, but to my mind she was transfixed. The next day she became excited when she saw me, using the same eye movements as Nichola towards the window, to me and back. We repeated the bird watching exercise again.

This child was firmly strapped into her wheelchair at all times. Several days after the bird watching I found her alone when I entered the room. She became extremely animated and told me with her eyes that she could use the walking frame. I unclasped her and stood her against the walking frame, taking all precautions to support her, just in case. She took a few difficult steps, and then a teacher charged in, whisked her into her chair and turned a tirade of abuse on me.

How had I known she had learnt to do this since my last visit. How could I possibly have known!? Unfortunately, I told the truth and said she had 'told' me, and from that moment, as far as that particular teacher was concerned, I was either an out and out liar or completely doolally.

There was one occasion that really turned my stomach. One day, I was walking down the corridor as a young boy walked towards me. He was carrying a small plastic bag and as he got close he grinned at me, opened the bag, took something out and popped it into his mouth. It was a colostomy bag. Did it give him a feeling of power, I wonder, to freak out any unwary adult he might encounter along his way?

My time with these children was one of the most profound learning experiences of my life. Many years later I read that very wise, very old souls choose to incarnate in these forms to teach compassion and understanding. Well, it certainly worked for me.

When we moved to Wales in 1978, the first year living in the Cottage, I began the teaching job at the High School and as I settled in I found that my pupils (everyone I taught always became 'mine' they were part of my extended family) would go to the Further Education College thirty miles away in Newtown, so I went along to find out what expectations their Business Studies Department would have for students attending their courses. I spent the day being shown round and treated with great kindness and interest. The following day, completely out of the blue I had a phone call offering me a part-time job in the Department, teaching shorthand, typing and Business Studies. This would be for one day with the offer of a couple of night-school classes.

Because of the travelling I said if they could arrange all into the one day then I would accept. I left home at 8:00 am and returned at 10.30 pm. It was a long and hard day. Don't ever believe that teachers have an easy job – carried out correctly, a teacher gives her all to her students. The more energy, commitment and enthusiasm the teacher puts in, the more the students will respond with effort and progress.

I was enjoying the teaching at the High School, the subject I was teaching had its advantages. I turned the room where the typewriters were to look as near like an office as I could with pot plants needing care, although desks and blackboards needed to stay as they were. I did my best to take away the old classroom look, the teacher's desk however was on a plinth set above the students, very old fashioned but had to stay. The typewriters were so old, a collection that someone, somewhere might have wanted rid of, at least one would have been accepted by a museum. The students drew lots to avoid the potential of favours being given for the 'better' machines.

When the students came to their first lesson I told them that this room was part of the outside world and it had certain rules and social niceties that needed to be observed as they would be in the adult world beyond school. I always dressed with care, offering respect as others needed to look at me and I would like them to do the same. Language, body language, noise and treatment of others was paramount in an office situation. On the whole they responded amazingly well.

Each year different students would be set to choose different subjects. One year I would have the more academic students and the next the less so. I was stunned and horrified with some of the less academic. In the days of typewriters, in order to centre say a heading, you would go to the centre of the page, count the number of letters and spaces in your words and divide by two. So a ten letter word would have five letters either side of the centre. Some of the less academic students could not divide by two, even something as simple as ten. Typewriting lessons began to cover a multitude of sins in trying to accommodate or fill these gaps in their learning. What an indictment of our educational system.

I entered my classroom one day and on the wall was a six inch word written in thick red felt pen, the students were all talking and giggling. I looked at this word and thought I must put a stop to the stir this was causing and said,

'Come on everyone, down to it, let's get on with it. Turn to page thirty-one and let's get started.' They all settled down and work commenced. Five minutes later the Headmaster and Deputy Head walked in through the door and stood over this word, heads bowed in a huddle and muttering and talking to each other. They kept looking at me with a look of admiration, respect even, as I continued teaching as though I hadn't a care in the world and as they both left they smiled and nodded at me as much to say – well done. I was left thinking I don't know what's going on here.

Lunchtime came and I went home to have lunch with Richard.

'Richard, what does 'masturbate' mean?' I asked. Richard coughed, choked on his soup and said,

'It's rather a compliment to know that you have never needed to know!'

It is a known fact that the 'quiet' children in a class can easily be overlooked. A parent trying to keep control of their own children can understand the pressure and the skills required not only to keep control of, but to teach, 25 to 30 exuberant youngsters who would rather, almost certainly, be elsewhere.

The disruptive children and the high flyers make themselves known. The 'quiet – middle of the road' children can then fail to get their share of a teacher's attention. I watched individual teachers at my school as they exercised their skills in their desire to give their class the best they could offer, whilst having to take into account the limitations and failings of the actual educational 'system'.

Discipline has always and always will be an issue; this is why I return again and again to it. Until we return to teaching self-discipline, authoritarian discipline will fight a losing battle. I am reminded of my experiences in Japan and know that this can be achieved. If authoritarian discipline is needed less it can then become a structure on which to understand our responsibilities. Yes, we all have rights but we must always balance these rights with the responsibilities that come with them.

Occasionally if a teacher was absent and I had a free period from teaching, I would be asked to sit with a class. Twenty-six Welsh twelve year olds in a Chemistry Laboratory demanded discipline and a no nonsense approach was the order of the day. The class went remarkably well and I dismissed them when the bell went for break. A small room at the back of the Chemistry Lab was occupied by six sixth form students carrying out experiments and work for their A levels with the obvious need of lighted Bunsen burners and other equipment. When the class of boys left leaving the sixth formers in the small room at the back, I heard a strange noise, quiet but insistent. I could have left it, it didn't sound important but there was a distinct noise, so I walked around the Chemistry Lab and discovered that all the unlit Bunsen burners were turned on to maximum pressure. The sixth formers along with that end of the school building would have been blown to kingdom come when the gas penetrated the small room with the lighted burners.

The then Headmaster chose not to follow this through and that class of young boys and their dangerous actions received no punishment, setting the scene for their future in believing that their foolish behaviour did not have consequences. This is the same Headmaster who brought me out of teaching a class to tell me of the heinous crime of James climbing onto a one storey flat roof to fetch a ball. An unusual choice of criteria for admonishment I felt.

I continued to extend my knowledge base and attended courses with the British Dyslexia Association which were excellent, informative and extremely well presented and I knew I gained a lot from them. I drove to Bath to attend a one week long course. It's a family joke that,

'If you take Mum twenty yards from the front door, twiddle her round three times, she'll never find her way home.' The journey from mid-Wales was complicated and Richard had written directions on a large scale map. It was a Bank Holiday, the British road system being what it was, and still is, road works were in progress with police everywhere and a major diversion. I was lost!

When I finally arrived at the B & B where I was to stay, I was literally stiff with tension, so I grabbed something to eat and went straight to bed.

At that time I had very long hair, down to my waist, and in the morning I would tip my head between my knees, brush it down, wiggle it into a big bun, put a hairnet on and that was it, done. The morning after I arrived for the start of the course, however, I couldn't get my arms to my head. They just hurt and refused to work.

I walked down to the college, my hair loose and I felt untidy. Every part of my body hurt. It was agony to take notes. My fingers hurt, my feet hurt, I felt exhausted, but I did the best I could and at the end of the day walked back to the B & B. I tried to do some knitting to calm myself down, but that wasn't possible.

Somehow, I managed to finish the course, which was a little over a week long. Then I had to drive home. I was in a state of dread to begin with, and then I got lost again, somewhere around Hereford. I called Richard in a panic. He set me straight and eventually I got home, but the whole experience had taken a toll on my nerves.

On my next scheduled visit to the doctor I remarked,

'My fingers are really sore.'

'I think you may have a touch of arthritis' she replied,

'Would that explain my feet, too?'

'Oh' she said, 'It could do.'

I told her I'd been thinking I was getting middle-aged and that it was time I got some flat shoes, but within weeks I was diagnosed with severe Rheumatoid Arthritis. I was unable to dress myself, unable to lift a cup to my mouth, and within six months I found myself bedridden.

They say that if your estimated saturation rate test, the ESR test, is over fifty there is very little they can do for you. I was having a test every month and it never showed below one hundred. I didn't know the significance of that at the time and only learned about it many years later.

In the meantime as I managed to overcome the worst effects I did my best to keep going and to continue teaching. I had developed a waddling kind of walk, rather like a duck, and some of the students found this highly amusing. One afternoon on my way to the classroom I heard giggling, I turned around and there were three girls behind me, all waddling and imitating me. They blushed to the roots of their hair, so I said,

'Listen. If we're going to play ducks we'll do it in a row. Come here.'

The girls burst out laughing, came up to join me, and we acted daft for a couple of minutes, waddling in a line to the classroom. Never again did anyone laugh at me. I understand, however, that those girls were not intending to be hurtful; rather, they were experimenting to know what it felt like.

It was the same when I began to use a wheelchair, I would find the boys careering around the house in the chair, not only because they wanted a bit of fun, but because they were experimenting to see how it felt. Eventually, of course, after much sick leave I had to give up the school and college teaching.

Alongside the Dyslexia training, I needed to learn Welsh, the language of our adopted country. I am ashamed to admit that when we decided to move to Wales I thought that the Welsh language was not a living language. I thought it was like Latin only the written word of times gone by.

Latin was taught at my school, I could never get the grasp of what went where:- subjects, objects, weird and inexplicable clauses, declensions and verb conjugations. All this left me confused and feeling stupid, perhaps this experience allowed me to be more understanding of dyslexia and other learning difficulties. School finished Friday lunch time, Friday afternoon was free for social time or homework or the dreaded detention. I was normally too timid to get detention for misbehaviour but I frequently got it to work on my Latin. I know that this perseverance, that at the time never seemed to pay off, became my grounding to manage enough to get by on our Spanish visits and enough French to get me through the journey through France. The Welsh are, like the Spanish, far more lenient of any errors than the French. I always say if you take one step towards the Welsh, and the Spanish in fact, they will take two towards you.

Welsh is a very difficult language to learn with its mutations, and not being able to say a simple yes or no. In Welsh you need to say I am; I will; I did; I am not, I will not; I did not, etc, choosing the tense of the required answer.

I found a ten day, full-time course being held at Aberystwyth University led by Dan Lin James, who was very highly respected in his field. I called to see him and explained what I wanted to do, particularly from a teaching point of view. He answered me with a stream of Welsh.

'I don't think I've made myself clear. I don't understand or speak one word of Welsh. I've only just moved to the area.' I said again. Another stream of Welsh. After three attempts I told him,

'If I'm to learn to speak Welsh at all, then at least until I attend the course we will have to communicate in English.' As a sting in the tail I added 'If you don't want to teach Welsh to someone who is not Welsh but English, then we won't waste each other's time and I'll leave.'

That did the trick. He explained that the other students were in possession of a study book prior to the course starting and had been for some months. I had only a few weeks and he didn't think that was enough time. However, he produced the book and I departed, with the date set for enrolment.

I brought the book home and started on page one. Ble mae eleffant? (Where's the elephant?) Mae eleffant yn y gegin; yr ardd. The elephant is in the kitchen, the garden, and so forth. I don't think I have ever given my family so much to have fun with and laugh at.

Enrolment day came and I proudly strutted off to do my stuff. We started with a quite complex written test, some of it multiple choice answers which made it easy – what would it be in French or Spanish and tick that. I knew a child who constantly used the phrase 'wedi lost it' meaning 'I have lost it'. This was easy. The tests were marked remarkably quickly and we were allocated our level of competence. My goodness, I was in the second to the top group. Quite scary.

Then came the verbal test. The lady smiled at me and asked me in Welsh how I was and what was my name? I answered –

'Pardon?' No longer scary – bottom class. It was an amazing course the only draw back for me was that I lived 'across the border' and had two vocabulary lists to learn each night. One to use in Aberystwyth and South and one to use in my town Machynlleth and North. Apparently I am told on good authority South and North Waleans can't understand each other.

I did learn enough to conduct sensible conversations, rude words being a priority! If I was teaching or looking after a class of twenty-six Welsh pupils when their teacher was sick I had to be able to jump on any nonsense or rude language. I didn't need to actually speak Welsh to them just understanding and responding made them wary so they would stay in control.

As the years go by I find I am losing so much of the language, if you don't use it you lose it syndrome; but it is still good to understand the daily chatter and understand the notices and posters. The lady who helped me in the house finally gave up our weekly Welsh speaking mornings as she said I spoke 'book Welsh' and she felt bad only speaking 'yr iaith y gegin' – the language of the kitchen. I couldn't convince her that that was the language I wanted to speak – the normal language of the people, as we do in our mother tongue.

Speaking of languages reminds me of a holiday we had in Sweden. This was a week over the Christmas period when the Caravan Park was closed and we were not needed. We were taken from the Hotel to the local Church for Candlemass. The Church was decorated with thousands of lighted candles. There were two 20 foot high Christmas trees covered in lighted candles and every ledge and niche was filled to capacity. No health and safety issues here.

The service was carried out in Swedish and the hymn book was all in the Swedish language. I applied my knowledge of Welsh and by the end of the first hymn had worked out that an 'o' with two dots over it made a certain sound and various other letter sounds were easy to identify. By the end of the second hymn I was singing with gusto, although unable to understand the meaning of what I was singing.

At the end of the service the people sitting in the pew in front turned round and started to speak to me in Swedish. It took a lot of persuasion to make them understand that I did not speak Swedish.

I was fascinated by what I felt must be the Celtic connection when I discovered that kirk meant church as it does in Scottish and again barn was so like the Scottish bairn for child. And then one day we visited a Tan Stikt Museet (forgive me if my memory for spelling is not accurate). In Welsh tan means fire, so the stick and the museum seemed obvious. We were visiting a Fire Stick Museum, in its literal translation, but actually translated as a Matchstick Museum.

Because of my background with teaching and alleviating the difficulties presented due to dyslexia, I became involved with the Head Master of the High School in Aberystwyth. Aberystwyth is a University Town and has a General Hospital and it may not be politically correct to say so, but the parents have higher than average expectations for their children. This school had a Remedial Department. Anthony and Edward were by this time attending this school as the local school where I was still teaching, did not have any form of effective help-line for children with difficulties. I might add sending them to this school was a difficult decision to make, bearing in mind I was teaching at the local school with the potential question of – isn't this school good enough for your kids then?

The Headmaster and I – he with his contacts and me with my knowledge and experience of the subject – put pressure on the Welsh Joint Education Committee who then allowed those students formally diagnosed with dyslexia, to have extra time to check their spelling when sitting their GCSE/O Level exams.

My work with and response from these children was being noticed by now and I was asked by the Pediatrician at the General Hospital to give a talk, as a parent with a dyslexic child, to an audience of some three hundred medical and educational professionals.

This was nerve-wracking to say the least. I kept to my remit of parent, thinking it would not be etiquette to encroach on the teacher's talk, despite this now being my field of expertise. I explained how Edward's junior school Headmaster had labeled him a rebel and how his school reports always stressed that he made no effort and could do better if he tried harder. What was really meant was that the teachers were fully aware of the discrepancy between Edward's obvious IQ and personality, and his performance. How many children have suffered from this over the generations? In fact the Headmaster explained, Edward was rebelling against the confines of his desk and would have done much better in an open plan classroom. I was stunned at this conclusion.

At the end of my talk I was inundated with questions and congratulations for the understanding I had offered to them and why had I not been invited to speak as the teacher? The main response was,

'You weren't nervous.' until someone said,

'You should have been sitting on the front row, you could see if not hear her knees knocking.'

Dyslexia requires continuous reinforcement of even the basic needs, such as constant structure, phonetics, rules, syllabification to name a few and what I call survival techniques. How do you spell beautiful? Well, if you can remember you are a Utiful (a bit like being useful) then just be one! 'Be A Utiful'. I know many of my students continue to use these survival tricks throughout life. Much has been made by the Government of the use of synthetic phonics, but nobody seems to know what that actually means. We don't need fancy names it is just pure sound. C – Kuh, A – a, T – tuh, no matter how fast you say it, will never say CAT, it will always say Kuatuh. But pure sound where the sound is clipped as C! A! T! when said at speed then says CAT. Too simple, if we taught all children as though they were dyslexic, all children would learn to read to their potential.

Credit must always be given, alongside encouragement and praise, for the sheer perseverance and hard work that these children learn to put in to overcoming their problem. Having realized earlier that our other two sons James and Anthony and even Richard all had dyslexia in different forms and in different degrees, it explained so much and helped remove at least some of the frustration of 'could do better' with them all.

The County Psychologist at one meeting regarding Edward gave me a rather patronizing and metaphorical slap on the wrist as he disagreed vehemently with my having told Edward that he was dyslexic and explaining the implications to him. By this time he had been formerly diagnosed by Aston University, who were at the leading edge of discovery of how to diagnose and teach this new phenomenon. In the psychologist's opinion he would not try now, he would just give up. I am astounded at the lack of practical understanding of these so called professional academics. The effect was the reverse Edward at last had a handle on which to hang his difficulties and differences.

At the age of seven I had been sitting on his bed reading him a story when he stopped me.

'I don't want to frighten you Mummy, but I think I may have something growing in my head that's stopping me being able to read as well as everyone else. 'Coz I know I'm not thick and I know some of the others aren't as clever as me, but they are good readers.' At seven years old this child thought he had a brain tumour.

As I think of it now I immediately feel the overpowering nauseous feeling that swept over me. I told the psychologist that I didn't care what he called it, he could call it 'flat feet' if he wished, but any child, Edward not least, needed a name for this hidden demon. The author Terry Pratchett says,

'Before you can slay the monster you need to say its name.'

Edward's dyslexia presented itself even earlier than this. He was a late talker and we always joked that he didn't need to as the other two spoke for him, which turned out to be far from the truth as the 'weverbewating washer' proved.

Aunty Ida was watching him writing and asked,

'Does he write like this often?' Well, indeed he did. She picked up the paper he had been using and motioned me to follow her. She held it up to the mirror and in the reflection in the mirror it read,

'I am Edward. I am five.'

Leonardo da Vinci is known to have written in mirror writing. When dyslexia was first discovered you had to be average IQ or above, so he clearly fits the profile.

A similar attitude to the Psychologist came to light when I first became immobile. The Head Rheumatologist at a well-known Orthopaedic Hospital in the UK said I should not use a wheelchair as I would then 'give in.' What he meant by this I wouldn't like to say, as I was at that time in great pain, unable to get out of a chair unaided and certainly couldn't walk. Fortunately my Social Services contact disagreed and set the wheels in motion – pardon the pun – for the National Health Service to provide me with a powered wheelchair, which at least gave me back the semblance of a life. A great example of which follows.

During one of my more active periods a large Function was held at the Hotel at Plas Dolguog attended by Lords and Ladies, MP's, famous names and faces. A Memorial Point had been organized by the BBC in memory of Wynford Vaughan Thomas. This was placed at his favourite view overlooking Machynlleth from the Plynlymon mountain range across the Dyfi Valley to Cadair Idris and the Aran mountains. We couldn't move for Rolls Royce cars.

I had been busy organizing flower displays for the tables and entrance, a job I loved even though I needed help to do it. I was bobbing about checking all was as it should be when a voice, and what a voice, said,

'May I talk with you? Is there somewhere quiet we could sit?' I looked up into the clear, twinkling eyes of Sir Geraint Evans. I guided him through into the beautiful Conservatory Restaurant and he sat down.

'Well, tell me who you are.' was his opening remark. I thought a moment,

'Er, I belong to the Hotel.' this was true the Hotel and land have never belonged to us, it is too special to belong to anyone. Anyway the Bank Manager would dispute any claim to ownership!

'I do the flowers, and check all the chair legs have been dusted and generally make a nuisance of myself.' I joked. He flushed.

'Oh, how rude of me. I didn't realize you belonged to this wonderful place. I thought you were a guest!' He lit a cigarette and I gently chastised him for jeopardising his voice. He laughed and said,

'I better tell you why I wanted to speak to you.' His smile lit up the room as he continued. 'I have never seen anyone drive a wheelchair with such panache!'

NLP (Neuro Linguistic Programming) was another teaching system hitting Europe and it was so relevant not only to my own situation, where health challenges were dominant in my life, but to my teaching, particularly of children with special educational needs. I attended a number of courses whilst in Spain and was fascinated with the impact that these quite simple yet strangely complex approaches could have, for instance to discover how to enter another persons world view. Some people view their world auditorily and some visually – this has nothing to do with sight or hearing but to do with the brain and its interpretation.

I could spend a day with a child using phrases such as – can you see how it works? Do you see what I'm saying? Look at what it's doing? and have no understanding or response. If the child is working on an auditory wave length and I change my language to – do you hear what I'm saying? Do you feel how it works? then an immediate understanding and response will be forthcoming.

I have been amazed on many occasions to observe the reaction. In a group situation the teacher needs to 'pepper' the conversation with visual, auditory, kinaesthetic and verbal approaches in order to catch the individual software of each child's brain computer. I could write a book on NLP alone and I acquired a Teacher's Certificate but never followed this through as I never felt I could fully do it justice other than using it as a tool in my own day to day situations.

The NLP training included sessions to help overcome nerves and loosen the tongue. It was called mouth flapping. Each participant was given a title and told to speak to the class on the subject for two minutes without repeating or stopping. The subjects included amongst others, chewing gum, peanut butter, string, and mine which was football. I didn't know anything about football, didn't like it even. So in I plunged and for two minutes told them about my dislike of watching grown men chase a pig's bladder around a muddy field. It was great fun and hilarious, each student becoming so wrapped up in the fun that indeed the nerves did disappear and the mouth did flap. At the end of the course, with this and other techniques, all of us were capable of standing up and speaking at a minutes notice.

At the end of the final session the tutor turned to me and pointed,

'You, finish the evening and the course with a meditation.'

Without stopping to think my mouth began to flap, without any preparation a meditation came and this process of learning to speak in any circumstances and in any situation has helped me on many occasions. Twelve of the students were Russian so the course had an interpreter throughout and this too became a lesson in how to speak through an interpreter which was helpful when I presented the Peace Scroll to the United Nations University of Peace some years later. The meditation also was very relevant to what was to transpire in my life in the near future. Here it is.

Our relationship with our home, the Earth.

Let's go on a journey. A long, long journey. A journey way out into space. For this you will need a space ship.

So climb aboard your space ship and fire up the engines. Listen to them roar into action.

OK LETS' GO.

Go – shooting out into space. Way, way out into space. Faster than the speed of light. Out into the black void. And as you slow your journey and come to a stop, turn around and look back at the earth. Way down below you – way, way down. The blue planet, spinning and dancing in the blue/black/purple void. Isn't she beautiful?

Now imagine, as a child would imagine, that the earth is getting smaller. Smaller and smaller. She is so small you can pick her up. So reach out and take her in your hands. Look at her. Beautiful jewel. Precious jewel. More precious and beautiful than any jewel you have ever seen.

Place her against your heart. Feel her heartbeat. Feel your heartbeat, and synchronise the two. Allow her to sink deep inside you. Place her in that special place where you keep all precious things. Because we all have a special place where we keep precious things, don't we? Remember she is you and you are she. Relax and leave this jewel there.

And now, look back at the real earth, way down below you, still spinning and dancing and go – shooting back. Down, down, faster than the speed of light. Back to your home, the Earth. Back to this town, back to this room. Feel your back against the chair, feel your feet against the floor. Feel your hands and remember your jewel, the Earth, she is you and you are she.

Take this experience into your life and live that memory, that relationship. Remember how precious and beautiful you both are.

As well as the school and college teaching, which was for just three and a half days a week, I taught individual children privately. The County were now paying me, unofficially, to do this against the Welsh Constitution, as parents were demanding that they had a choice and the results I was achieving no-one else, certainly in our area, was.

One of the teachers in school approached me one day,

'I know what you're doing with Edward.' she said, 'My nephew, who is Welsh speaking and attends a Welsh speaking school, cannot even sound his alphabet let alone read. Will you teach him?'

'No, I'm not qualified for remedial work, I can't possibly teach him.' I replied, but she virtually got down on her hands and knees and begged me. In the end, I relented.

'Well, I'll do it, but bear in mind I'm not promising anything. We'll just give it a go and see what happens, on the condition that I teach him in English, because that will follow through into his Welsh (he attended an all Welsh school and his family language, his first language, was Welsh) but if I attempt to teach him in Welsh it will not follow through into his English.' I proved this over and over again with different students whatever their ages. Welsh is a phonetic language and once you know the alphabet is far more logical than English.

The child was highly intelligent. He knew all the names of the planets and could tell you the distance between them. He had two pet goldfish, called Jaws and something else – the name eludes me now. So we started by creating a scrapbook, cutting out pictures and I wrote names underneath them.

After a few lessons and once I had gained his confidence I said,

'I've got a blue felt pen and a red felt pen, which would you like to use to draw over my writing?' Using the word draw was deliberate, my theory was that I hoped to take away the decision of whether he would or wouldn't write and turn it into a decision of which colour he would choose. It worked.

'I'll do it in blue.' he said, this was the first time he had used a pen for writing in a long time and the mental block was cleared. He was eight years old.

We progressed from there and I'm delighted to say the boy eventually went on to get all his A levels and works in the University at Aberystwyth. I have many similar tales about children whom the education system totally and utterly failed, because their 'software' was different to other people.

Another little helpful trick was to offer a red pen to an older child and say,

'What's this and what is it used for?' The reply was inevitable,

'It's a red pen and it's what teachers use to find and mark all your mistakes.' This was a powerful instrument, a weapon of mass destruction to a dyslexic child.

'Mm, well today you're going to be the teacher. You can look at your work and find what you would like to change, if anything. That pen is very powerful – now you have it you have the power.' This little trick was always a winner. The children, from that moment on, began to cultivate the habit of looking for and finding their own errors.

One young girl I taught had spina bifida and needed teaching at home. She had had an operation implanting steel rods into her back and was lying on a flat bed in the farmhouse kitchen. She spent four hours on her back and four hours on her stomach, so her lesson had to be planned to fit. She hung over the end of the bed with the typewriter in front of her on a small table where she could reach it. She was a cheerful young girl and my task was to persuade her and encourage her to learn to type. She liked poetry and to help Mummy with baking. I showed her my anthology and she decided she would like to make one. She chose the poems and then chose her favourite recipes We gathered an anthology of her favourite poetry and built up a recipe file, all of this typed by her.

At the time I was in so much pain that I didn't know what to do. Richard would drive me to her house as even with an automatic car it had become impossible to drive myself. I continued to go to teach this child even on really bad days because I only needed to take one look at her and that made me think,

'How dare you, how dare you feel sorry for yourself?' She did me so much good and taught me not to wallow in self pity.

Another young child came to the house for dyslexia lessons. His dedicated and devoted mother drove him a sixty mile round trip twice a week for this. He had mild brain damage and it was very difficult when it came to holding his attention, even his eyelashes when blinking distracted him and broke his concentration. Attention Deficit Disorder at its worst. Richard was this young man's hero and he would work in exchange for half an hour 'playing' with Richard – you see bribery does have its place. His mother was a wonderful person and determined that her son would have enough help to be able to reach his full potential. She brought me a letter one day from the school Psychologist.

'I want you to tell me what this means. I don't understand it. It's a report on John's progress.' I took the letter and read it, once and once more before I burst out laughing. The letter read,

'John is reading to a level of which he is not capable.' I looked at her and she looked at me. I didn't have a word to say, I didn't need to. The acknowledgement of the work put in on all our parts was praise indeed in this strange sentence.

As I gathered more and more students I set up a small business ploughing the money back into the different resources needed for each individual child. I called it 'Frogs into Princes'. As a child started I would read them a story I had written and send it home to be read by parents. Alongside the story I gave them a tie pin of a jolly green frog. This they were to wear at all times, particularly at school.

The story told them that the reason they were having difficulties learning to read was because deep, deep down inside them they weren't children, they were frogs, and now they were having lessons that were designed for frogs they would soon catch up. It explained the wonderful qualities that frogs have because of their problems such as understanding, compassion and the ability to help others experiencing difficulties in all sorts of different ways. The frog pin was for the bad days. I told them,

'If you are finding things hard, being bullied, or just tired through having to work harder than normal children, then look at your frog pin and smile. All is well now you are having frog lessons. You <u>are</u> different, will always be different, everyone is different. When you look at your frog pin and smile you know you will come through, shining above others with your special understanding. That is when the frog will become the Prince, you won't even need to be kissed by a princess.'

It had an effect over and above for one young man. He was sixteen and I hadn't given him the story or a frog pin, because I thought he would find it condescending and belittling. At sixteen he was a man not a child, but he saw them on my desk, asked what they were and proceeded to read the story (severely affected young people don't <u>read</u> for pleasure!) As he read, he passed comments and made funny little noises. He slapped the story down onto my desk.

'Why didn't anybody tell me. I never knew. All these years and I never knew I was really a frog. Where's my frog pin?'

Our youngest grandchildren, who live close by, have two sets of grandparents who are fully involved with their daily lives. They hear stories of themselves when they were small, their parents as they grew up, their grandparents and what life was like in their grandparents young lives, their great grandparents and the progress of technology, the cost of goods …. with food rationing, war and peace and so on. They develop a history, a context in which they can find where they fit, where they came from, how today fits into what has been and how it will fit into what is to come.

Each generation is born into what is to them normal. Today's excesses of technology, food, entertainment take their toll in laziness, obesity and a lack of personal imagination. Bearing in mind Einstein's saying 'Imagination is more important than education' this has the potential to be serious.

Christmas and the New Year are a time for family and especially grandchildren who are a great joy, with so much to teach us in their advanced and profound way of looking at the world and our relationships. Our three year old granddaughter spent a number of weeks in the run up to Christmas, declaring that she was going to have a rocket from Santa. This was so that she, Grandpa and Grandma could go to the moon. The details she had worked out were amazingly complex – such as where we would keep our coats and what we would eat. What was even more amazing was that she was fully aware that this was pretend. My spiritual training has included working with 'what if' or 'pretend' and it fascinated me that this was inherent in her understanding.

When I tell my grandchildren little anecdotes of my childhood, they sit wide eyed and fascinated.

'During the Second World War I was a baby and when the air raid sirens sounded everyone had to go into the underground air raid shelters. Aunty Jillian was old enough to have a Mickey Mouse gas mask, but I was too tiny so my Mummy, your Great Grandma, had to put me in a box with a glass lid and she couldn't take me out, even if I screamed or needed feeding or my nappy changing. Not until the all clear signal was given and the danger of toxic gas had passed and we were safe.'

The questions that this brought forth encompassed all human emotion, the greatest though was compassion. I was interested to see recently that the Dr Who series featured Winston Churchill and the Second World War and the children came to talk to me about the relationship with the stories I had told them and Dr Who brought this alive in their eyes and became a practical point of learning and knowledge.

I tell them about rationing. I tell them that when I was thirteen just one hundred and twenty five grams of sweets were allowed. Not each day – each week. How houses were not heated as they are today and my sister and I would get dressed in bed under the covers because the room was so cold. In a morning an inch of frost and ice would be clinging to the inside of the bedroom windows. They don't know what chilblains are! When I was twelve I attended an all girl school, at that time two out of every three of the girls in my class did not have a father. Single parent families, not through choice or disagreement but the horrors and fatalities of war.

The grandchildren come to me for craft play, particularly making greetings cards, a hobby of mine as I became less able in other fields. They bring imagination and flair in full action and I provide the materials of every description to fulfill their ideas. I am the 'sitting down' Grandma whilst Nain (Welsh Grandma) is the active Grandma who takes them on trains and double decker buses and to playgrounds. Their lives are full of so much that their elders have to offer, extending and expanding on parents and school, creating a web of past, present and future on which to build their own life experiences.

When grandson Robert was just five he told me,

'Grandma you are really, really old.' I teased him saying I was not and anyway how could he tell? His answer was something that lives with me to this day.

'Oh, I can tell by all your crinkles and you are so wise.' We have lost that Native American tradition of honouring our Elders and benefiting from their wisdom gleaned over their lifetimes.

We were once taking two of the grandchildren to Anglesey for the day to a dinosaur exhibition; they were about six and eight. They were sitting in the back of the car and they started talking about which came first, the chicken or the egg? Richard and I left them alone thinking what good pals they were, and they continued to chatter away.

'Well, it would be the chicken, because if it wasn't the chicken where would the egg come from?' pronounced Taionee.

'Yes, but where did the chicken come from to lay the egg in the first place' responded Kiera. The conversation went on like this, round and round and back again.

'Perhaps it was an eagle. Perhaps God laid the egg and the eagle sat on it.' This must have gone on for twenty minutes and was getting rather intense.

My patience was running out and I turned to them and said,

'Look, God laid the egg, God sat on it. That's an end to it!'

A quiet voice responded,

'I told you Grandma knew everything.'

Wisdom is just another perception!

Education is not 'pushing in' information or knowledge, but it is often just that through all the checks and tests. Education comes from 'educare' which means to draw out. This is the drawing out of inherent knowledge to complement presented information. Our education system works on the principle of 'no child left behind' in this way we have no losers but nor do we have any winners.

Self discipline is something learned through perseverance and it is the ultimate discipline, an essential tool. Authoritarian discipline has no effect without self discipline, incorporating responsibility, not only to oneself but to others. This kind of education teaches collaboration, integrity and respect. If due respect were given to our Elders and our Elders took their role seriously then evolution could progress on a very different route to greater becoming. Respect for others is of paramount importance but it is often forgotten that we need self respect, self worth in order to be a whole human and interact with others and our world in a positive way.

Elders embody through experience, that perennial wisdom so needed in today's hectic pace of life. By honouring the input, experience and wisdom of the Elders, society, particularly the young members, will become rooted again. They will have a sense of place, a sense of history, a sense of where they belong. Interchange and family values can then become normal with a giving and taking, a sharing and an understanding, taking the time to stand and stare, to become as a child and link hands.

Teaching and learning could become so integrated that we would have to ask the question, who teaches whom?

Chapter Fifteen

Plas Dolguog – Destiny Presents Itself

In 1991 we were faced with another major business challenge. Our property was bounded by a small river on two sides and across the river was Plas Dolguog, a Grade II listed building. This had been part of the Londonderry Estate, in fact the house provided for the Manager, as the Londonderry family used The Plas (Hall) in the centre of town for their holiday home. Plas Dolguog bears an inscription testifying that it was renovated in 1632. Written history tells us that there has been a residence here since the 6th century and was to be found marked on maps before the town of Machynlleth itself. The local doctor and his wife and daughter had lived there for many years and eventually sold to a couple from the South who had given up a Residential Nursing home to semi-retire in the country.

The house was in dire need of further renovation and David and his wife Eileen, who now owned the property, began to renovate the old building.

We became good friends, they would come to us for a shower when they were without, and 'baby sat' the two teenage sons left at home when Richard and I took a break. Early one evening they rang and we went round. Behind the boarded up fireplace and fitted three bar electric fire was a small but beautiful inglenook. They had only rolled the carpet back a couple of feet not expecting to find such a gem. We all sat sipping coffee and tea whilst Richard and David exposed the beam and stonework, sipping to slake their dusty throats.

After eighteen months David and Eileen had to resign themselves that they could not carry on. The evening meals and the B & B were just not enough to make it work and it was beginning to affect their health, still renovating in among the guests. With great sadness, they would have to sell. They offered it to us first as it was more valuable to us than to anyone, bordering our property as it did. We couldn't even put it in 'the thinking box'. We had nothing to sell and no means of raising that kind of money, so it went on the open market. Sadly for David and Eileen it did not sell and they turned and returned to us as their only hope.

Richard and I were already besotted with the place but explained the amount we might, and it was a big might, get the Bank to consider would be an insult and ruin our lovely friendship. They came back again – they didn't say 'insult us' but that's what it came down to. We were always conscious that it could be bought by some big business which would ruin its peace and energies. We knew the answer to our offer would be a refusal and all would be well.

We've made some miscalculations about situations in our lives and this was one of them – they accepted. Oh my goodness what were we to do now? We were led by our hearts and not our heads. What experience did we have of running a small hotel?

Those well-used thinking caps were wearing thin. We concluded that the only way to make the extra nine acres of property viable would be to put in wooden chalets as holiday homes, discreetly placed amongst the trees and in the old orchard. With carefully planned and sensitive positioning, permission was granted for us to move ahead.

We advertised and interviewed for a Manager and basic staff to cover the seven day week. We settled on a couple who appeared to have the required experience and CV's and a date was set for their arrival.

I had decided the only thing we would change was the dining room at the time painted blue, blue carpet, blue tablecloths and serviettes. It was always cold in this room and people dining would always whisper as though in a cathedral. I wanted it pale, pale pink to warm it up and make it less intimidating. I called in the services of a friend who had been an interior designer and owned with her husband their own hotel at one time. We chose the colour and Richard had thirty to forty litres mixed. He and Anthony, who had a day off, set about painting as we awaited the arrival of the Manager and his wife.

I went home and brought the soup I had prepared earlier. On my return, I gasped at what I saw, half the ceiling was painted – fluorescent, candy floss pink! I defy anyone to choose a colour from a shade card but this was truly exotic and quite, quite awful. Back to the shade card and start again. Anybody want a tin of pink paint?

The couple duly arrived and started to organise the attics where they were to live. As Anthony and Richard had been painting I had sat with this couple, discussing menus, costings, expectations, and asking for their input – my, had I done my homework in the last six weeks. The couple went to the attics where they were due to live and started to organise their possessions.

When lunch time arrived a half hour or so after they had gone to settle in we called them to eat. They didn't come. We called again – Anthony said,

'That's funny they've just driven out, their trailer attached.'

The immediate reaction was why? Or more dubiously, what have they taken? Richard went up to their quarters to find them unchanged with none of the couples belongings and he set off to see if he could find them to see what on earth was happening.

They had gone – never to be seen again. We sat in stunned silence. What was all that about. Anthony turned to me and said,

'It's all your fault Mum.' Open mouthed, I asked what could he mean?

'Well, six weeks ago you knew nothing, you were exceedingly inexperienced in this field. I don't know how you did it but I was listening to you as you talked to them and you have learnt so much in the last six weeks. They thought they were going to take you to the cleaners, and suddenly discovered that was not going to work anymore, hence their hasty departure.'

I didn't know what to say except to take it as a compliment. This was Anthony's trade and he knew what he was talking about.

Well slowly it dawned what a predicament we were in. Easter coming up and accommodation and rooms already booked. Richard was way out of his comfort zone and I was too disabled to be of use to man or beast.

Anthony said,

'I'm going back tonight to start work tomorrow. I have holidays owing, I will hand in my notice and come home and we'll do what we can.' All three of our boys have taken the upbringing we gave them and with their own personalities, used it to achieve the maturity to make decisions and stand on their own two feet. I don't know how we survived those first weeks and months but we did. Anthony became twenty one during this time and repeated history by doing what I had done and catering for his own twenty first birthday party.

Anthony, at such a young age helped by André, who had stayed on when David and Eileen left, did a remarkable job. Waitressing staff were found, with housekeeping staff and people to wash up. Young people from school on Saturdays were a bonus. This had been Edward's job cleaning brasses and helping David, having waded across the river in his wellies with his shepherd's crook – payment for working with the local doctor tending his sheep. Anthony was putting in very long exhausting hours and it was imperative that we found help.

Richard had been invited to join the Rotarians some years before and I had therefore become a member of the Inner wheel. I had done my stint as President and one morning I had a phone call from an Inner Wheel member, it was common knowledge we were looking for a chef. The lady concerned gave me a phone number of someone working locally, she mentioned the business, she gave details about him and that he was looking for a change. She knew him well and could recommend him not only as a chef but as a thoroughly nice person.

I rang the number she had given me. The man that answered said he did not know the lady concerned, he was not working where she had said, in fact not working at all, as he was at home looking after two very small children. After a short rather strange conversation he said he would come to see us as we did sound to be in a pretty difficult situation.

Gary arrived for our meeting, tall, good looking, sense of humour and a CV to take our breath away. We all hit it off straight away and he asked what we were looking for. It was obvious that our struggling start meant we could not possibly afford someone of his calibre and sadly we had to say so. He thought a few moments and said,

'I'm allowed to work for sixteen hours without affecting my benefits. I would be willing to come in and help Anthony with Sunday lunch and prepare steak and kidney, lasagna, whatever, to fill the freezers.' This would definitely take some of the pressure off Anthony.

The universe works in such unexpected ways, but what a blessing from such a strange and inauspicious start. As Gary became more involved and his children went to live with their Mother, he came to live in the attics as the original Managers had been due to do. As the weeks went by he brought a lady friend carrying a small boy and a little girl holding her hand. Slowly, but not too slowly this relationship became permanent and Sharon and Gary married and moved into a chalet which they bought and fit out to their needs.

By this time Anthony had met a local girl, Tina. She was planning to go to University to study Hotel Catering and Management in Huddersfield. Anthony wasn't prepared to lose her and so enrolled as a mature student and they went together.

Sharon and Gary took on the job of Managers. Obviously they couldn't work seven days a week, twenty four hours a day, so Richard and I spent many hours sleeping in. We tried every bedroom in order to check its user friendliness, every hotelier should do this; booking guests in, and my special job – keeping guests entertained – I may not be capable physically but I love to talk!

One evening I was sitting in the small residents lounge with the inglenook fireplace, always thought of as the heart of the house – in Spanish a 'housewife' – ama de casa – is called 'soul of the house' so much nicer and so much the truth, when an older gentleman in his eighties, tall upright and inevitably Scottish, (a recurring necessity in my life is the Scottish connection) with his lady companion, she was younger in her sixties, both smartly attired and elegant, arrived to stay in the Hotel.

The gentleman took a pendulum out of his pocket and it began to swing gently and inconspicuously at his side. When he had finished, I asked about his use of the pendulum. His reply was so matter of fact,

'Oh, we are going to see George Chapman and I couldn't remember whether to turn left or right so I just asked.' George was a famous internationally renowned healer living locally.

Our conversation continued and I remarked about the stone heads and made reference to the devas in the healer's garden. His reaction was immediate,

'Devas, what do you know about devas. People don't talk about such things, don't even know about such things. What's your involvement with devas?' Devas are the spirits and gods of the elemental kingdoms.

After much quizzing and talk, his companion interceded to say,

'Of course, she was a Cathar.' And he responded that it was not important at this juncture. He managed to draw out of me my spiritual journey and understanding. Richard and other guests had joined us by now and he turned to Richard and asked if there was anywhere he could speak to me privately.

The bar room was now closed and we could sit in there with the required subdued lighting. We talked some more filling out details of my understanding and experiences and he proceeded to lay his hands on my head – only for a matter of seconds.

'Right, these are the books you must now read.' and he wrote out a list of more than twenty books and authors on various esoteric subjects. He then passed it to me. I asked in what order should they be read? He looked at me with a look almost of disdain,

'The books will present themselves, in order, when you are ready to receive the information.' Suitably chastised I took the list and wondered how it would all work. The two visitors left, although he said he would return, I have never seen him again. Richard teased me and said perhaps he was a spirit being who came just to set me on the next path. What if ?

Immediately, the first book presented itself. A friend said he had a book I would be interested in. One down, nineteen to go! Over a period of some eighteen months the books appeared. Sometimes I found them in a bookshop, others were lent, an odd one discovered at a second-hand book shop or Bring and Buy sale.

When visiting Glastonbury, Richard wheeled me into a large esoteric bookshop.

'Good grief, I'll never get you out of here. I should have brought a picnic.' he said. I found a couple of books that I wanted. The shelves were full to capacity, every nook and cranny from floor to ceiling packed with books.

With a wheelchair you are always at least a couple of feet in front of the pusher. Richard was reaching for one of the books as he was behind me.

'Third shelf from the top.' I said. Suddenly of its own volition a fat green book leapt, there's no other way to describe it, from its snug position packed between the other books on the shelf and landed cleanly and directly on my lap.

'I think I'm meant to have this one too!' It was 'A Course in Miracles'. I studied this course for the full year, one page every three days. I had to overcome the initial read, absorb, don't question, just do attitude, in order to be able to do this but found a lot of help and insight within its pages.

Spiritual understanding, thinking you've found the way, joining like-minded people, frequently leads to disappointment and disillusion. Some years later whilst attending the Millennium World Summit for Religious and Spiritual Leaders in 2000 I came across a group of 'A Course in Miracle' followers.

I was in a wheelchair, tube fed – obviously not a perfect specimen of a physical human. We sat with them in a casual layout for lunch. I thought I was imagining it when I was left out of the conversation, or would catch a glance of fear? contempt? I wasn't sure. Until Richard told them he was just my facilitator and I was the delegate. Oops, not the best move, they rounded on me.

'Why would you be invited? You are physically imperfect, maimed, a reflection of the inner spiritual soul.' I would not achieve nirvana or whatever names they gave it. I was doomed to oblivion as a warped, unusable specimen.

Needless to say we did not sit with them again, they wouldn't have allowed it, even if I had wanted to, just perhaps to fight my corner. There was no point, they were absolutely convinced that they had interpreted this Course exactly as it was intended and anyway I must have been lying saying I had completed the Course in one year, alone and without group assistance, they had never heard of that being possible.

I can't judge them because if I do I would have to use words like, fanaticism, arrogance, closed mindedness, fear, the need to be told what to do, being unable to make their own judgements through experience. The words can stay on paper but not be applied or I fall into the same trap.

So many interesting guests came to Plas Dolguog Hotel. We joked that there was a belisha beacon at the end of the lane announcing,

'If you are weird come here!' They say – like attracts like.

I remember two older, very conventional ladies. It was my job to sit by the log fire in the Residents lounge and keep guests occupied and entertained. Richard said,

'No ghosts tonight don't frighten them.' We talked generally for a while about the weather and what there was to do in the area, when one of the ladies broke in and said,

'What about ghosts, my dear, how many ghosts do you have?' Wow, what a surprise.

'First there's Mary, she sits here in a rocking chair by the fire, just where I am sitting, I didn't know why I chose to sit here until I learned about Mary. A young lady psychic told me about her. She said she was 'the soul of the house' and had great love for it. When I asked the psychic the ghost's name she said,

'I'll tell you tomorrow when I've consulted my guides.'

When tomorrow came, I knew what it would be. It would be, Abigail, we had enough history, and there was a plaque on the outside wall F & A, to know that the house had belonged to Francis and Abigail. Well, my psychic lady told me the ghost's name is Mary. What a let down, she'd obviously got it wrong. However, I went to do a little research. I shouldn't have been surprised, the house had been given as a wedding present to – Mary – on her marriage.

We also have a 6th century poet Llywarch Hen, who wrote a very melancholic twenty six stanza poem during one of his visits whilst suffering an illness. He was supposed to wander the grounds at night.

Then there was my Godmother, who I am told, appeared standing beside me one night, I was given a full description and what she died of. Mind you she didn't really count as she has never been seen before or since.'

The old lady smiled sweetly,

'There's one you've missed dear, there's old Charles. We pass him regularly on the staircase. He has a bad leg and a limp and comes here because he had such happy times visiting when he was alive. They are all benign, my dear, and have only the interests of the house and its occupants at heart.' Lessons in how we see people, not just people with disabilities, and preconceive who they are, are always around if only we notice them. Fascinating people disguised in ordinary bodies with normal faces.

Later in the evening a third lady arrived, they were all sisters. This one read the tea leaves. My Maternal Grandmother 'read the tea leaves'. She read a neighbour's leaves and was unable to tell her what she had seen. A young child would die in an accident of some sort. The neighbour's child survived into adulthood. My Grandmother's two year old son Stewart, however, died following an accident with a boiling pan of potatoes. She never read the leaves again. Perhaps I inherited my psychic abilities from my Grandmother.

As a young child I eavesdropped on a session with a psychic who had come to do a reading for her. I hid behind the curtain, there was no door, as this lady went into trance. Her introduction stressed that she must not be interrupted, no loud noises, telephone, door bell or such because she would leave her body for the spirit to enter and whilst she was gone she would be attached by a silver thread, that is how she would find her way back. If she was startled the thread would break and she would be stranded unable to return to her body. She went into trance and her normal voice became as deep and resonant as the deepest man's. Either I don't remember the rest or I fled, terrified at the prospect of a disembodied person being left with no way for the spirit to find its way back.

A little more humorously was when a man working for British Telecom was staying at the hotel, long term, during a specific job. He sat up many a night drinking the odd beer, talking to the staff and locals for company and no doubt the ghosts cropped up. It was the habit of this dear soul to go to bed with the remains of his beer and a whisky chaser. Some ten minutes after retiring he came dashing back into the bar, ashen faced and shaking,

'I've just seen the ghost. He was floating down the garden – all white and eerie.' The poor man was never told. Chefs wear white tops and blue check trousers, in the dark and at a distance their bottom half seems to disappear and they appear to be floating. That night as Anthony had been locking up he had walked his dog down the garden, the dog loved to dive into the bushes, which would leave this floating apparition alone and in full view. I have no doubt our guest dined and drank well on recounting his real life ghost story and only if he reads this will he know the truth.

Richard and I were on duty booking in guests, it was late afternoon, dark, very wet and miserable when a charming couple arrived. They were wet and cold and ready for some warmth and hospitality and Richard booked them in and offered to make them afternoon tea. As they sat by the roaring log fire they visibly relaxed and started to talk of their trip. The gentleman was American and the lady was Hawaiian. I asked how far they had traveled today before arriving with us.

'Oh quite a long way, taking into account the weather. We came all the way from Peewhillie.'

When I recovered I explained my laughing response. 'Well that's a new one on me. Actually it is pronounced – here I will write it phonetically using the Welsh alphabet – Poothhelli.'

I spent the next half hour teaching them the Welsh alphabet so that they could at least pronounce the names of the places they visited. We will always call it Peewhillie, (Pwllheli) how can we resist?

Chapter Sixteen

A Decade of Change

The 1990's heralded a decade of enormous change in my life, from the deaths of both my parents to the start of an initiative that would ultimately take me to the United Nations in New York as a delegate to the Millennium World Summit for Religious and Spiritual Leaders.

Mummy and Daddy enjoyed their garden and Daddy needed to move the greenhouse. The neighbour had allowed his leylandii hedge to grow so tall that it blocked the sun and light to the greenhouse. This caused Mummy and Daddy much distress as the neighbour refused to listen to their requests that the hedge be topped to a more reasonable height. The concrete slabs on which the greenhouse was sitting were the old fashioned kind, thick and extra large and Daddy in his early eighties was moving them, single-handed to another area of the garden where the greenhouse was to be repositioned and thus benefit from the sun.

Daddy came in, he was cold, and Mummy went to make him a cup of tea as he went to bed to warm up with the electric blanket. When she took the tea in to him, without any warning Daddy lay back on his pillow closed his eyes and took his final breath. She ran to the neighbour who came and sat with her awaiting the arrival of the doctor.

Janet and Jillian were away with their husbands and the neighbour rang me to tell me of his death. I would have none of it however. Richard and I were at the Hotel as it was Easter, the busiest weekend of the year for caravanners and hotel guests. It was noisy with the bustle of happy thronging people. One of the young waitresses called me to the phone in the small packed Hotel foyer. As I took the phone Mummy's neighbour told me that my Daddy had died. I'm afraid I argued with her and said she must have the wrong number, she'd got it wrong, it couldn't be <u>my</u> Daddy. If anyone was going to die it would be Mummy with her intensive care visits every year due to a heart condition.

Poor girl, it took three attempts for her to persuade me that it was me she wanted to speak to and it <u>was</u> my Daddy. I had to accept it.

Our car had delivered us to the Hotel in a cloud of black smoke and probably wouldn't get us the two miles home never mind to Yorkshire. I sat in a state of oblivion not understanding what had hit me and still suspecting that they had got it wrong. Our dear friends Joan and Ieuan were dining and Richard told them what had happened. Without ado, Ieuan put his car keys on the table and said,

'Don't argue, take them and go, and don't come back until you have to.' The world provides us with an abundance of wonderful people who are most appreciated when a crisis is in flow.

We drove to Wakefield. Mummy was very distressed at sleeping alone and anyway with her medical condition her being alone was a worry. So, I slept in Daddy's bed beside her.

Richard returned to Wales to return Ieuan's car and sort ours out as we were going to need it. Janet, Jillian and I remained to support Mummy and carry out the necessary arrangements and organize the funeral. Daddy's body had been removed by the Funeral Director and my request that I visit him before the autopsy was honoured. It is thought in some traditions that the spirit visits the body after death during the transition period, so it was important to me that I see him before any medical intervention of autopsy.

I read a passage to him from Stephen Levine's book Who Dies? It was the first dead body I had ever encountered and I have to admit that to kiss someone who is cold and unresponsive is a disconcerting experience. It was, however, a wonderfully releasing and forgiving time and helped me immensely in coming to terms with his death.

Nowadays, we don't visit the body after death as we used to but it is a very spiritual experience as, as you look at the body, the shell of the person it once was, you have to ask, what happened to the essence, the part that animated the body and made it who it was? In acknowledging that essence, that is no longer there, I found I could very easily accept that although the body had died the essence, the soul or spirit cannot just have evaporated. It became obvious to me that the essence had departed to another dimension.

Think of water, fluid, running and mobile. Water is still water even when it is frozen, apparently lifeless. Or think of steam and evaporation that dissipates into the unseen, still existing but no longer visible, it is just a matter of frequency.

We had returned home when Mummy rang to say that she was organizing an appointment to scatter Daddy's ashes. The process of cremation had been delayed due to Easter and the need for an autopsy. She rang back to say that the only available appointment was 2.30 pm that afternoon giving us three and half hours to do a three and a half hour journey. If I took into account that I was not yet dressed, a slow process in my case with the difficulty of mobility and particularly my painful and deformed hands and the fact that Richard was out working on site – this meant it was impossible.

I was distressed that I would not be present at the final goodbye. Being there in spirit is true but not quite the same. I was unable to do the physical things that Jillian and Janet could do and now I would not be present at the spiritual.

At this point Richard came in and in my distressed state I told him what had happened. His reaction was the obvious one, to drop everything, again, and take me up there. We asked Sharon, Gary's wife managing the hotel, to ring to say that we had left (before the time of mobile phone excess). It was in fact half an hour before we did leave because of going round in circles, getting dressed and putting petrol in the car, which was by now repaired. Richard told Sharon,

'Tell them to wait for us.'

We arrived, having been accompanied by a Guardian Angel, all traffic lights green, all road works in our favour and the traffic loading light, with ten minutes to spare. I was glad I was there although it was only a ten minute affair it was good to be able to say a final farewell and a final releasing of Daddy's spirit.

Too shy to photograph

We three sisters
Safety in numbers

Daddy, Mummy, Jillian, Diana, Janet

Young Love

Our Wedding Day

Playgroup in session

Winston Churchill, Pete the Pirate, Liberace

Calves and pet lambs were great companions

Never quite made the Boy Band

Daddy, Mummy, Jim, Edward, Diana, Anthony, Richard

Jim, Granny Rhodes, Diana, Richard,
Grandpa Rhodes, Edward, Anthony

A Kimono transformation and authentic Japanese experience

Honouring Budha and a lost baby

Hiroshima – the central building left as a forceful reminder

Granny's cousin
William Lesley
Isle of Orkney

Elizabeth Rob his wife

Manifestation!

The ride of a lifetime

The Gathering – our sacred space and the Seed of Life symbol
cut into the turf

Honouring the new Peace Pole

Professor David Bellamy dedicating and opening
Grandma's Garden 2004

My fairy fully baptised

Views from Grandma's Garden

A Celtic Vision

Elephant God Ganesh fountain

Cheque presentation from Grandma's Garden proceeds

Children are just some of the beneficiaries

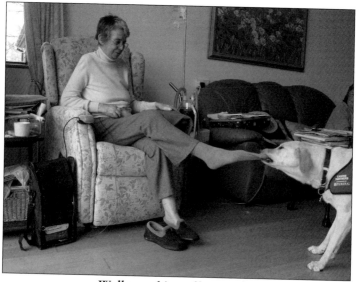

Wallace taking off my socks

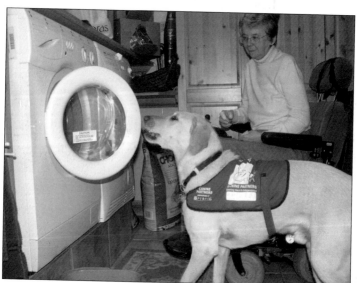

Opening and emptying the washing machine

The men in my life!!
Edward, Jim, Anthony, Richard

Jim, Christopher, Sylvia, Robert, Mandy, Arron

Conall, Tina, Anthony, Taionee, Deri, Kiera

Edward, Michelle, Jessica, Alex, Chris

Shortly after Daddy's death, Richard and I were visiting friends who had just come back from attending an Event in America.

Janet and Toby had bought a cabin at Dolguog and we immediately became firm friends. Their conversation encompassed the practical, the physical, the esoteric, a wonderful combination of interest. I was fascinated with their spiritual background and pressed for more information. They attended an Ancient School of Wisdom in Yelm, America. It claimed to be the only open Ancient School of Wisdom in the world.

Somebody once gave me a tape, it was Louise Hay and the tape started off with,

'If you are reading this book or listening to this tape you have drawn it to you and whatever illness or problem you are suffering it is through karma. It is something you have done in a previous life and you are now suffering for it.'

In that case I felt I personally must have beheaded and disemboweled approximately three quarters of the world's population. Louise Hay was anathema to me. When I attended the Ancient School of Wisdom I discovered Ramtha's past.

Ramtha is a 35,000 year old entity. In his lifetime he had been a barbarian, his army leaving a trail of killing, pillaging and raping. One day he was wounded and sat on a rock for seven years being tended to by his entourage. It was during this time that he became enlightened. He had returned, to teach the path to enlightenment and was channelled by a lady by the name of JZ Knight, known simple as JZ (Jay Zee).

OK, maybe – what if – I did behead and disembowel all those people in a past life? That is then and this is now. Get over it, get on with it and realize I can't live in the past for this life time or it will be wasted. I have never quite come to terms with Louise Hay for what she put me through however.

As Janet and Toby told me about the teaching of the school I became transfixed,

'I'm going to the next Event.' I said

'I don't think that's a good idea Diana.' said Janet.

'Yes, but I'm going.' I said.

'It's very physical, Diana, you wouldn't cope, and who would push the wheelchair? It will be a Beginners Event as the teachings are progressive so Janet and I won't be attending.' responded Toby.

'I'm going.' I said with a sort of dull insistence as though I wasn't really in control of what I was saying.

Richard chirped in,

'We can't afford it, where will you get the money?' I was teaching privately, but I had allowed this source of income to decline as I was limited by my health. I had had to give up my teaching jobs at school and college, but still worked with individual children with special needs who came to our home.

'I'll teach more.' I responded.

'And where are the kids going to suddenly appear from?' Richard quizzed.

'I don't know, but they will and I'm going to the Beginners Event.' I stubbornly replied.

I think the three of them got the message that my mind was made up, although none of us, me included, could understand why or how. This was Sunday afternoon.

Monday morning at half past nine the phone rang. It was a parent requesting help for a child. Half past eleven that morning another parent. By the end of that week I had five new students requiring specialist teaching to help with their difficulties. The money was starting to materialise.

The Event was due to take place in May and as the date got nearer I realised that I would not reach my target to cover flight and Event costs. About three weeks before the due departure date I had yet another phone call, this time from the School. The May event was postponed, it would be held in September! Was this just for my benefit, longer time to earn the money? I certainly felt something was at work.

That first Event was a short Event. Once a year an Event lasted three days and once a year, the second Event lasted nine days. Richard accompanied me, to the first three day Event, staying at a local B & B and awaited my return from the Event, just to make sure I could cope with the difficulties of travelling in a wheelchair. That first Event confirmed that these were the teachings for which I had been waiting all my life.

As I continued to attend the School, Richard would accompany me to the three day Event and as I attended School he relaxed and did some sight seeing for the three days. We would then spend the rest of our week to explore and use as a holiday. When I attended the nine day Event I would travel alone. Airports can be scary when you are alone and in a wheelchair, but I worked on the premise that if they had checked in my luggage they wouldn't go without me. I was able to relax and await my 'pusher'.

When I look back, it's no wonder the doctors thought I had a psychiatric problem. I was having trouble swallowing even then, so my diet for the duration of the event consisted of Weetabix soaked to a specific consistency with a high energy milk supplement, dried split green pea soup to which I added boiling water, soft white bread, avocado, bananas, Barleycup and dried milk to make a drink. Food had to be eaten lying down on my left side to control the swallowing muscles to prevent choking.

One rather amusing incident was arriving in Seattle to go through customs when a large, weapon carrying uniformed security guard (I don't know why the uniformed guys in America are larger than life) approached me.

'Ma'am, I need to look in your Fanny bag.' Oooo! I was taken quite by surprise. I know English and American words for the same thing can be different like boot – trunk, and bonnet – hood, but Fanny bag? – this was quite unexpected and at the time a little disquieting.

During this Event Ramtha (the entity being channeled) greeted us. We were the group who travelled farthest to attend from Europe, Australia even as far as South Africa. We would be tired from our journey and needed to recuperate. Ramtha explained that we were to take part in a Candle Meditation. Over a thousand people sitting cross legged gazing at candles.

The Events were held in a horse arena, built entirely of wood, no metal fixings or screws as the metal was not conducive to the work being carried out. There could be one thousand to twelve hundred people attending the Event and the floor of the room was marked into rectangular areas measuring 4 ft 8in x 2 ft 4in with walkways around the perimeter and through the centres. Each rectangle was allocated to an individual, this was your living area for bedding and belongings, and sleeping space for the entire period. In those early days there were four ladies toilets indoors and three wash basins with cold water only. The gentlemen had similar facilities. Otherwise it was Portaloos and hosepipes in weather that could be as low as minus 10/15 degrees centigrade. Oh, how I wished I had shares in wet wipes! All clothing and food were taken in with you at the start of the Event. There was no leaving the Event for any reason; it was a pure retreat of surrender.

He explained to us that this was the hardest thing we would ever have to do in our lives. The power of concentration, the ability to sit in one position – unmoving, unblinking, was a huge challenge of endurance. The evening started with much shuffling and manoeuvring as everyone tried to prepare themselves for the extended period one, two, four hours or more, we never knew. After some time, probably after the first hour people were fidgeting. As the second and third hour came round grown men were crying. Many people left the arena unable to continue the meditation exercise. I had already reached what I thought was my limit of pain endurance when I suddenly realised I'd been here before. What was I playing at? Too much to bear? Then flip out! I flipped out, which meant I became an observer, my body was in excruciating pain poor thing, but I wasn't, 'I' was fine and continued the meditation. It was an amazing enlightenment that my years of coping actually had far more effect than I could have realised. Never did I think I would be more physically capable than a 6ft 2in strapping, athletic male. There was so much I couldn't do, this I could.

Whilst attending the Ancient School of Wisdom all that was asked of us was that we should participate. There were many quite amazing happenings that I will cover at a later time but many are relevant to life after death or at the least energy after death if the former is too challenging, although I guess if it was, you wouldn't be reading this book.

Wisdom flowed from Ramtha like an endless river as he spoke for hours without notes, encouraging us from time to time to turn to our neighbor and repeat his words, to make sure we understood the teachings.

Sometimes other speakers and teachers would attend to introduce us to what was happening in the world that was not covered by our oh, so closed minded media. I wonder do they have closed minds or are they closed for them by others?

We were continuously taught 'mind over matter', and to be sovereign – meaning survival. When Margaret Thatcher came to power she was interviewed and appeared on television showing the country her pantry. As a grocer's daughter she had a stock of food to last two years, and she encouraged everyone to follow her example as closely as possible. Obviously she was laughed at as many people, even more now, shop from day to day or live on take aways.

Some years after this the Channel tunnel was blocked by the French with some strike demand or other. I went to the Supermarket to find that their large vegetable section contained one bag of potatoes, a few hands of bananas and a small box of tomatoes. The Manager told me that the strike meant that food could not get into the country and he didn't know when his supplies would resume. A three day strike caused these dramatic shortages.

How long could we each survive without daily supplies or utilities? Can you eat, drink, keep warm if there were a shut down for an extended period?

There's more to being sovereign than eating and drinking though. How often are we owned by adverts telling us what we need to be happy or what we must do to be socially acceptable. Hypnosis is a state of mind in which the conscious controlling part of your mind temporarily moves aside and suspends the critical function that it has.

Natural hypnosis occurs when you become totally absorbed in reading a great book or watching a movie or something on TV that you are absorbed with. Only when someone speaks to you and has to raise their voice and break through your focused thought pattern – waking hypnosis – do you respond.

The same thing can happen when you are driving and can't remember driving to your destination because you are on auto pilot, and your conscious mind is then free to wander – day dream – unless an emergency calls you back to attention.

Neuroscientists are well aware of the impact of television on, particularly but not confined to, the young brain. Not least Attention Deficit Disorder, behavioural problems, language difficulties and weak problem solving skills. It is now proven that higher levels of television viewing correlates with lower academic performance. Television engages the brain's attention involuntarily and puts it into a state of hypnosis similar to the one when driving on auto pilot or daydreaming, where the brain's attention is not available for an awareness of what is going on in the real world.

The subtlety of advertising or even the blatant 'ramming it down your throat' advertising pays. Whether consciously or subconsciously, you are persuaded to, hypnotized into, buying that product. Check your shopping list and ask yourself,

'Why did I buy that product or that brand of product?' and see if you have a plausible answer.

My friend's child rang her on her mobile and asked,

'Mummy is Woolworth's on the left or right side of Darkgate Street?' On another occasion an eight year old rang her friends on their mobiles to see where they were. They were playing hide and seek at the time! This has the potential to be a generation unable to make decisions or problem solve.

Hypnosis is definitely not sleep although the Greek word hypnos means sleep hence the confusion. Hypnosis causes changes from an alert beta brain wave state to a predominantly alpha-theta brainwave state. It is the predominant theta activity that is associated with hypnosis. Research suggests that a hypnotic state creates changes in the brainwave of the subject; changes in brain waves vastly affect human behaviour.

Is your life, your 'parade' dictated to by an Emperor with no clothes? Or do you make sure your Emperor, the Lord of your Being, is fully clothed? You can choose not to be manipulated, you can choose to be Pinocchio. Lose the strings, become real, make your own decisions with open eyes. You can choose not to go where your strings are pulled, our lives need not be ruled by advertisements and soap operas etc if we so choose.

Our journey at this School required dedication, participation, and to be humble enough to overlay the empty table with abundance. Want to know how? Then watch Peter Pan and the lost boys. They overlaid their problems with another reality, they stayed happy, they didn't blame others for a situation or condition. True masters don't blame others, holding grudges might take pressure off us but holds us in its grip. We need to do what the lost boys did and overlay the empty table with a banquet. We need to remove the attitude of 'it's just the way I am, I can't help it' syndrome. We can. Suffering on any level is never rooted in someone else. I was taught that it takes a great person to admit they have been in error but a fool clings to attitudes that take them to the grave, and you can't change others you can only set an example. Easy to say, less easy to do I think but worth a try.

Richard was flying off somewhere on a business trip and found himself walking alongside and then sitting beside an older lady. She turned to him and said,

'Oh, do forgive me. You must be thinking how dreadful I look. Well, you see I have to wear flat lace up shoes because I have arthritis in my feet and I know how bad I look.'

Richard smiled at her and hoping to put her mind at rest replied,

'Don't worry. My wife is only in her early forties and she has to wear flat, lace-up shoes due to severe RA I never even noticed yours.'

She didn't seem too pleased with this reply so she came back with,

'Well, she's lucky getting it so young. She has time to get used to it.' Richard was so taken aback the conversation came to an abrupt halt. I tell this little anecdote to stress how life can be negative and depressing if we concentrate on what used to be and not what is. In this lady's case the loss of her smart court shoes dominated her life, overriding the pleasure of her forthcoming holiday. Those lost boys could have helped her see things differently.

A fascinating talk was given at the Ancient School of Wisdom, by a former CIA employee. The CIA was concerned about the experiments being undertaken by the Russians on parapsychology. Remote viewing was developed by the military and he had been part of the Remote Viewing team. Governments used, probably still do, this technique to explore military installations half way around the world. This was the largest spy programme ever attempted using clairvoyance.

As they experimented in shielded rooms, and even the shielding offered by a submarine that would block all, even low frequency, electromagnetic waves, they came to the conclusion that the only way remote viewing was possible was through the quantum effects and this suggested that we have a constant interaction with what is now known as the zero point field.

In other words, we may not be normally aware of it but we are everywhere at once. Einstein said that 'The Field' is the only reality. It explains the interconnectedness of all things through quantum physics. This collective consciousness has been known about for centuries, theologists call it the Holy Spirit! Lynne McTaggart explains in her book 'The Field' that the theories of Darwin and Newton and their contemporaries left us with a vision of life as separate, mechanistic, without soul. Everything was predictable, reliable in a way that was measurable. In the Field view we do matter, offering the means by which we can learn to understand our world and ourselves and our place in it. It is a view of unpredictability such as sub atomic particles that can be both a particle and a wave at the same time. She describes the Field as a heaving sea of energy, an ocean of microscopic vibrations in space and between things, one vast quantum field.

The remote viewer working in the equivalent of deep meditation is given a set of latitude and longitude co-ordinates – nothing more. Accurate information can then be obtained by this specialist practice of clairvoyance. Remote viewers are asked not to interpret or evaluate just to report what they see, hear and feel.

This speaker gave us the opportunity to try this out for ourselves. After his talk he gave us a set of questions as a template for our meditation focus. He then held up a brown, sealed envelope, our target.

During the period of focus and meditation I had perceived the following things – a mountain with a snowy top, at the base of which was a river or lake and a sandy shore with trees like palm trees. I perceived my senses to move from a cool environment to a hot environment. I perceived a low table, an eye within a bright light, a yawning big cat. I perceived a sight of natural beauty, a savannah landscape of wild animals, a serene and poignant state.

When we had completed the exercise our guest speaker, David Moorhouse, opened the envelope and showed us the photo and as it was revealed much was as I had perceived it to be except for the water. It was not water, it was a vehicle and the sun was reflecting in its windscreen, bright and shining like a mirage of water! What was truly amazing was that at least seventy five percent of the audience had at least some of the target scene correct.

David has recently been in a documentary presented by Michael Aspel saying that the reason he left the CIA Remote Viewing Team was because they were being asked to target Saddam Hussein in order to eliminate him. In actual fact Saddam Hussein complained to the World that he was being targeted and of course nobody believed him at the time. David's involvement with Remote Viewing was to make the world a better place and deciding who and who would not be in that world was not part of his vocation so he left the team.

On another arrival night Ramtha told us we were to start with meditation as we often did. It might be an hour, it might be four hours, it might be all night, but we were to stay as we were, in meditation pose, until he came to fetch us, as he phrased it. The wall at the end of this huge horse arena was covered in black plastic, a vast expanse. I assumed they had a water leakage problem and thought no more about it. The group settled down (not an easy procedure with over a thousand people) and the meditation began.

As I went deeper and my mind gave up its chatter I began to see pictures. Here was the picture of The Creation by Michael Angelo – God straining to reach man, pointing and reaching with his finger in his effort to make contact. Man reclining, nonchalant, with a limp wrist reaching, but without strain or effort, in the direction of God. God symbolically portrayed as an old man with white hair and white beard, an intense, enquiring expression in his desire to touch and awaken man's latent spiritual passion. Those surrounding him seemed to be so relevant to the whole meaning of the picture. They floated within a cloud. Or was it a cloud? No, I looked closer; this was the shape of the brain, even the spinal column protruding from the base. I was seeking God, Creation, Mother of All, whatever we call it, it is there, and I had just discovered the truth of all the ancient texts,

'Seek within. Be still and know that I am God.'

As I retreated from this vision another one began to replace it. A sepia photograph of a man in WWI style uniform, I suspected this was my maternal Grandfather, and as I watched he became younger and younger until a small bouncy boy stood before me, jumping and bouncing and laughing, clapping his hands in excitement and glee.

'I'm Stewart.' he said. The older man in the sepia photograph his Father, my Mother his sister. When he was three he had pulled a pan of boiling water onto himself. My Mother, who was about fifteen, was sent to scour the streets to find someone who knew where a doctor could be found. This was long before phones, mobile or otherwise were available and certainly before NHS and ambulances or casualty departments. She and Stewart were so close, my Mother always said they idolised each other. A doctor duly attended and prescribed an ointment for the burn. When applied the ointment was so cold that it sent him into a convulsion, from which he died, fulfilling my Grandmother's tragic prophecy.

My Mother's health had been poor for ten years, each year she spent time in intensive care with heart problems.

'I've been chosen to meet Marion.' Here Stewart used a nickname for my Mother, which to this day, once I had told my Mother, I cannot remember, perhaps I am not mean to.

'Tell her, I'll be there.' and with a double somersault, a spring in the air and a clap of his little hands he disappeared.

The third vision slowly appeared.

'It's me and I'm coming back. Watch for me. I'll be there.' Details were given and then that vision too disappeared. I remember nothing else until Ramtha came to 'fetch us'.

He talked for a while and then issued the instruction to remove the black plastic from the wall. As the plastic dropped on its ropes it revealed a huge painting – The Creation. I was awestruck I had not registered that my visions might be prophetic but this was amazing proof. The odds were too ridiculous to contemplate a coincidence.

The event concluded as the days passed and I went back to stay with my friends Toby and Janet,

'We've had a phone call from Richard today, your Mother's in hospital and your sister thought you ought to know what she had said.' Mummy had a habit if one of we three daughters was away. She would say,

'They'll be back on Sunday', or 'back in three days'. When I spoke to Richard he said Mummy had matter of factly stated,

'Diana will be home in 4 days 8 hours and 30 minutes.' I came off the phone, rang the airline and changed my ticket. The cost was unimportant, I was just grateful there was a seat.

Richard picked me up at Heathrow and drove me straight to Wakefield, a five to six hour straight drive. I was exhausted. The events and conditions of the School throughout the week had taken their toll. The flight, being unable to eat or drink had left me dehydrated and the drive was the final straw in my feeling of absolute inability to cope physically. How I accomplished it I do not know but we visited my mother in hospital, she was sitting up in bed surrounded by visitors and waving as we arrived, she was rosy cheeked and she looked in her elegance like the Queen Mother. As visiting hours came to an end we had time for an exchange of sorts.

After the visit we went to my sister's house. Jillian and Janet had been told that Mummy must no longer live alone and they had been looking at Nursing Homes. They were due to visit one the next morning and another in the afternoon, all unbeknown to my mother.

The next morning we all set off to check out the Nursing Home. It was awful, old people, sitting in rows, just waiting to die. It smelled of urine and could have been cleaner. On one wall was a board with Christmas photographs of the inmates.

'Look what Santa gave Phyllis',

'Here's Eric pulling his Cracker.' It was so bad you couldn't even see the funny side. It was now Easter. What had they been doing in the meantime, I wondered? We left feeling totally depressed. There was no way Mummy could endure the indignity of a place like that.

At 2.00 pm. Richard and I presented ourselves for visiting. It had taken a long time to park (Richard and I have a lifelong record of always being early for everything). I walked into the ward.

'Where have you been, you're late.' I couldn't answer. I had never known what 'the cloak of death' meant until that moment. She was sitting up in bed no longer the lady she had looked yesterday, but enveloped in what I cannot describe physically – but spiritually was nothing less than the cloak of death. I was the only visitor for the first few minutes and we talked and talked and talked. Mummy had always been an emotional person and often fell back on emotional blackmail in our upbringing. Not once that afternoon did she shed a tear. I did though. I kept collapsing into tears at anything and everything and tried to convince her it was jetlag and tiredness.

Visitors would come and go and our train of conversation would be interrupted. As they left, she repeated our last sentence and picked up the thread again, her main questions being about my latest visit to America and the School of Wisdom.

'I came to see you.' she said. This from someone who was terrified of dying and most things unseen. 'You were sitting on plastic grass and it glistened in the sunlight.'

'No, Mummy. The floor of the arena is dirt. Just plain soil marked with tape. That's why we get so dirty and dusty, especially when it's wet and we drag in the wet and the mud.'

Three times we had this conversation. Three times Peter denied Christ. Three times I denied her, until suddenly the light dawned. Oh, my goodness. That Event the whole inside of the arena had been carpeted with plastic grass, albeit covered with sleeping bags, pillows and people's belongings. How could I have forgotten! She just said,

'I told you I came.'

Mummy had never acknowledged the spirit of the body or life after death. I told her about Stewart coming to see me and his message. Instead of crying, which would have been normal for her, she became animated.

'I've been wondering whether it would be your Daddy, or perhaps Granny. I never thought of Stewart. Oh, how wonderful. That's perfect, just as I would have wished.'

I was dumbfounded with this new Mummy and continued with my intermittent bouts of crying. When I look back this time was a great gift. I don't like the phrase closure, but we did bring recognition and closure to so many things in our lives.

When I left the ward at about five o'clock I met my two sisters in the corridor. They thought they had found the right place.

'Don't tell her.' I insisted. 'Whatever you do, don't tell her, she doesn't need to know.'

My elder sister was very agitated and understandably distressed. My younger sister had been present at my pronouncements before. When Mummy had been in intensive care some ten years earlier, the doctors had called us in to say our goodbyes and Daddy was distraught and talking about what the doctors had said as we surrounded her sleeping body.

'She isn't going anywhere Daddy don't talk like that.' He was very cross. Couldn't I understand how serious it was? Yes I could, but for some reason I knew she wasn't going anywhere.

Hearing is the last sense to fail, never talk negatively to anyone, near death, in a coma, or under anaesthetic. Always talk of peace, happiness, something uplifting because even if they die the last thing they will hear will be an upliftment that can help set the tone for the next phase of a very different life.

Richard took me back to Wales that evening. I told my sisters I would come back, but for now I needed clothes, my own bed, and a period of recuperation, however short.

During my conversations with Mummy I had told her that everyone dies and I wanted her to know that when she decided to go and meet Stewart she had our permission to go, in her own time, it might be today, next week or ten years down the line, but when she decided, if she was afraid she must call me and I would be there. I gave no further explanation.

We arrived home in Wales and I had a bath and went to bed. I could not sleep – not one wink. I talked to Mummy all night in a state of alert wakefulness. How long could my body go without sleep? I looked at the bedside clock. 6.00 am What a busy night. I turned over and immediately fell asleep.

Someone was calling. Calling my name. It got louder and stronger. Mummy was walking towards me. We clasped hands facing each other, smiling, as I walked backwards, guiding her on, I turned and stood beside her in the dark, a great black-blue void before us. Irreverent as ever, I shouted,

'Stewart, where the hell are you? You promised.'

I woke with a start just half an hour had passed. The phone was ringing. It was my sister Janet.

'The hospital has just rung. Mummy has taken a turn for the worse and Jillian and I are on our way. I think maybe we're too late, Diana.' It struck me immediately this was the second of my meditational visions to happen within two days. From where do these energies emanate?

Sometime later, the third of those visions was also to manifest and complete the trilogy.

To continue this theme of the energy of other dimensions, I go back to a party we three girls organised for Mummy's seventieth birthday. Janet living closest as usual bore the brunt of the work, Jillian made and decorated the cake and I did very little on the physical level except turn up. Mummy's birthday was New Years Eve, Hogmanay. She was Scottish and this always held nearly as much importance as Christmas for us as a family. She loved the bagpipes and a good pipe band. We organised a lone piper to come and play for her. He was a member of the Wakefield Metropolitan Police in full Scottish regalia. As we were anticipating his arrival, a closely guarded secret from Mummy, she said,

'I can't understand why all this fuss.'

'Well, it's not everyday you're seventy.' Her reply was unexpected,

'I'm not seventy, I am only sixty nine.' Three of us and we got our sums wrong. Jillian rushed into the kitchen to scrape the seventy off the cake and change it to sixty nine!

The Piper arrived, he was a massive man, must have been at least 6 ft 6 inches with a girth to match. He unwound himself out of his mini, put on his bearskin helmet, picked up his bag pipes and played as he marched the full length of the street. Mummy went to the window as he marched past all the neighbours, who had come out to look, and up to her front door. Her face was something to remember. He came in had something of the party food to eat and downed two thirds of a bottle of whiskey.

So this was one icon for her memories. The second was when she and Daddy were confirmed, both in their seventies, and a red admiral butterfly flew round and round them during the service. After her death we three sisters saw butterflies under the strangest circumstances. The Christmas after she died we were dining in the hotel after all the guests had left, the children and grandchildren. I was at the head of the table, always the most convenient place to put a wheelchair. Remember this was the middle of December – a red admiral butterfly appeared from nowhere and settled on my head. I didn't know until the children told me, when it flew off and settled back on to my shoulder.

Even more amazing was the Piper. At times in my life when I was facing a challenge, needed encouragement, or was feeling low he would appear. During the trip in Holland when Grandmother Parisha announced my imminent death I was obviously stressed that such a thing could be in the planning. At the end of this conference style weekend, which was taking place in a Woodland Centre for Conferences and situated in the middle of Holland, there were eighty people sitting in a Native American medicine wheel circle and we each were invited to sum up in one minute our weekend experience. Richard was sitting opposite me in the circle and he was the last to speak. As he prepared to speak there was a long wail, I really thought I was hearing things. The circle of people waited until it progressed into a full blown bag pipe recital. Richard's response was delightful, he looked around the surprised circle,

'Don't worry,' he said 'it's just my Mother-in-Law, telling Diana all is well.'

Another time when I was trying to make the decision to leave the Ramtha School of Enlightenment we were with Janet, my dear friend who was living in America and who had introduced me to the school. We were meeting Dave, her prospective new husband, for lunch. We were early so parked in the back streets of Olympia, away from the docks, until it was time to meet him for lunch. As we sat there, a large office block on one side and a demolished and cleared block on the other, a young man walked into the centre of the spare ground carrying a bag, he took out his bagpipes and started to play. As I sat, my head in my hands in disbelief, Richard got out of the car. A young lady came out of the office block and Richard asked her did this piper come here often to practice?

'I have worked here for fifteen years and have never seen or heard him before.' was her astonishing reply.

The last time I was to experience the Piper we were on our way to Costa Rica to present the Peace Scroll to the United Nations University for Peace, and then on to present it at the UN to Gillian Sorensen Assistant General Secretary to Kofi Annan. Miami airport, as usual no doubt, milling with people, security guards, airport staff, when the crowds filling the concourse parted, striding down the centre was a lone piper in full Scottish regalia playing his pipes, we never did find out the significance of his presence, although we enquired, no-one knew.

After Daddy's death at the next Event I was again in a situation of not having enough money to attend. Daddy had died a few months before and I received an unexpected call from Mummy,

'I'd like you three girls to have a little something, so I am sending you each a cheque for £1,000.' She was thrilled when I told her what I would use it for and what that would mean.

The Ancient School of Wisdom was taken to Court, accused of being a cult. It went through the Courts and came out with flying colours. It was agreed that the teachings were Gnostic principles and mind over matter. The Gnostic beliefs were very different to modern Christian beliefs. Sir Laurence Gardner and others believe the Gnostics to be the true pre-christian Christians. They believed the individual could have a relationship with God without a need for an intermediary. Gnosis means knowledge or knowing, the knowledge of Christ, Christ here being the Christ consciousness. Gnostics believed that the spirits of men and women had become trapped in material bodies but belonged to the spiritual world as beings of light, which were perfect. They described the human condition as 'gold in mud'.

Independent thinking was encouraged in Gnostic teaching causing a problem within the Church's teachings and they were therefore branded heretics and went the way of all heretics where the church abolished them by whatever means.

At yet another Event we were given instructions to draw on the small rectangular cards distributed for this purpose. We had been receiving teachings regarding the blue body – the healing body. The area that surrounds the physical body contains not only the physical, emotional and mental light bodies but also the etheric. The blue body is the etheric light body, the blue print of our being. Our other teachings also included the raising of the Kundalini. This is the serpent energy housed at the base of the spine as it raises through the seven chakras or energy centres of the body which follow the route of the spine. As this energy raises it is the precursor of achieving enlightenment.

I had drawn my card showing a crayoned blue, etheric healing body with a red line portraying the Kundalini surging up the spine and through the head to enlightenment. The next day the cards were due to be passed around the thousand plus throng of students when they would be taken and taped to the fence in the field, picture to the fence and duct tape securing them.

I had decided that to honour Ramtha's request that students participate I should try to go onto the field rather than stay on the side lines, which I had done previously. With over one thousand people on this field it was impossible to stretch out your arms and not make contact with someone and yet despite wearing a blindfold very rarely did people bump into each other. The intense focus seemed to keep each individual in his/her own energy bubble. Knowing my fear, young Gary, my good twelve year old friend at this Event, was busy talking me into it.

'What you fear you draw to you, don't worry Diana. Just go for it, sleep well and be ready for the morning field exercise.'

That evening the students were called outside to participate in another exercise. I stayed inside, I was extremely tired, in a lot of pain and worried about whether I would attempt entering the crowded field.

Some of the students had stayed in the arena, they were playing music, singing, dancing, eating and drinking. I was feeling annoyed that they could physically participate and had decided to party the night away instead. I went to sit in the corridor on the way to the toilets next to the drinks machine. I sat with my head in my hands, wondering what had possessed me, thinking I could meet the challenge of living and sleeping on this 4ft 8in x 2ft 4in rectangle whilst being so disabled.

As I sat there I heard a voice. When I looked up Ramtha was standing there in his greatcoat for warmth and a baseball cap.

'Not participating, Master? You have come a long way and are not here for long. You will soon be back home and no longer able to participate I would like you to participate.' He turned on his heel and disappeared into the dark.

I do not like to admit it but I was angry and disillusioned. How could he? How could he single me out like that? The noise and merriment from the Great Hall as it was known could not be ignored. The revelry was loud with music and laughter, why not speak to them? How had he found me hiding in a dark corner, alone and lonely in my fear of participating?

When the others returned from their outdoor exercises I spoke to one or two of them and told them of my visit from Ramtha. He must be a fraud, it was all a con job to get our money. Didn't he realise the extent of my pain and disability? Because if he did he wouldn't pick me out, particularly when so many able bodied students were partying and certainly not participating.

The answer from each of those I spoke to was the same. Ramtha had never left the field or them, not even for one second or one minute. Either I had dreamt it or Ramtha had bi-located. I knew the ancients talked of being in two places at the same time but I had not thought of it being possible in modern times.

All I did know was that I hadn't dreamt it. Sitting on a very uncomfortable folding seat, in the dark and cold, with my mind racing, meant there was no way I had dreamt anything. I rested fitfully through the night. In my opinion Ramtha was a fraud; I'd wasted my time, money and precious energy. How could he not know my condition if he was what he claimed to be. This was it, next day I would leave the school and not return.

In the early hours of the morning my Yorkshire bred stubbornness (bloody mindedness my Father called it) had surfaced. I would make one last effort and go on the field, leaving my wheelchair behind, to find my blue body card. I owed it to my young friend Gary.

I passed my card to be taped on the fence and waited to be the last to go to the field. I was frightened, there were more than 1,000 people, many big burley men and the prize of finding your card was the overriding thought. Care for others was sometimes neglected in the desire and power for the prize. Ramtha came to the field and set us off, turning and spinning, for those that could, to disorientate the brain. With blindfold firmly in place, breathing technique in action, off we went. It is amazing how quickly deprived of one sense – sight – we all became accustomed to entering a fully focused thought – the card, our card.

I don't know how long it took until I found myself flat on my back unable to breathe. I came to gasping for breath, realising someone had literally ploughed into me and knocked me down. I felt the 'guards' appear to help me.

'What can we do?' they all knew my disabilities. I was furious with my situation.

'Go behind me, put your hands under my arm pits, lift and push me up.' I snapped.

'Do you want to come off the field?' one of them asked.

'Like hell,' I replied 'let me go.' Gary was right his prophecy that I would draw it to me had manifested.

Back into deep focus, it's amazing how quickly I achieved that, I set off never to make contact with anyone again. Obviously I had learnt my lesson. I 'hit' the fence, at which point we had been instructed to lift and turn over the card immediately in front of us to see if it was our card or not. If it was, bingo! If it wasn't we were to return it to its position and continue our focus. Some of the twelve hundred people in the field after four to eight hours might never even bump into the fence let alone find their own card and some would find the fence but not their own card.

I looked at the drawing on the card that I had turned over and thought 'Goodness, someone's drawn a blue body just like mine. Goodness, they've got the same name as me.' Then it dawned on me I had found my card, first time on actually bumping blindfold into the fence and the first card I had turned over. When people found their cards they shouted and screamed with delight and everyone responded. I just half whispered,

'I've found my card,' those within earshot picked up the chant and the field exploded in excitement.

. 'She's found her card.'

I made my way off the field avoiding the more than 1,000 blindfolded people with my card as my prize. As I left the field Ramtha was entering,

'Well done, Master' he said 'see what happens when you participate?' How could he have recognised me from the night before out of twelve hundred students.

The idea was to draw another card and start the process again. I was exhilarated yet exhausted physically. I sat at a picnic table where three or four others were drawing new cards having found theirs too. It was suggested by Ramtha that we didn't wear watches. Time was irrelevant where we were. I noticed one person wearing a watch and asked the time.

'No, your watch must be wrong.' I said. Someone else produced a watch and confirmed the time. It wasn't possible, I had been in focus walking on the field for over four hours. No wonder the elation was tempered with exhaustion. Medically twenty five yards was my limit for walking without seriously damaging my health.

In the evening Ramtha would send round a microphone for people to tell short stories of their experiences and inspiration. This night he pointed to the back and at me. I was given the microphone and I proceeded to tell them that I had spent four hours on the field and supposedly should not be able to walk more than twenty five yards. I told them I had been afraid and had drawn my fear to me.

This was a breakthrough for me for truly the only thing we have to fear is fear itself.

I passed the microphone back but Ramtha insistently kept pointing at me. I told the person with the mike,

'I don't know what he wants me to say, what am I supposed to say?' The mike lady said,

'I think he wants you to tell them you found your card.' I took back the mike and said,

'Oh, I forget to tell you, I found my card today.' The hall erupted and I shrank back into my seat, amazed by this response. Then Ramtha began to speak. I will tell you what I can remember and what others told me after, as my brain as usual in a crisis, be it good or bad, shut down much of my memory.

'This woman is the epitome of the student I wish you all were. She forgot to tell you she found her card because to her the journey was more important than the prize. You all think you have suffered discomfort here. I assure you, you have not. If you had the aggressive pain and the limitation of mobility that this woman has continuously then you would realise how insignificant your inconveniences are. When you are incessantly prodded by pain you cannot be distracted, your spiritual path is constant and ongoing. If you find a distraction or wish to rest, the pain nudges and prods to keep you on the straight and narrow. Use her as an example, don't turn from her because she appears not to be whole. Your path of spiritual evolution will be far slower. She will be a Light unto the world.'

Humanity as a whole tends to have problems with self worth and remembering these words bring mine to the fore, I have difficulty seeing what is truly worthy when I know all my faults and things that are not worthy but I did try to use it as a tool not to give in.

As Ramtha's talk finished and the evening was left for us to socialise, young Gary was my first visitor, beaming from ear to ear.

'Told you didn't I, conquered the fear and won out didn't you?' he said. He truly was an old soul in a young body.

Then the others arrived. I was surrounded by students who had not even noticed me before, calling me Master, asking me questions, treating me like some golden deity. I was shocked, I have to say turned off, by their attitude. I was exactly the same person I had been before Ramtha's talk, nothing had changed in me. I was cross again, that some of these people had not even seen me worthy of a good morning before and now I was a Guru, a Master.

It was whilst I was writing this book that Richard allowed me to see these people differently.

'Think of a picture turned to the wall or in a dark corner or corridor. It's not noticed, no-one can see it unless its face is turned away from the wall or a light is shone on it. Then you can see it for what it is.' So I then had to forgive myself for harbouring thoughts I had had about people needing to be told what to see. However, I still cannot come to terms that a Guru can be appointed on someone's say so just because the someone saying so is considered to be prestigious. I have found the most profound teachings come from children and ordinary men and women with no claim to a superior spiritual path.

I attended this Ancient School of Wisdom twice a year for seven years. I worried that if I left I might blow my chance of learning all there was to learn. If reincarnation was on line then I wanted to achieve enough learning to keep my next incarnations to a minimum. I didn't fancy returning into another body like mine or a third world starving body or a body in a war torn country. By my reckoning the odds weren't good to get a healthy, strong body without major challenges of some description.

So when I came to contemplate leaving school it was a difficult decision. The First Sundance/Gathering was in the offing and I could only do so much, no matter how committed I was. Something would have to go.

I was sitting, one of the few chairs allowed, on my space amongst everyone's belongings, spaces piled high with sleeping bags, pillows and belongings.

After a particularly good session of teachings the students paraded with Ramtha, chanting and praising. Normally, Ramtha's procession stuck to the walkways but tonight they had spread out trampling everyone's spaces, the group fully surrounding him. The large group in front were walking backwards hiding Ramtha from my view and totally oblivious to where they were treading or going.

I could see them getting nearer. I knew I could not get out of the way. I knew I was not capable of climbing over the things around me.

Two of the guards were screaming at me,

'Lady, get the hell out of there. You are going to get trampled. They'll kill you, get the hell out.' I just spread my hands and smiled at them, I knew what I was in for but I had no way to get out. My thoughts were,

'Well, I was thinking of leaving and couldn't make up my mind. Perhaps this trampling is the way I am to leave.' When the group were about fifteen feet from me, they suddenly, for no reason, parted and turned round, seeing me and avoiding me. I saw as they parted, Ramtha, he gave a smile and a small nod and the procession moved on.

I looked around, nothing was out of place compared to before. I was sitting exactly as I had been. That smile, that nod, was I felt the approval, the permission to go out into the world and take up the next quest.

Chapter Seventeen

Native American Sacred Sundance Ceremony

The residence of Plas Dolguog was renovated in the 1600's. During the 1900's more renovations were carried out and there hidden in a dark and sealed cupboard was the exposed tip of a huge monolith, perhaps 3 ft by 3 ft. In ignorance, it was contemplated that its movement to a more prominent position would be an attractive addition to the house. Only when the mechanical digger reached approximately 12 feet was it decided that this was no ordinary stone but something special, which at some time had been incorporated into the structure of the building. It was brought out of its dark, dirty cupboard into the light. It was as if it began to breathe.

Hamish Miller (International author and dowser and Founder of Parallel Community) in his usual charming and enthusiastic way 'talked' to Richard's standing stone It has also been pointed out that the stone is not of local origin and was in its past part of a twenty eight stone, stone circle.

When the Conservatory was built on to the hotel it was discovered the old house did not have any foundations. The Building Regulations man was very disturbed and wanted the foundations for the new addition to go deeper, until Richard pointed out that that would destabilize the whole building by undermining it and causing subsidence. Richard does remember that although there were no foundations there were huge stones laid under the building as a base plate and the old house appeared to be built on these. The new foundation for the new extension was then laid alongside the huge stones in order to keep them in line and act as a solid foundation. It seems logical to suggest that these stones are the stones from the old stone circle.

Someone asked how the energy at this site compared to other sites in Britain and Hamish replied,

'On a Richter scale of one to ten of powerful sites in Britain, it is probably about six or seven. This is a powerful site and a powerful stone.'

Whilst in Tahlequah Richard accompanied me to a meditation, not something he did very often. He saw the stone in a small room with small lines of light coming from it. He could tell the size of the chamber because as he moved away the colour faded and became black and white and when he went towards the stone the colour returned. He realized that the colour fading signified the size of the room and the lights symbolized the ley lines. This room has eventually been built within the hotel function room in accordance with his vision.

People were fascinated, even asking what was behind the Restaurant wall because they felt a powerful energy. One gentleman who he told us absolutely did not believe in anything he couldn't see, feel or hear asked to look at what was causing the excitement. He approached the stone and reached out to touch the tip. As his fingers made contact he appeared to leap backward and ended up leaning against the wall some eight feet away from the stone.

'What the..... was that? I got a terrible jolt.' Anthony was present and he jokingly said,

'Oh, we've got it plugged into the mains, to add to the experience.' It wasn't funny. This gentleman turned scarlet,

'You could have killed me! You could have killed me! I've got a pacemaker and a dicky heart, you imbecile.' The more everyone tried to convince him it was just the energy of the stone and he must be very sensitive, the more he was convinced that Anthony's 'joke' explanation was real.

His was an extreme case but others were more open and believed what they had felt. This stone has now been exposed more fully, although still only partly exposed, perhaps 5 ft high by 5 ft wide, it is housed in its own small room. A small sacred space as seen in Richard's meditation, designed with a Moorish influence where people can sit and experience its quiet, peaceful, healing energy. It is known simply as The Stone Room.

In November 1996 a series of amazing synchronistic events began to unfold. A long awaited destiny was to come into fruition. Tom, you may remember we met in Spain, came to visit us in Wales. Tom was very sensitive to the energies of certain tracts of land and as he walked with us around Dolguog and the Caravan Park he not only saw the past but also had visions of the future. The visions of the future were a new phenomenon for him. As we explored he gave us a running commentary. There was to be a huge gathering, an event of great celestial significance and healing, involving the whole world, hundreds of people would come to this sacred place.

This was hard to take in.

'Why here?' I asked. 'Why not Stonehenge, why not Lourdes?' The answer was that this place had been kept hidden, kept sacred and unpolluted, its power was centered at the monolith where many energy lines, known as leys, converged.

Later, as we talked with Tom, he would mention other things including an ancient yew tree. We are in possession of a Certificate signed by Professor David Bellamy and the Archbishop of Canterbury stating that the yew in question is at least three hundred and fifty years old, validated by a survey of yews in Great Britain. Apparently, yews are almost always found on religious or pagan sites and very rarely in gardens or fields as the yew is highly poisonous to animals and humans alike. This site has at least eight yews – should we ask why?

The next thing Tom mentioned was a freshwater spring. Richard's face was a picture.

'There is a well,' he admitted, 'that not many people know about, as it needs excavating. As far as I know, it's fed by a freshwater spring, and to the best of my knowledge, I'm the only person alive who knows that!' This well has now been renovated and is functioning again, renewing its role in the landscape.

'I also saw a circular building.' said Tom. Good heavens! Spooky! There was on the land a small circular slate shelter. It originally comprised of a circular building with two windows, a fireplace and an entrance or door. Unfortunately some years earlier, before our ownership, a group of children decided to use the slate from the walls as missiles, throwing them the 60 foot drop into the river.

For many years it has been known as the Summer House indeed that was probably what it had been used for. A local lady sadly no longer alive told of sitting round the back of this summerhouse overlooking the two rivers, the South Dulas and the Dyfi (Dovey), and doing her homework. She also talked of fetching water from the well for use in the house.

It is greatly significant from a spiritual and religious point of view that this building is situated on a high promontory above the confluence of two rivers, as this has religious and spiritual connotations, within a grove of ancient oaks. It has been mooted by a local Reverend and a local amateur historian and linguist that it is possible that this was one of the first religious cells in the British Isles. Perhaps a lone monk from Ireland would have set up his cell at this spot, spreading the word in his self-enforced retreat. Even as we talked with Tom, another part of the puzzle was unfolding and the two pieces of the jigsaw would soon come together.

I felt that Tom's visions and pronouncements needed to be shared with someone and my first thought was Geraint. I rang him and told him the story so far and he came straight over. We sat over coffee and Tom filled in the details of his visions and as I was sitting listening I thought how weird and far fetched a lot of it sounded. When Tom came to the end of his story I looked across at Geraint.

Geraint is a very open minded vicar but this was perhaps a step too far. He was sitting hunched over, his head in his hands enveloping his bushy beard.

'On no,' I thought 'here comes the end of a wonderful twenty year friendship.' After a while he lifted his head and said,

'Now, I've got something to tell you. I've been back from Oklahoma just three days and what is occurring now is absolutely incredible, but here goes.'

His amazing story follows.

Over the previous ten years I had been a member of a group called the Order of Sancta Sophia. This was run by Geraint, who is the rector of Pennal and Corris of the Church in Wales. We studied everything from Celtic Spirituality, the wisdom of Sophia, the Cabbala, the Grail legends and King Arthur. We used different forms of meditation techniques and kept individual journals of our progress and dream time.

Geraint told Tom and I he had received an invitation to lecture at a New Age Church in America by the name of the Church of Sancta Sophia. Sophia played an important part in the groups understanding. Philo meaning the love of or study of something, and thus philosophy, meaning the love of Sophia or wisdom.

The church was based in Oklahoma. Geraint began his story.

'The night before I left, a member of our Order rang to tell me about an unusual dream she had had. In the dream I would meet a Cherokee Indian who would have a message for me. I had no reference for this information and just filed it in my memory. I was too engrossed in packing and preparing for an early flight next morning. Neither I nor Karen, the lady who had the dream, knew anything about Oklahoma's place in Cherokee history.

So there was I being taken to my destination of Tahlequah, when I saw a sign for Cherokee Turnpike. A few miles further on I was even more surprised to see an even bigger sign. Cherokee Nations Headquarters. My destination village, Tahlequah, quite unbeknown to me, turned out to be the capital of the Cherokee Nation. What might have been a coincidence continued to evolve.

Two days into the conference I felt so much at home that I shared Karen's Cherokee dream with some of my new friends, one of whom was Robert Johns, a member of the village. Robert had both Welsh and Cherokee blood in his veins. As I led a meditation following a service Robert had a vision of a Celtic cross on Sundance grounds – the Sundance Ceremony being particularly sacred to the Native American Indians.

Robert asked me if there were any stone circles in my country of Wales. What a question! Wales is covered in them not least those connected with the National Eisteddfod. Robert then shared his vision with me and also the congregation that the Sundance was to come to Wales in the near future, linking Celtic and Native American spirituality. Robert was told to hold the vision in prayer that all spiritual paths would come together for twelve days in August 1998, with the Sundance as its focal point. Robert's vision quest leader, a Lakota descended from Horn Chipps, the spiritual adviser to Chief Crazy Horse, also 'saw' Native American sacred ceremony in Wales.

As the conference progressed it became apparent that the Native American people had their Ceremony but didn't know where the land to carry this out would be. I was sent home to find the land on which this Ceremony could take place. A land with stone circles and a Celtic connection to spirituality.' Geraint fell silent as we sat transfixed.

This was only the beginning.

Here I would like to quote a prophecy taken directly from the ancient chronicles of the Native Americans:-

My people were told of the coming of the Europeans to this continent ... and we were told that if they came here in a sacred manner to learn the spiritual teachings from us, then we would come together and live in harmony. Each one of us would bring a gift ... and it would be a beautiful thing between us. But if the people from across the great water didn't accept our great teachings or acknowledge them, then a time would come where the native people would lay as if they were dead in the dust ... and our teachings would be forgotten by many of us and even our young people wouldn't listen to us. Then after a period of a hundred years or more, we would stand up again, we would be walking on our hind legs and we would be as if we were earth spirits that had sprung up from the earth again. We would have power again to work with the natural forces, with the beings and powers and at that time our children would run to us and seek this knowledge. Not only would they do it, but the people who had come from across the Great Waters, their sons and daughters would be doing it and they would say to us,

'Teach us, because we have destroyed the earth.'

The Sundance is a Sacred Ceremony carried out by various tribes of Native Americans with their own variations of the Sundance. It is a very strenuous and challenging spiritual ceremony and in its true form is only open to full blood Native Americans. It consists of four days of purification including fasting, visioning and spiritual preparation, four days of dancing and piercing and four days of teaching and learning. This is how it was described to me and how I understood it would proceed. The central focus of the ceremony is a tree, the Standing Person. Participants can choose to be pierced in the chest area and then dance attached to the Standing Person, the tree. Piercings are the most sacred part of the Sundance Ceremony as it is the sacrifice that the individual makes for the good of others. I was told that this was the man's offering for the people and also to honour the pain of women in childbirth.

As I learnt more about the Sundance I worried about the piercing and the suffering but had to concede and balance this with my Christian upbringing where Jesus also hung from a tree and suffered.

The time was imminent – before Geraint's visit the Elders had been informed through their dreamtime meetings that a guide would come to show them where they must 'cross the Great Waters' to perform a sacred twelve day ceremony for the celebration to the Sun. Was Geraint this guide?

This was where our story took another turn. Richard and I have always considered ourselves guardians of the land on which we live, but with the purchase of Dolguog we truly felt we had taken on a sacred trust. Richard and I had an answer to the question we had held for so long, even as we were teetering on the verge of bankruptcy and thought we would lose the land – why are we here? There is a destiny for this land. But what is it?

The decision was made. There would be a Global Prayer Ceremony incorporating the Celebration to the Sun and including worldwide Star groups to work at the same time towards the same end, the healing of Mother Earth and the unifying of consciousness of all peoples, to live and work in peace with each other.

I was given the job of running the office, gathering participants and coordinating everything. That couldn't be too difficult could it?

The word went out and people began to respond. In fact the response was amazing. As the organization progressed we had reason to travel, encouraged by Richard's Uncle David.

When he came to live near us after his wife died he became a surrogate Grandpa. Where else would you not only be allowed but welcome to take your muddy bike into the living room and mend a puncture in front of the fire?

He went to visit his cousin who had lived in Australia since she was ten years old. She was a widow and during his visit their relationship blossomed to the point where he emigrated and went to live with her. Richard sold Uncle David's bungalow avoiding the cost of an Agent and one morning we received a cheque in the post with an invitation –

'Come and see us.' We had adopted the philosophy 'Do it today, you don't know what tomorrow holds', as we didn't know when my disability would prevent it. Today I have no regrets as I can look back and say,

'I have been there, or done that.' and no longer being able to loses its sting.

This trip to Australia was to be the first of a number of visits over the years and when we started to travel to other countries following Ramtha's school and the peace work, we incorporated the trips together. We found that it cost less to keep circumnavigating the world than to go to one destination and then another, which meant we got to visit some wonderful places such as Hong Kong and Fiji.

We booked a few days in Fiji, it sounded so exotic, and arranged a three day cruise on a small island boat. The boat carried approximately thirty passengers with berths and cabins on the lower level, an open deck above with a roof and an area at the front of this deck for the Captain for sailing and navigating. The open deck was where we spent our days and ate our meals, enjoying the scenery and enjoying the blue sky, sea and islands.

The Fijians are a beautiful, carefree, happy people and the men have, certainly on our cruise had, enormous feet. As they piped us aboard they wore sparkling white uniforms, some with short trousers and long white socks. They looked spectacular.

We sailed from the mainland and visited an island, where the inhabitants prepared us a typical island lunch and showed us their homes and culture, selling us their hand made carvings from masks to coconut bird houses. I was nervous of leaving the boat to go to the island, but the Fijian crew had no such inhibitions. One of them picked me up and another folded my wheelchair and 'threw' it to be caught by yet another crew man in the eight man rowing boat below. Before I knew it I was also following that same route to be caught and seated on the bench. I was enthralled, I have never been handled with such gentle compassion in such a dramatic situation, it was an amazing experience.

When we returned to the mother ship it was dark and raining. The crew just balanced on the edges of the small row boat, helped by a small outboard motor, holding umbrellas over us all as they sang at the tops of their voices and swayed with precision to keep the boat balanced and on course. Back home to a superb meal on board our cosy mothership.

The following morning we had been at sea less than forty-eight hours when the Captain called a meeting. His opening remarks were,

'I have something very serious to tell you. I have heard from the mainland that a cyclone is heading our way and will reach us within hours. As the Captain I have been ordered to take the boat straight back. However, I wish to ask you to trust me. I do not wish to return to the mainland. In my opinion it is far too dangerous and I would like your permission to head for one of the small islands and find shelter until the cyclone passes. I have to warn you we are in a dangerous situation.'

No one challenged him, we were all out of our comfort zone and had no point of reference for such a danger.

The Captain set off to find his hideaway as we all sat rather subdued and looked at the beautiful scenery wondering how and when it would change. Richard who always wants to be involved was in the open cabin at the front talking to the Captain. The Captain had been all night at the helm before telling us and was awaiting his chance to move as safely as possible and make our way. Trays of food and drinks lay strewn around him as he sat cross legged on the work bench watching the sea ahead. By this time all the crew including the Captain was in much more casual gear and all barefoot. Their large feet gave them a great advantage in balancing and giving them purchase on a swaying ship. As Richard stood talking to the Captain he said the sea just parted, literally parted, as in the bible. A huge opening appeared in the sea and our boat slid at speed down the side of this sixty foot opening. Trays, maps, anything loose, flying out of the door – not really a door just an opening with not even a gate. Richard braced himself in this opening as things went skittering between his legs.

Everyone else in the open cabin was thrown around, I managed to grab a support pillar as I in my wheelchair, brakes full on, slewed across the deck. I sat with my arms and legs wrapped around the pillar as if my life depended on it – which in fact it did. As we hit the bottom of this huge trough the boat had to right itself and get us out into more open water, albeit rough and turbulent. In the cabin we couldn't see what was happening, but it was blatantly obvious that something dangerous and dramatic was in progress. I feared that Richard had probably been swept overboard. I was so relieved when he appeared and began to help the crew with the passengers.

One young lady on her honeymoon was extricated from her foetal position under the front bench of the deck, having slid from one end of the deck to the other.

She was bruised and traumatized but all the members of the crew were wonderful with her and treated us all with great concern and compassion. The Captain steered us somehow to his island shelter where everything was calmer and as the news came through we discovered we were in the eye of the storm. The anchors were dropped and everything gathered and tidied.

The next day dawned and we were still safe and reasonably calm.

'We are running out of food and water.' The Captain said, 'Some of the crew need to go to the nearest occupied island to buy supplies.' As they set off and left the shelter of the island harbour in such a small boat, in their bright yellow storm coats, with the put-put of what to us seemed a feeble outboard motor they were still singing and laughing. The waves were so high we kept losing sight of them. When they returned some hours later the goods had to be transferred from the small boat as it bobbed up and down with a twenty foot difference in height between the two boats as the waves rose and fell. Stacked trays of eggs appeared to be thrown as one boat went up and the other went down until the crew were eventually back on board and the cheers resounded their welcome and bravery just so we could eat and drink.

As the news came through the Captain chalked it up on a blackboard for us all to see and keep in touch with the cyclone's path. After three days things began to settle and the Captain decided it was now safe to make our way back to the mainland.

The crew set about releasing the anchor, or so they thought. The anchor had different ideas. The motor for the winch jammed and the anchor remained firmly in place. We all watched in trepidation as they went through the routine. No amount of engine revving and pulling back and forth would release it. The mainland engineers said 'Do A, then do B, then do C.' Over and over they repeated this procedure, with an occasional clout with a very large hammer, with no results. The company on the mainland had no information to help free the anchor or mend the engine that wound in the anchor cable. We were unable to move.

The Captain made a decision to cut the cable loose and leave the anchors where they were, embedded on the sea bed. If we met rough weather however we would find ourselves in a severe predicament unable to drop anchor.

I was amazed Richard had waited so long, but this was the final straw. He jumped down to join the crew. They were still singing no matter what the situation a little less enthusiastically however. He found that the clutch mechanism to one of the anchors wouldn't work, so he organized the crew to move the anchor from the non working motor across to the working motor of the other anchor and the problem was solved. Up came the anchors leaving us with the possibility of dropping anchor again if we needed to on our trip back to the mainland.

Although it was a bit rough we had an uneventful journey back. As we approached the mainland we passed the boat which had gone out before us, its Captain had returned as instructed. She was laid on her side, a sad spectacle, how they had got the passengers off without injury or worse was beyond imagining. At least fifteen people had lost their lives in the storm. As we berthed in the harbour, the quay was covered in people selling t-shirts 'We survived Cyclone Gavin.' The island had been devastated.

We could not return to our Hotel, although there were a flight of six or seven steps to the Foyer the waves had entered and completely flooded and devastated the Ground

Floor. As we were transferred to a less damaged Hotel we passed electricity telegraph poles, snapped clean off about six feet from the ground. Houses semi demolished, small boats swept half way up hills and the Fijian population waist high in dirty water rescuing their belongings from their wrecked homes – still singing.

On our return to the mainland I discovered I had lost a large filling leaving a substantial hole in a back tooth. We had a number of days before getting back to the UK and I didn't want to lose the tooth so made enquiries as to where to find a dentist.

'You need to go to the local hospital. They'll deal with it for you. I'll call a taxi you can go straight up.' said the Receptionist.

The taxi driver was a typical happy Fijian and asked if he could take us a small detour to see his new house. He was so proud that we gladly agreed. Twenty years he had been saving for this day. We drove up to this corrugated iron garage style building with a dirt floor, and he beamed at us.

'This is it, and I even have a little garden, so I can grow a few vegetables.' We were non-plussed, we were staying in a four star Hotel with everything we could wish for and being waited on hand and foot. Many of the Hotel guests complained incessantly about minor, in their opinion major, inconveniences. We did our best to enthuse and congratulate him as he continued to beam at us with such pride.

The hospital had about thirty women (I don't know where the men were) sitting on benches waiting for their turn to be seen. I reported to Reception, I don't think they had seen a wheelchair actually in action before, and asked me to wait. Almost immediately I was called into a tiny dental surgery. It was fairly obvious that hygiene was not a priority. I opened my mouth for the dentist to look, and as he stepped aside, someone else looked and then someone else until I realized – these were other patients just checking to see if I was the same as them.

The dentist was very apologetic that he could not fix it immediately, he could put in a temporary filling, but it was a big one and he would have to charge me double.

Before I left the dentist's chair he insisted on calling the taxi back to take us to our Hotel and as we left I paid the 'double' bill. It was the equivalent of seventy-five pence.

Fiji was so beautiful despite the devastation caused by the cyclone but I felt uncomfortable throughout our stay. The contrast between the inhabitants of the island and the tourists, some of them extremely rich and demanding an affluent life style, was something I found difficult to cope with even though I knew the presence of tourists allowed the taxi driver to earn enough to buy his house, I couldn't help but think his wage was probably a tiny percentage of the cost of a holiday on his island. The inequalities of life were extreme and for any one with eyes to see beyond their own protected hotel and beach, stunningly obvious and disturbing.

We continued our journey, Richard and I were visiting Uncle David and relatives in Australia and incorporating this with the Sundance arrangements, of course my passion went with me, with amazing results. In Perth, having written to one supporter to say I was coming, I arrived to a ninety strong audience at a local community centre. From that meeting my contact, Brett, organized a meditation group and distributed over 10,000 leaflets.

In Adelaide we met Roger and Glenda, founders and members of Fountain International, they lived in Adelaide. I gave another talk in the Rose Garden in Adelaide's beautiful parkland; this was a superb setting for an inspirational future.

Roger and Glenda told us that Fountain International in Adelaide were, amongst many other things, working with the police force to cut the crime rate. If a very small percentage of the population meditated, in other words entered a state of consciousness that allows mental activity to settle down into a deep relaxation and coherence in that individual or group, then that state can be picked up at a distance by those not practicing Transcendental Meditation and do not even have any knowledge of the experiment personally.

Science actually calls this phenomenon the 'field effect of consciousness'. A bit like a mobile phone picks up microwave signals, the electro-magnetic frequency of the thought process can enliven the electromagnetic field in a specific manner and transmit waves to be received at a distance, imprinting the receiver.

The Adelaide experiment was one of the first, there have been many more since and the results show that this technique creates a dramatic reduction – up to 25 per cent to date – in the crime wave, including assaults, murders and incidents of rape. The phenomenal results are backed by rigorous statistical analysis which rule out alternative explanations.

We returned home and as the plans progressed it was arranged for Robert Johns to come from the USA with his thirteen year old son and we set off on a tour of the UK to tell people about the Sundance Ceremony. Richard drove us a total of 4,000 miles, having a wife who gets lost in her own garden made planning the itinerary a little fraught! We spoke at fifteen different venues starting in Walsall. We traveled up to the Findhorn Community in Scotland, then back to Norwich, Ipswich, Haverford West, Sutton, Newport and Cornwall, where Robert and I were invited to speak at the Fountain International Conference. We travelled back home to Wales and then to London.

The talk in Ipswich was the first time I had ever used a microphone. There must have been about eighty people present. Robert Johns spoke first about his involvement and his vision of the Sundance, but he found it difficult to speak and soon passed the presentation over to me. This is where my NLP training helped – that and my passion for the project banished all traces of nervousness, and when we returned to our lodgings I was as high as a kite!

Richard and I were staying with a young couple who had recently moved house, so the sleeping arrangements consisted of one single bed, a mattress on the floor and a room full of packed boxes. At about 3:00 am my internal telephone rang. Words were tumbling and turning in my head and I knew I would never remember them in the morning.

"Richard! Richard! I need a pen and paper, but don't turn on the light!' I was still half asleep, as if I were sleepwalking.

We won't dwell on Richard's reply, other than to say he did find me a pen and paper after stumbling and fumbling in the dark. I scribbled down the words as best I could and promptly went back to sleep. Next morning at breakfast I tried to decipher my handwriting, and as I wrote the words more clearly I discovered what I had been given; a poem.

'Dreaming the Vision.'

Dream the dream of man uniting.
Dream the dream of man held dear.
Dream the dream of life unfolding.
Dream the dream and hold it clear.
Bring your soul and give it freedom.
Bring your love and let it share.
Make your choice and let it blossom
Spreading joy from here to there.
Bring your thoughts and give them power.
Plant the seed and let it grow.
Bring the grace of choice and prayer
Helping nurture what you know.
Dream the dream and take its knowledge.
Watch your thoughts and keep them true.
Step inside with faith and courage.
Live your life in every hue.
Take the dream into experience.
Make it yours to live and own.
God is joyous, full of beauty.
Create your path as he has shown.
Spin the dream upon earth's axis.
Watch it form as it revolves.
Yours is choice and yours is freedom.
Take that choice as it evolves.
Dream the dream as love intends it.
Dream the dream of man's release.
Here's the chance to own your beauty.
Live in love and light and peace.

> Dream the dream as you create it.
> Dream the dream that is foretold.
> Own the fact that you are holy.
> Dream the dream you now can hold.

Ten years after these talks I received a phone call from a lady in Cornwall. She said she had attended one of the talks I had given. At the time she was not into all this spiritual stuff but had merely accompanied a friend. She continued to attend with her friend when they cut the Seed of Life symbol in the turf in Cornwall and had become more and more involved. She now helps organize four ceremonies a year around the symbol in the spirit of the original Seed of Life teachings. As the group has got bigger they have extended their venues and were going to Glastonbury to hold a ceremony there this year. She wanted me to send her information regarding the start up of this work,

'I've visited Australia, Germany and America where Seed of Life symbols have been created along with active groups in those countries and I know for a fact they are all over the world. I want to remind everyone how it was started and the legacy you have left behind, Diana.'

I sat down when I came off the phone and contemplated that conversation. What I had started, to replace the Sundance when it did not manifest, with the Gatherings taking over, had evolved into what I had set out to do. The members of each group had gone away and done their own thing, no dogmas, no creeds or beliefs set in stone. It was a great enlightenment to realize that I had achieved what I had hoped and wanted to achieve.

The next big event on the calendar in the lead up to the Sundance ceremony was a trip to Tahlequah, where Geraint had been presented with the vision of the Native American and Celtic traditions coming together.

We scheduled this trip to follow immediately after my attendance at what was to be my last Event at Ramtha's school. Richard accompanied me to America and we flew on and met up once again with Robert Johns, and all the wonderful people in Sparrowhawk Village in order to further the plans for the forthcoming ceremony planned for August 1998 and our discussions and planning put things well in hand for the Sundance. Elders, dancers, drummers, cooks, organizers and other participants totalled about sixty people. An ambitious undertaking, as you might agree.

All week, one of our new friends, Pattie, had been urging me to undergo a past life regression. I steadfastly refused. I was not interested in past lives as it seemed everyone had been Cleopatra or Henry VIIIth, and no-one ever cleaned the toilets! But Pattie insisted. She persuaded me that I would not be hypnotized, just very relaxed, so I finally agreed to a session just before we were to leave for the airport.

That morning, Robert and his lady friend invited Richard and I for coffee. They had a gift for me. I unwrapped the most exquisite deerskin pouch, decorated with small beads depicting a beautiful red rose. And as I took the pouch in my hands I was overcome by a devastating and uncontrollable attack of weeping. I shook and wept and couldn't speak, to the great consternation of Richard, Robert and his friend. When I eventually gained control, all I could say was that I had owned it before. I did not know what that meant.

We went to the Church of Sancta Sophia for a service. There was a picnic table outside the church, surrounded by children talking to a tall man. As I approached the children turned to look at me. Standing on the table was a wolf and although it was a pet, it retained the

271

magnificence of a wild, free spirit, with eyes like pools of liquid knowingness. Wolves are wonderful animals, with strict social and moral codes within their pack and rules for survival. I stroked the wolf and talked to the owner before heading down a path not designed for a wheelchair and into the church for the service.

It was a beautiful service and did a lot to help calm my turbulent emotions. Afterwards, I accompanied Pattie to her therapy room, where she sat me in a comfy chair and told me to relax and just tell her what I saw. I was still dubious about the whole thing, but decided to go with it.

'If I say I was Cleopatra, I'm out of here, okay?!'

I started by seeing a wolf.

'Oh my goodness, here we go. I'm only saying that because I've just met him.'

Pattie encouraged me to just go with it and keep on describing what I could see.

'Well, he is smiling at me and wants me to go with him.' As the session continued it transpired in my visions that the deerskin pouch – or one identical to it – was something I had given to my wife on our wedding day.

The visions took me through my life until the day of my death, when I handed the future over to a grandchild. Without doubt the whole experience felt totally real and true, even though I had interjected throughout with derogatory remarks of disbelief.

When the session finished Pattie took a satin bag from under my seat. It contained small coloured glass stones with symbols on them, and these she proceeded to lay out on a circular purple and silver glass tray in a flower petal design. She began a reading and Pattie became very excited. One of my stones was special, she said and indicated the manifestation of great things. She took this as a sign that I was indeed the right person to be working with the Sundance project. For myself, I was impressed with the insights this particular technique had into my own personal situation, so I went to the village shop to purchase a set of this game.

Time was pressing for us to get to the airport and the girl in the shop seemed to be taking forever. Suddenly, Robert burst through the door.

'Stop! Don't buy it.' he said. 'Come with me.'

Robert had a tendency to be impetuous so I was a bit annoyed with his interruption, but duly followed him out of the shop. He rummaged about in the back of his pick-up and came out with a pristine box containing all the essential elements of the game.

'Here. This was given to me. I don't use it, but you will and you should.' he said. 'It will give you guidance.'

I accepted graciously and we rushed to the airport just in time. My energy depletes easily and I was more than ready to sit back and gather my strength. As I sat quietly thinking over the events of the last few hours a poem began to form in my mind. It turned out to be an accurate rendition of my past life memory.

25th November 1997 – flight home after past life
regression with Pattie.

White wolf greets me, laughing and happy,
Journeys me on to a life long forgot.
Memory jolted, remembered, awakened,
By a deep red rose on a gift just begot.
Beaded with love and compassion for tradition.
Exquisitely placed on white buck skin.
Memory flooding, as the valley remembered,
Horses corralled, yet free as the wind.

Children are playing, laughing and singing.
Memories strange, yet haunting and true.
I stand there, surveying the tepees, the village,
My people, my children through guardian's view.
They see me as awesome, a powerful being.
A father, protector, to guard and to guide.
A woman so beautiful, hers is the buckskin
Embroidered with pride for her future life.
In the picture before me, we stand in the circle,
As she walks toward me to take as my wife.
The scenes that follow are darkened and clouded.
Fighting and violence enter the scene.
Wounded and dying, sickly and elderly.
Decisions to take that no man should dare.
Who shall decide, those to stay or to follow?
Whose karma, the choices here offered will bear?
To forsake the few that the rest may continue.
Tomorrow the sun will rise as our cue.
My people will see it, their future to build on,
To search and to find a new home, a new land,
Decisions, decisions of love and compassion,
Yet streaked with remorse for the need to disband.
Carry the burden, my wife always by me,
Beautiful, beautiful, pure as a dove.
Yet even her love is tinged with her knowing
Violence begets violence, even in love.
The scene quickly changes, tiring and tired.
The future revealed in my dreams and my prayers.

How will I warn them, protect them and guide them,
Give of the knowledge of a future that's theirs?
Stories are precious, told to the children,
They are the ones who will further the dreams.
Resting, releasing, a grandson stands by me,
His is the task for the future I see.
I leave for my grandson a wide new horizon.
A time of change and a new path to emblazon.
Leaving, releasing, I no longer carry
Burdens entwined in the heart and the soul.
A future where leaders join for a parley
Sharing decisions they take now as a whole.
Relaxing, releasing, learning the lessons.
All lessons and experiences awaiting my owning.
Forgive all that's gone in reciprocal fashion.
How many lifetimes recessed in my mind?
Know the soul's journey was to live life with passion.
God's love and compassion reward that I find.
White wolf is laughing, remember, awaken.
He greets my memory and joy for my life.
The mystery unfolded – remember, acknowledge.
Never forsaken, lost sight of the goal.
The Source of my being has given me courage.
I carry this with me deep, deep in my Soul.

Note: I had been convinced that the wolf in my vision was the same wolf I had seen outside the church. Until I had my photos developed. He was not even the same colour!

Chapter Eighteen

The Seed of Life Peace Foundation
Gathers the World

The build-up to the first Gathering continued. During our annual winter visit to Spain I held a final meeting of the video club, with fifty people present. I told them all about the project and from this meeting we enrolled seven translators to translate the information into seven European languages.

It soon became obvious that we would need some kind of formal organization to run this event. The name came about as a result of my search for a symbol that held no preconceived connection to any particular creed, dogma or religion.

The Seed of Life, together with its counterpart the Flower of Life, was flash burned into the rose granite walls of a temple, in Luxor Egypt, in fact the foundations of a later temple, the later temple being dated at 6,000 years old. By today's technology our scientists do not know how this was achieved.

This symbol is humanity's template. It is the hologram that we live. It forms a three-dimensional Star of David. When you look at the symbol as a three dimensional image it will appear as a star tetrahedron – a tetrahedron is a diamond shape – (two interpenetrating tetrahedrons). A star tetrahedron is one of the five platonic solids and one of the building blocks of life, in ancient texts such as the Bible these platonic solids were described as the Codes of Creation. This is the same pattern that is created at conception by cellular division – the first eight cells of a human being, immediately after conception, also form a star tetrahedron.

This symbol resonates deep in the soul as a memory or potential. When you look at the symbol, where the circles overlap is the blending, the balancing of the male/female energies, the yin and the yang, the visible and the invisible worlds, the conscious and the unconscious. Here is a mandala for life in all its creativity and diversity.

Observe this symbol – the six unified circles/cycles of expression. 1. the first circle of expression – the law of right human relations – faith. The faith to work for this aim. 2. the second circle of expression – the principle of good will – surrender. To surrender to the act of good will regardless of outward events. 3. the third circle of expression – the law of group endeavour – service. The sense of working together in service. 4. the fourth circle of expression – the principle of unanimity – abundance. Unanimity, one for all and all for one, enough for everyone to experience abundance. 5. the fifth circle of expression – the law of the spiritual approach – temptation. To stand up to temptation and approach it head on knowing the spiritual consequences. 6. the sixth circle of expression – the principle of essential divinity, overcoming. Overcoming temptation and challenges to approach divinity and understand spirit union. Revealing, generating the seventh sphere of perfect spirit union. I am you and you are me.

Using this symbol as our point of focus the word spread. Months of networking resulted in the formation of many Starseed groups around the world. Men, women and children from forty countries came together with prayers and meditations as they focused on peace and healing for the Earth.

After many requests from people for help in order to spread the word or set up a Starseed group Richard suggested I ran a seminar.

'Who me?' I said. Twenty six participants undertook the process of learning how to inspire others with the vision. It was fun to discover wonderful phrases such as,

'The indivisible (God) divides in order to appear, but only appears to divide.' 'The purpose of living is to discover the purpose of living.'

It was around this time that I met Jane. I was on my way into town and met Mo, who was to become a stalwart of the Gatherings. She was a friend of Jane who was then told of what was being planned. She cheerfully said,

'I'm not into all this 'woo woo' stuff, but I am a fast typist. If you need any help I'm your person.'

She certainly was and quickly became my right hand and third sister, taking the 'woo woo' stuff in her stride.

At the end of May I wrote to a total of two hundred and forty seven world leaders, inviting their support. I also emailed schools, organizations, groups and children, hundreds of people from around the world requesting their words for a Peace Scroll.

Six weeks before the Sundance was due to take place, I got a casual phone call from America telling me the Sundance group would not be coming as the funding was no longer available.

'We'll keep in touch anyway.' they said.

This was unreal. The work and energy that had gone into getting it all to this stage was immense, not to mention the phone call from AIM, the American Indian Movement, threatening my life if I proceeded to help facilitate the Sun Dance being brought into white man's territory.

'Guns will be present, if not before.' I was told. Help, I was only the office. Had others been threatened also?

I could not believe it. The office was festooned with charts and paperwork, the business relegated to a small corner, one wall taken over with a large chart containing more than a hundred names and addresses of people planning to attend.

If someone hands you a wet baby you have two choices. You either put it down because it's not yours and it might get pneumonia, or you wrap it in a warm, dry towel and nurture it. I decided to do the latter and contacted all one hundred plus people. To my amazement, they all decided to come anyway. One lady even hitch-hiked from France with a six year old child. People came for the twelve days and held the focus and energy and others came for eight, four, two days or even a few hours depending on the time that they could manage to allocate. They were coming from Europe, Australia, Canada and America as well as the UK over one hundred people in total.

The planned Sundance had been the catalyst, but The Gathering now had an energy all its own. Letters of support from many world leaders were coming in on a regular basis as a result of my letter and email campaign. I had grown more than one grey hair over the work involved and the responsibility but I always remembered Ramtha saying,

'Every grey hair is potential wisdom.' The secret though is to fulfill that potential!

Richard stripped out two old caravans and installed gas cookers and a sink. We brought in portaloos, arranged rotas and menus. Food was bought in bulk so that little time needed to be spent shopping for necessary items during the Gathering. The charge to attend was kept to an absolute minimum and included all food. Part of the experience was to practice Raja yoga, the yoga of service, two ladies, Linda and Dot, took on the job of organizing and supervising the vegetarian kitchen. Vegetarian not just to keep the cost down but to help keep body and mind clear and focused.

By the time animals have been taken to slaughter their bodies are flooded with adrenalin, fear, fight and flight chemicals and hormones of aggression – then we eat them. In years gone by, a pig say, would lead a contented outdoor life, perhaps down the garden, until it was required for food. When it was slaughtered it would be done quickly, without fuss and the need for this influx of fear chemicals. Might the mass slaughter and influx of chemicals be part of our aggressive society today?

We drew up a set of guidelines for the Event, which was to be a sharing, a coming together with sweat lodges, drumming, song, prayer and meditation, healing and teaching. We gathered in a large tepee, honoring the Native American tradition of teaching in a circle with no hierarchy or superiority. Participants were involved at whatever level they felt drawn to offer their wisdom and knowledge.

Many of the Starseed groups around the world chose to set up and organize events to run in conjunction with the main Gathering. In Cornwall there was the synchronicity of an identical size Seed of Life symbol, on similar sloping land, being cut in the turf. In Ipswich a full camp experience on very similar lines to the Gathering in Wales was organised. A Peace Festival was held in Hawaii under the banner of the Seed of Life during the twelve day period. In Spain, a specially designed dome in Alcalali was open for a week of toning, song, prayer and meditation, at the Findhorn community a symbol was created in flower petals and in Western Australia, in drought conditions, forty people round a gum tree managed rain! Native American tradition says if it rains on your prayers the gods have heard. ... just a few of the wonderful ways in which the event was celebrated throughout the world.

We were ready or as near ready as we would be. When participants started to arrive it began to dawn on me that what had once been a dream, a vision, with no expectations and no limitations, had on this beautiful sunny day become a reality. I wandered about in a daze, proclaiming, much to the amusement of my grandchildren, that I couldn't even remember my own name. Suddenly, the database of participant names, the beautiful shared letters over the last weeks and months, had faces and personalities. We were creating a new extended family.

A sacred village awaited its inhabitants. The 28 foot diameter tepee had been erected as a sacred meeting place with beautiful verses set at points of special energy around the land to inspire meditation. The old, circular, vandalized summerhouse structure had been cleared out and made available for Reiki attunements. Toilets and showers had been brought in and plumbed into the existing septic system, timber stacked for the sweat lodge and camp fire.

It was a magical time. I could easily fill several pages with memories. I remember vividly seeing my friend's husband

Dave from America, with my eight year old grandson, marching off with buckets, mops and spare toilet rolls to clean the toilets as the eight year old remarked,

'I'd rather do this than peel potatoes all day.' We had music and dancing, meditation and ceremony. Each day from 11:00 am until 12:00 noon we held a world linking, reading messages of inspiration and support from across the world. These were sent in response to my world wide request for contributions for the Peace Scroll, links from so many individuals, groups, organisations, not just Seed of Life Starseed Groups but many others. An A4 file bursting with these physical links was passed around for people to read or use during this time. Many countries were involved, Australia, Barbados, Belgium, Canada, Czechoslovakia, China, Cyprus, Denmark, England, Egypt, France, Granada, India, Ireland, Japan, Lithuania, Mexico, Netherlands, New Zealand, Nigeria, Oman, Russia, Scotland, South Africa, Spain, United States, Wales. Each contributor was asked to approximate how many they represented, astoundingly the final total was five million.

We cut a thirty foot, Seed of Life symbol into the turf of the land and everyone present took part in the placing of pure white stones around the outlines of the interlocking circles. This created a permanent energy centre that continues to be maintained. We had planned to use this symbol for ceremonial work that night but it created an energy field so strong that even the children would not go into it they just hovered around its edge. It seemed to be saying,

'I am taking root into the earth grid – honour my space until I am fully connected.'

By the following day the symbol was 'open' and a Peace Pole was planted in the centre, with the word PEACE on its four sides in eight different languages. At this time we all unfurled a Peace Banner – one hundred and forty four languages proclaiming Peace, one hundred and forty four feet in length. It was quite emotional as everyone walked the banner, reading the words and linking with the culture and people of each language. One participant throughout his life had used a word he had been given by his Native American guide, not understanding the word or the reason it had been given. At the last minute he decided to attend the Gathering and confirmation of his decision came when he read 'his' word on the banner. It was the Blackfoot word for peace – a moment of revelation and high emotion for him.

One final note on the power of the symbol – on the evening of the day we created the symbol in the turf, Richard was sitting with our grandson Robert and Big Bob around the campfire as the main group meditated in the tepee. Richard left them to go to collect rubbish sacks from the lower camping level when he was startled by a cacophony of noise. He turned to see Bob and Robert pointing at the sky. A huge group of between sixty and one hundred crows was flying down the valley and as they approached the symbol their noise was deafening. As they came to the symbol they split into two groups, flew around either side of the symbol on the ground, and then joined up on the other side to resume their flight in silence.

It was not just us that felt the earth energies but the crows certainly did also.

Grandmother Falling Leaves of the Blue Moon Lodge Tacoma, through the Gathering preparations, became a friend and great inspiration. She fully endorsed the Gatherings despite the eventual non fulfillment of the Sundance Ceremony. She taught me different forms of meditation and gave me confidence to believe much of what was happening to me and in my life.

I came home from visiting her to practice her teachings on a vase filled with water, holding a bunch of roses. The meditation was to focus on the roses and send their love and compassion around the world. Although the roses were standing in water, within three days of the meditation they became dry and brittle, maintaining their colour and even a little of their perfume. These dried roses were then removed from the water and used as a dried flower arrangement imbued with the essence of love and compassion. It was, in a small way, a life changing experience to watch this happen.

Grandmother was the adopted daughter of Grandfather David a former leader of the Hopi Nation and was thus given instruction in many of the ancient beliefs and ways. She had a collection of audio tapes as in Grandfather's later years, aged 104, she had taped her conversations with him.

These tapes she gifted to me with the words,

'One day you will know what to do with them.' His voice is rather weak and not very clear but fascinating all the same. One day I will know what I am to do with these tapes, until then I keep them safe.

The first Gathering received one hundred and forty visitors from around the world. During this time a huge cross was seen in the sky for six consecutive nights. It was seen by people on site, in the town, in the countryside. Richard had just delivered a young lady into town to her B & B and came dashing in to fetch me, in my nightie, to see it. He had spent ten minutes gazing at it trying to explain it logically – cloud reflection, laser lights (in the country?) but he did not find an explanation. It measured, or the ground area it covered, was a mile long and half a mile wide.

and three days later received a letter from a gentleman in a US state penitentiary, he had a life sentence of seventy five years. He had used his time in incarceration to discover and follow his own spiritual path knowing that his path would always be in a confined community. I was in this way forcibly reminded of our remit to cross boundaries, cultures, creeds, how more profoundly could this have been shown than these two letters.

Even today men and women choose a path of strict confines such as in monasteries and convents. We are learning to remove judgment and understand the myriad paths we humans choose to learn and express our spirituality.

Our times in Spain, I think because we didn't have the distractions of business, became times of profound growth in spiritual development. Two young people who lived in Holland and had attended the Gathering organised a meeting in Holland to continue the work from the first Gathering. Grandmother Parisha attended (Grandmother is the leader of the Yunsai White Buffalo Society and would have been the Leader of the Sundance Ceremony). She had been approached by a number of people to intervene concerning Tom's behaviour, his patriarchal insistence that his channeling must be acted upon, not only to the word but to the letter, was increasing, and his negative and often unpleasant attitude towards me. This was why we had parted company so that we could each follow our own path. I was sending love energy to him, all day, all night as all the books and spiritual people were telling me to do.

There were eighty people at this meeting and one afternoon Grandmother Parisha asked those with a direct link to Tom and me to attend a separate meeting. There were thirty of us, sitting in a circle in the woodland. She announced that she could now intervene as Tom had written to her and as he had involved her she could now proceed. She read out his letter, which was negative, demanding, unpleasant. All I could think was how sad. What she said next I was totally oblivious to. Everyone else looked shocked and Richard had moved to sit beside me. I couldn't understand what I had missed, but it turned out that my brain must have shut down and refused to acknowledge her words.

'Tom is working toward this woman's illness.' she said again as she now stood in front of me facing me.

'If you love her you will pray continuously for her well being, if you don't she will be dead in three months.' My first reaction was as though I had been hit by a large wet fish; my second reaction was – she doesn't mean <u>towards</u> my illness, she means towards my illness getting better. I could not, would not even, take it on board.

She continued to explain to everyone the meaning and consequences behind Tom's actions. I remember very little. She asked me to join her alone afterwards.

'Stop immediately sending him love, stop immediately thinking about him. Place a mirror around yourself until things have eased. Placing a mirror is a difficult choice and must be undertaken only in dire circumstances, as by reflecting everything that comes in you reflect the good as well as the bad.' She said.

How could I do this? because if as she said he was set on my demise than by reflecting it back to him I would be the cause of his. Her explanation was that I could not be responsible for others' thoughts and actions, if he was sending good then he would be blessed with his own goodness, if he was sending bad then he would be the victim of his own thoughts. I could not be held responsible for not accepting his 'gift'. I had a choice, I could succumb or protect myself. She was right, the choice could not be in question, the spiritual mirror must be erected. We returned home.

The next Gathering was due to be held, our son and daughter in law and grandchildren from away were visiting and we were outside in the pleasant sunshine having a cuppa. They were teasing me, ever the talker, I had lost my voice. Two hours later that afternoon my temperature soared and I became really ill. On admission to hospital pneumonia was diagnosed and Richard was told they were worried that I may not be strong enough, even with the help of antibiotics to fight the infection. That night was a difficult night.

Richard had a visit from Syd, one of the stalwarts of the Gatherings and as they sat talking Syd referred to his diary. It was a full moon, perhaps more to the point, it was exactly three months since Grandmother Parisha's pronouncement in Holland.

I can only thank all those who devoted their time and energies to my well being, as after ten days I left hospital and continued my journey. Sad to say the gentleman (Tom) who had decided to send his negative thoughts and emotions died within the year. What effect the mirror played in his demise can only be conjecture, the spiritual and emotional energies do not give us proof. We are encouraged to have an open mind and I can only refer to my life question 'what if?' In the meantime more was to surface.

As I languished in hospital three angels came to the rescue. Syd, Carol and Lyn, who had attended the first Gathering and stayed in touch, now dropped everything to come and help Richard and my friend and right hand

Jane complete the arrangements and set everything up So much so that when I asked for a notepad to send home messages and jobs to be done, the one I received measured 3in x 4in! I left hospital to run the Gathering as though nothing had happened.

Grandmother's traumatic pronouncement was followed by another. During this time I was visited by four ladies with an interest in the Gatherings and the philosophy behind them. I had met and become friendly with two of them but the other two I did not know. The discussion turned to Tom and the problem that had arisen. One of the ladies asked me if I owned anything that he had given me. Well, yes I did, not exactly given but bought from him. He had made me, over the period of our friendship, two necklaces. One was a string of beads made from carnelian, the other was a collection of beads in jade and carnelian. Jade is a healing stone and I was very attracted to the colour. Tom had a collection of beads, dating back up to 2,000 years he said from excavation sites, from which to choose. Amongst them was a large, modern, engraved carnelian pendant approximately 1in x 2in. I loved it immediately. What I saw was an angel with large wide spread uplifted wings. Tom explained that he had bought it as a phoenix. It didn't matter; perhaps the angel together with the phoenix would raise me from the ashes. I wore this necklace a great deal.

'May I look at them?' said the lady concerned. I fetched them and they passed them around for a good look. I was asked what was on the pendant, so I explained thinking they could see both a phoenix and an angel.

'This is no angel, Diana, you better look again and tell me what you see now.' What I saw brings shivers to my spine even today. The angel/phoenix had gone and in their place was a hunched, evil looking individual with a stick over his shoulder and a bag on the end, like Dick Whittington carries over his shoulder in the Panto.

'That I'm afraid to tell you is an evil magician, the bag on his shoulder is a bag of spells, and they are all directed at you.' The feeling I felt was indescribable, I was holding something in my hand that not only defied logic but defied physical possibility. There was more to come.

'You must bury it, six feet down, wrap it in cotton or linen but under no circumstances wrap it in plastic or aluminium foil.' By coincidence, Richard was repairing the septic tank and the hole was well on its way to the specified six feet. In the necklaces went. The job was done; we could relax and leave the rest to the earth to clear whatever energy was creating this situation.

Some ten days later I received a phone call from the lady who had instigated the burial.

'I've had a dream,' she said, 'something's wrong. You must dig up the necklaces and throw them into the sea.' How could I query her she had been right so far, but how to tell Richard that the six foot hole needed to be re-dug! As usual Richard responded to the crisis. When he brought the necklaces into the house, this dour Yorkshire man looked shaken and jumped on me,

'Don't ask me about the plastic, it wasn't me. God knows what's happening.' The necklaces were firmly wrapped in cling film. The only two people who had handled them were Richard and I and I had explained fully about the consequence of plastic or aluminium foil not allowing the negative energy to be absorbed and transformed through the earth.

The next few weeks were to prove how difficult it would be to throw something into the sea. Richard stood on cliff tops, we visited beaches, but could not find access to a deep enough section of the sea. After three weeks we found a dilapidated pier and Richard carefully got as far as he could and slung them out to sea. It wasn't particularly deep but nor was it frequented by people. Our final option would have been to go out in a boat or pleasure craft and that might have caused a few raised eyebrows as we carried out our little ritual. I sometimes wonder, if in years to come, the beads will be found and cause speculation as to how they came to be there. One thing is for sure the sea will have cleansed and purified them from whatever they carried.

I was out of hospital and the second Gathering was upon us. I had another visitor, a phone call from someone who wanted me to meet a gentleman by the name of Son Eagle from Canada. Son Eagle had come to the attention of a group of people who had attended the Gatherings. They had raised money to bring him to the UK – a lot of money – I know of two people who actually took out second mortgages to finance this man's trip and even then as he came through customs they had to bail him out and vouch for him whilst in this country. He claimed he was going to bodily ascend, and those who wished to join him would be carried along with him into a mass ascension. The people who had committed so much, on many levels not just financially, had done so with great sincerity and belief in his claims.

The two gentlemen duly arrived in time for coffee. I was really taken aback as Son Eagle was a small, unkempt individual with Rastafarian style hair, and eyes that couldn't keep still. To be truthful his clothes were dirty and beyond shabby. Was I to judge or discriminate or for the short time I was with him just to allow? We talked for a while and he picked up the paperwork we were discussing and held it two inches from his face and moved his head from side to side in order to read it. He explained, although he assured me he was now clean, he had been a drug addict and it had badly affected his eyes.

I had been wondering for some time if I was actually the right person to be doing the work I was doing. Physically severely disabled, unable to eat or drink other than by surgical intervention, at that time the machine and pump and artificial liquid food was carried in a back pack with a plastic feeding tube leading to my stomach connection point. Not an example of how to heal body and soul in the conventional sense, exactly the opposite in fact. What was I doing tying to encourage and lead others?

As we sat talking my lack of conviction that I was 'in the right job' came to the surface. This strange man looked at me, although his eyes were going in different directions and looked totally unfocused, and said,

'I want you to imagine – can you disassociate from yourself? Pretend you are someone else looking at a stranger.' Well, yes I could, this had been a big part of the NLP training. 'OK,' he said 'You are watching this middle-aged, very disabled woman, with a back pack with tubes coming out of it and into her, being helped onto a stage and telling you what she is involved in and the work she is doing. What do you feel about her? Tell me – stay looking at this stranger and tell me.' My reply came without my thinking about it.

'My God, if she can do that in her condition, what can I do?' He just smiled.

This strange individual had given me the gift that most people never find in a lifetime. Dear old Robbie Burns 'to see ourselves as others see us'. We have to have the integrity to see the good and the less good however or it doesn't work. Most of us know our not so good points and need reminding of our good, or is it sometimes the other way round?

The story of the ascension goes on. The group gathered and was placed in specific positions as they performed their ceremonial ritual. As this story was recounted to me the young man telling me became agitated.

'Then the black helicopters arrived, flying low above our heads and as I looked up I was staring into a high powered rifle.' he said shuddering a little.

The ascension didn't take place. The group was told the energy had been spoiled; their focus had not been strong enough to facilitate the required vibration to allow the ascension to take place. Son Eagle was devastated blaming his supporters and followers.

Son Eagle returned home leaving the UK group financially and spiritually bereft. They had learned the hard way that spiritual leaders don't create financial hardship for their followers or brag about their powers. True spiritual leaders teach by example.

For all this man's strange ways and ideas I can never forget that he gave me the boost to go on doing what I needed to do and for that I can only thank him.

The first two days of the second Gathering were 'button pushers', with peoples' personal issues and perceptions high on the agenda. After all, 'it was different' to the previous year and change challenges us all. This year we had a large marquee for meeting and eating allowing us to reserve the tepee as a sacred space. The food was provided commercially, wrist bands were worn to show who had paid and was entitled to food.

'Starving people should be fed, not have to prove they have paid.' Was one response, although there was no explanation as to who would pay.

'The sweat lodge hasn't been built to my sacred tradition, how can I use it?' this from a 'white man'.

'I don't like the marquee, I liked the tepee better.' This until the deluge came. All these and many more rippled through, in fact a minority of the people, but you know what ripples do to a calm pond.

These ripples, however, were beautiful, as just like in a pond, they added vitality and movement, allowing people to air their views and perhaps see things from a new perspective. I stood between people as they aired their grievances, coaxing them into the belief that there were no problems, only solutions. How to find the solution to each grievance needed tolerance.

Usually these individuals are sitting on the side lines, afraid and unsure of where they fit, or how change will affect their lives. My 'mistakes', your 'mistakes', in doing or not doing, are not mistakes, they are 'experiences'. Remember, as my Grandmother often reminded me (it's up on my office wall) – 'A man who never makes mistakes, never makes anything.' I have learnt to, had to learn to, risk making the odd mistake and when I do I try to turn them into experiences through which I hope I grow and heal into a higher being.

The daily World Linking between 11:00 am and 12:00 noon continued as in the previous year and a continuous fire provided a focal point for meeting, singing and drumming. A point worth mentioning – we had a 24 hour candle that had been lit from a flame originating with the Peace flame lit by His Holiness the Dalai Lama and sent around the world. This candle inexplicably burned for three days and three nights.

The World Peace Prayer Society is an NGO recognised by the United Nations. The World Peace Prayer Society's Peace and Flag Ceremony with representatives from the European Division were present at the Gathering to conduct this Ceremony. It invites people from every race, religion and culture to join in one voice and spirit to pray for peace in every country of the world. It is a simple activity in which all participants recite the prayer for the peace and happiness of every nation around the world in turn and simultaneously the national flag of each country is presented. There is a flag for each country recognised by the UN and words are offered 'Peace to the country of.... Peace to the people of.....' For those countries not recognised they are acknowledged at the end with a large flag hanging above the proceedings showing the earth from space. The simplicity of this Ceremony allows everyone to participate. The Brownies came to one of these Ceremonies along with Kiera who at three carried a flag, they all so enjoyed their involvement..

The first year this Ceremony was carried out in a tractor shed as the weather was abysmal with torrential rain. We were presented with the great temptation by the photographer of the local paper. He begged that the eighty people come outside for a photograph with all the flags, explaining that if we did so the colour and spectacular scenery would make it not only to the front page of his local newspaper but he could also sell it to the tabloids and it would be spread all over the country. He didn't understand that this ceremony was not a gimmick but extremely serious with the intent of having an effect on world peace. I explained that you wouldn't bring people out of a wedding or funeral service for a picture and that this was just as sacred. His reply was,

'My bosses won't understand I am devastated. All I want is that picture.' The ceremony continued with our integrity intact.

Another year, we were invited to conduct this ceremony in the local chapel in the centre of town. It was inspiring to hear remarks from people who sought me out to tell me such as,

'I worship here every Sunday, and have all my life, and have never seen the chapel look so beautiful.' and,

'The energy raised here today will change the energy, not only of the chapel building but of the whole town, for higher good and higher consciousness of the population.'

The World Peace Prayer Society also presented a Peace Pole to the Seed of Life Peace Foundation in 2001. The Peace Pole Project was started in 1976 as a way to spread the prayer *May Peace Prevail on Earth*. The message inscribed on the four-sided Peace Pole is available in every language. Peace Poles can be found in town squares, schools, places of worship, parks, gardens, businesses and homes, acting as a constant reminder for us to visualise and pray for world peace. 200,000 Peace Poles in 160 countries have been dedicated to places such as the United Nations and many major cities in many countries around the world and to Nobel Peace Laureate Mother Theresa in Calcutta, India.

Another Fax was to arrive and honour our work. My ability to access the Dalai Lama came when I was speaking with a young lady. She had been blessed with two audiences with HH Dalai Lama and was telling me of her experiences. I must have said how wonderful it must be to have that contact I would love to ask him to contribute to the Peace Scroll, perhaps she could do that on my behalf.

'Well, I actually have his phone number but I couldn't possibly give it out.' she said. After a while she frowned, 'I'm getting such a strong impulse to give you his phone number, I think I should.' From that beginning came his involvement.

As I had presented a copy to his representative, who was attending the Millennium World Summit of Religious and Spiritual Leaders, I emailed to ask if he would write the Foreword for the next edition. They emailed back, saying they had mislaid the presented copy would I please send another. I did, but felt this was just telling me that my request was not a priority – a gentle brush off? Some weeks later on the fax machine one morning was the fax, not Dear Madam, or Dear Mrs Rhodes, but Dear Diana, informing me that here was the Foreword with the Dalai Lama's blessings and informing me that the hard copy was in the post.

Another contributor was HRH Prince Charles. I rang Geraint,

'How do I contact Prince Charles?' His response was,

'Ring Directory Enquiries.' Gee thanks.

Anyway I had no other ideas so set about it with my best telephone voice. The operator said did I want the hotel Kensington Palace?

'No, I want the Royal Palace.' This in my best Sunday voice. I received the number and rang. I needed another Department it seemed, and another. After three Departments I was told I should try St James Palace. Another response.

'Well, that does sound important you better speak to His private secretary, Stephen Lamport.' He personally took on the job of securing Prince Charles' contribution to the Peace Scroll. I continue to smile when such absurd answers to what can I do? turn out to be so obvious, so simple and so practical.

We asked ourselves as the Gatherings came to an end, were they a success? And what is a success? People came carrying fear, anger, rejection, many emotions. At the Gathering they found a safe haven in which to confront and release these limitations. Is that success? People came and found knowledge, information, sharing. People came lonely perhaps a little lost, they found new family and friendship, caring and love. They came seeking and found hidden depths to their being, strengths that they didn't know they had, adding meaning to their lives. People came and linked millions round the world. They returned home with potential and ambition to be more understanding, more compassionate more aware of the impact of their thoughts, words and deeds on the whole of humanity. They left determined to foster the self discipline to be aware of every thought, word and deed, not to be depressed if it doesn't always work but to try to cultivate this way of living until it becomes second nature. Was this success? How do you measure success?

As this Gathering came to an end I contemplated the state of the world in the months leading up to the new Millennium. Little did I know that I would be spending this much heralded event in hospital contemplating 'You are going to die!'

Well – was it the predicted change or was it a damp squid? At first it may seem as though nothing happened as we entered the Millennium. Y2K problems were minimal if at all noticed, and everyone still walked about as before. No-one seemed to have lost density and be walking about semi-transparent, and nobody I know floated about two feet above the ground. Joking apart, let's just look back to the run up to this phenomenal time.

Did you notice all the parties, the gatherings, the quite unprecedented meditations and ceremonies? There was an exhilarating sense of joy and vision for the future. Even where I was... in hospital.

There were no major glitches. Stored food, water and fuel were redundant for that time. Were we wrong? Did we panic? Or was there some other energy at work?

Look at all the energy we put into Y2K, having been told our technology would fail as the Millennium came into being. Individuals, communities, nations, the World in general would find themselves in turmoil. The Millennium situation meant that people took the time to work together. Creating a common enemy brought everyone to the realisation that each of us needs the other. A global network of co-operation and from this we have all realised that being part of a world community means that every person benefits far more than by holding onto their 'I can stand alone' mentality.

The Millennium and this awareness of All is One, the interconnectedness, the interdependence, the awareness of others' misfortune is the healing that has brought people together to problem solve, to think things through, to be responsible for action and consequence.

We saw people in denial – 'it won't happen – I won't prepare', people in fear – panic buying and survival issues uppermost; people who said 'what if?' who prepared as the proverbial boy scout to be sovereign and help others less prepared. Whatever words we use there is only one that covers it all. Change. In an unprecedented display of concerted and concentrated effort which included so much work, service and commitment – the message went out.

'We are prepared to change.' The change is internal, the external preparations were merely the symptoms of what has and still is happening on an internal level.

Those who watched the World linkages on TV realised the spiritual and emotional leap that humanity made. People of all faiths, laughing, singing, dancing together.

Meditations, prayers, candle ceremonies. So many people saying,

'I don't want to boogie and drink this year – it just seems too special.'

The year 2000 held many more challenges for us, not the least of which was the weather. But what the build up taught us is that we do have the ability to think differently, to act radically, to change for the higher good of wo/mankind and the earth. We did and do make a difference. Don't be fooled into thinking nothing happened – the change was acknowledged, realised, accepted. We have made our choice known and the future is ours to dream.

The best prophets never receive the accolades, because the best prophets predict what will happen, and by predicting they give humanity the opportunity to change. When humanity changes and the predictions don't come to fruition, then the people say the prophets were wrong. Predictions are warnings and the best prophets and the best predictors are those who warn the people well in hand to give time for change. We may have to cope with changes, there is no point in going into denial but this is our opportunity to acknowledge our contribution to the process.

My own millennium was one of great challenge and change with the fitting of the PEG. Challenge is the form we humans find most efficient for spiritual growth. When I was five I fell off a swing. I sat in a muddy puddle wowling as the swing struck me from the front and then from the back and continued unabated as I sat there non-plussed. If my sister hadn't rescued me I might have sat there for longer. I have recalled this event many times as an example of, well certainly of how I, need pushing and pulling, sometimes even screaming into the next learning experience.

Greg Braden describes the Mandlebrot set as an image portraying the point at which order and chaos converge. This chaos theory and the mathematics required to describe this point are so complex the mathematicians were only able to show us graphically after the development of high speed computer capabilities and the development of massive computer memory capacity. These graphics portray these beautiful mathematical fractals that are truly awe inspiring and breathtaking. A fractal is a spectacular geometric object which repeats its structure on a smaller and smaller scale. Fractals are exquisite, a snowflake is a fractal. It's worth taking a look on the internet. The Mandelbrot reaches a point of perfection, holds it for a second and then plunges back into chaos for the next beautiful experience. Chaos is no longer chaotic but moves from chaos to perfection and back. In these chaotic times are we heading towards that point of perfection?

During this period I was invited to join with Professor Thomas Daffern of the International Institute of Peace Studies and Global Philosophies and Prince Frederick von Saxe-Lauenberg in organizing a Peace Conference – 'Peace and Justice, or War and Terrorism? The Implications of September 11th to Faith and Education Communities'. The venue was at St Deiniols Library, Hawarden. Dr Jane Goodall (now Dame) was the main speaker, inspirational, practical and sincere. The same group of people with the organisation and help of Lembit Opik then MP for Montgomeryshire, held the first meeting in the Houses of Parliament where it was established that an All Party Parliamentary Group was to be formed to study Peace and Conflict Resolution/Transformation. After many meetings, even in Westminster, this All Party Parliamentary Group is now up and running as the Ministry for Peace.

After getting to the House of Commons for one of these meetings and then through the Security checks

I thought I should make a visit to the ladies before the meeting started. The stair lift platform to take wheelchairs to the floor where the meeting was to be held was at the top of the stairs with a lady in a wheelchair waiting to descend. The platform was stuck and would not work. Richard forever the practical engineer went up the stairs, took over from the two men working on it and mended whatever was causing the problem. As the lady descended she said to her partner that she needed the 'ladies'. She told me there wasn't one upstairs, so the two of us were taken, for security reasons, by a guard. As the lift would only take one of us at once and we travelled so far down corridors this process took twenty five minutes. This is the 21st Century with a Disability Discrimination Act and this is a Parliamentary Government building. As I joined the meeting, the Chairman not only apologised for the fact that they had not waited for me but also the disgraceful situation regarding accessibility of the toilet facilities.

The British Holiday and Homes Parks Association (BH&HPA) is a Trade Association for the holiday home leisure industry. It represents 80 per cent of all holiday home parks and petitions and lobbies, works with, and tries to ensure Government legislation is practical and works at the grass roots level in setting standards for Holiday Parks to follow.

One of their emphases is on eco/green tourism with Professor David Bellamy as the figurehead and his involvement with the Conservation and Sustainability Awards nationwide.

Richard is Director for the Mid Wales Branch and in this capacity is involved at all levels with the work. Each year a large Conference is held with approximately seven hundred delegates attending for meetings, high level speakers and information exchange sessions. One year this is held in London and another in the area of the BH&HPA Chairman, Torquay, Edinburgh, Blackpool, Harrogate, wherever a hotel with the Conference facilities required and accommodation for at least the main participants can be found.

In 1995 the Disability Discrimination Act (DDA) came into effect and the Conference emphasis was on the need for implementation of this Act. As a long term wheelchair user I was eager and full of anticipation for the results this would achieve.

The DDA came out of the Disability Unit Office with the First Minister and Deputy Minister heading this Unit. The First Minister, Minister for the DDA was a lady MP. She was booked as one of the main speakers at this very large Conference. The main Conference Hall was a large room, sloping towards the stage. Access was down the side of the seating rows, three or four steps, a slope and so on down to the bottom. At the back of the Hall was a small curtained level area, perfect for anyone wishing to remain 'incognito', and seated perhaps six people. This was my only option and Richard and I sat awaiting the talk.

This lady came onto the stage and, pardon the expression, waffled for around twenty to thirty minutes, finishing with a beaming smile that she had managed to hold her own for the allocated time. She asked for questions and someone walked around with a microphone. Richard had to stand up, lean out of this boxlike area and wave his arms about requesting the mike before he was noticed. He handed it to me. I thought my question was pretty simple and held the key to the whole Act.

'If a business, individual or organization does not comply with the Act is there a follow up, some way of ensuring that the Act will be complied with?' The guy with the mike could not reach me in my little box area and kept motioning for the mike to be returned. I kept it firmly by my side awaiting the answer.

Well, if I thought her talk was waffle, I don't know how to describe her reply except to say it was interspersed with many more 'ers' and 'ums' than before. When she finished answering, I spoke again,

'It would seem I didn't make my question clear so I'll rephrase it if you don't mind.' She responded with even more nonsense and yet surprisingly kept her composure. The microphone man was gesticulating more wildly for the return of his mike, but I held on.

'I'll try again as I'm not receiving an answer to my question. Perhaps if I phrase it where it just requires a yes or no answer – does the DDA have any teeth, is there retribution for non-compliance, such as this hotel where I cannot attend three quarters of the Conference due to steps?'

I handed back the mike. The audience erupted into disarray at my third attempt to receive an answer, realizing that the DDA was a long way off from being ready for application, particularly when the First Minister was not able to answer my question satisfactorily without acknowledging the DDA's inadequacy.

The Hotel, because of its design and lay out of the land was a nightmare of ups and downs and two or three steps at every turn. Designed with wide corridors this should not have posed a problem.

We returned to our room, difficult as the lift was only large enough to squeeze the wheelchair in if I lifted the footrests and Richard used the stairs.

An hour later we came back down for the evening – every step in that Hotel had a ramp. I could get everywhere. The

Hotel had obviously responded to the embarrassment if not the law. The DDA with its recommendations however was proven to have no teeth, not even a nasty suck!

Some years later the Conference was held at this same venue so I rang to book our places. I had upgraded my wheelchair to a slightly larger model and asked about the lift. I had been assured by the BH&HPA that when checking their booking the Hotel had proudly informed them that they had spent a lot of money installing a new improved second lift. I asked for the measurements to ensure that it would take my new wheelchair. Not only would the old lift not take it but the new lift was even smaller. How much money was spent bringing forth this Act that was almost useless, the Hotel's inaccessibility even after housing the Conference with its emphasis on the DDA, meant I could not attend the Conference or even stay in the Hotel that year. What had it cost to put this Act in place? It meant nothing when it was unenforceable.

Another year in a Hotel in Bristol I was approached at breakfast by the Duty Manager. He was charming and apologetic that the lift stopped at the mezzanine floor causing major problems for a wheelchair. He handed me his personal mobile phone and said,

'You will need to use the service lift. The doors are difficult to open and you will need assistance. In order to maintain your independence you can use my mobile and I or one of my staff will come immediately to assist you. Please just ring as often as you need to. Enjoy your Conference.'

The one thing the DDA had not taken into account was attitude. As a wheelchair user I don't expect to have access to everywhere but where I do not have access the attitude of those concerned is what makes the difference between feeling compassionately helped or discriminated against.

Back home and learning to live with the PEG, I focused on the compilation of the second Peace Scroll, dedicated as promised to the UN University for Peace in Costa Rica to acknowledge the United Nations Year of Peace. An invitation had been extended to the Seed of Life Peace Foundation to present the Peace Scroll to the University later in the year. How could I refuse?

Another invitation would soon be forthcoming. I had chosen to include the Earth Charter in this year's Peace Scroll and one day I received an email from Mirian Vilela, Earth Charter Executive Director, The Earth Charter Secretariat, asking if I would like to attend its launch. She had looked on the map, she said, and we were quite close. She had not understood the barrier of the Channel, but after all, what's a body of water between friends?! Without hesitation, Richard said,

'I'll take you if you want to go.'

If I wanted to go? No question about it.

The Earth Charter is devoted to a process of change rooted in the values and ethics promulgated by this document and through commitment of people from different nations, cultures, communities and professions – clearly fostering a new sense of global community in which caring for the environment and respecting all life, provides the foundation for a more hopeful, secure and sustainable future. The principles are drawn from international law, science, philosophy, religion, UN Summit meetings, and the international Earth Charter conversation on global ethics. The goal of sustainable development is full human development and ecological protection.

The Earth Charter recognizes that humanity's environmental, economic, social, cultural, ethical, and spiritual problems and aspirations are interconnected. It affirms the need for holistic thinking and collaborative, integrated problem solving. Sustainable development requires such an approach. It is about freedom, justice, participation, and peace as well as environmental protection and economic well-being.

The day arrived and off we went. After forty five years of consultation and ten countries taking part I thought it would be a huge affair, but in fact there were just two hundred and fifty invited guests. The ceremony took place in the Peace Palace at The Hague in the Netherlands. Mirian had given me permission to ask for contributions for the next Peace Scroll and I had come prepared. She quickly sought me out to introduce me to Bawa Jain, Secretary General of the World Millennium Summit of Spiritual and Religious Leaders to be held at the UN in August 2000.

We sat awaiting the honoured guests, the main speakers being Mikhael Gorbachev, Queen Beatrix of the Netherlands and Maurice Strong of the UN University for Peace. As Queen Beatrix was speaking, someone came and squatted at my side (my wheelchair was in the centre aisle approximately ten rows back from the speakers). It was Bawa Jain. He thrust something into my hands.

'These are my words, dedicated to my spiritual father. When I leave here I will be so busy I might neglect to follow through, so by giving you my words now I will not miss this wonderful opportunity.'

With this, he crept away.

During the lunch break, Maurice Strong was brought to meet me. Maurice Strong has amongst his roles Senior Advisor to the then General Secretary to UN Kofi Annan, Senior Advisor to the World Bank, President Chairman of the Earth Council, Chairman of the World Resources Institute, Co-Chairman of the Council of the World Economic Forum, he was a busy man. As Mirian brought him towards me he declared,

'She's there. There she is. I've been asking after you. You're the lady I want to meet. I've been wanting to meet you since I received your letter about the Peace Scroll. Do you realize without people like you, I wouldn't have a job!' It makes me realize that when we say,

'What can I do?' then here is proof that there is something, however humble. The following inspirational little story says it all.

An old man walking the beach at dawn noticed a young man ahead of him picking up starfish and flinging them into the sea. Catching up with the youth he asked what he was doing.

'The starfish will die if they are still on the beach when the sun roasts them with its mid-morning heat.' came the answer,

'But the beach goes on for miles, and there are millions of starfish.' countered the old man. 'How can your effort make any difference?' The young man looked at the starfish in his hand then threw it to safety in the waves.

'It makes a difference to this one.' he said.

I sponsor a child in Peru and when I worry about all the other children that I am not able to sponsor, I remember this story and feel better.

Then Bawa Jain sought me out again. As if the wonders of the day had not been sufficient already, he asked during our conversation,

'Would you like to attend the Summit?' It was all I could do to nod my mute acceptance.

Back at home the weeks sped by and I heard nothing. After all, Bawa had said he was a busy man. I was not to be disappointed however and the invitation duly arrived requiring registration. The security forms made those for the Earth Charter look like something to join a local club!

Yards of penetrating information and a request to write a paper that would be included in a book along with those of all the other delegates and leaders. I spent a long time writing that paper as I felt a great responsibility for the words I would be putting in black and white for the world to see.

With a third Gathering behind us, Richard and I set off for Costa Rica, to present the Peace Scroll to the United Nations University of Peace and then on to New York to present it to the United Nations. When we arrived in Costa Rica I had an appointment with Mirian Vilela, The Earth Charter was in the same building as the University. Mirian's secretary had arranged our hotel and car hire so we were truly pampered.

The Presentation was arranged to be held at the University which in fact does not house the main body of students, they are taught through outposts some of which are in different areas of the world. The students were bussed in and I gave an introductory few words in Spanish and followed in English with a Translator. The students were very receptive and the Chancellor, Professor Budowski was very enthusiastic and happy with the Dedication. Richard and I were given a tour and met up with all the people working with others around the world; I was particularly impressed with their outreach programmes for young people.

I then met Dr Robert Muller, he has been given the title Father of the World Core Curriculum. Robert believes, as I do, it is the media who are 'informing' us and should in fact be educating us about the major, very rapid changes which are taking place in the world. But, he says, the media do not recognize their role as educators, they are simply communicators. He believes that the world will not change and find peace unless there is a new education, a new media that educates and presents objective, unadulterated and uncensored facts.

Robert has been, amongst many other roles, Assistant Secretary General to the UN, Chancellor of the UN University for Peace and Senior Advisor Emeritus of this University. In his eighties he is inspirational in his thoughts and ideas and asked if I would become the UK representative of the Bench of Dreams and place a bench and plaque, which he presented to me, in Grandma's Garden. The Bench of Dreams is the child of Robert, he and his wife live on Mt Rasur in Costa Rica, the site of the United Nations University for Peace. Robert says Mt Rasur is a place where dreams have a way of simply manifesting into reality. The original Bench of Dreams is located at the base of Mt Rasur where visitors are asked to place a pebble or small stone in each hand, press the two hands together, and, with eyes closed, to dream. When opening the eyes, one stone is thrown to the Earth, so that the sacred Earth will remember the dream, and the other stone is taken home as a reminder of the dream. He says to check your dream after two years and see if it has manifest.

Costa Rica is a beautiful country with the most exotic plants and beautiful butterflies. We took an aerial ride through the rain forest (I dare not take anti-malarial pills so was being treated with Homeopathy as malaria is quite a threat, particularly to tourists). What an experience! Travelling through the tree tops over two hundred feet above a ravine. At this height there existed another world of plants, wildlife, insects and birds all designed to live in this unique band of the ecological environment.

Then we were in New York. It was time for the Millennium World Summit for Religious and Spiritual Leaders.

As we registered I was given a briefcase with symbols of
the twelve major world religions emblazoned on its front,
an acrylic plaque celebrating the event and other small
items. Richard was given a blue badge and I was given a
red. I tried to lighten the atmosphere a little by saying,

'Oh, blue for a boy and red for a girl.'

'No, madam.' came the stiff reply. 'You are a Delegate;
he is only an Observer and is only admitted to certain
areas and sessions because he needs to push you.'

That certainly put poor Richard in his place and set
me thinking yet again – how does a disabled, yet ordinary
middle-aged woman find herself in these circumstances?
To sit in the horseshoe of the United Nations conference
area with paper, pens, microphone in front of me and
surrounded by all of these important people. There were
twelve hundred Delegates with the addition of Observers
and one hundred and ten countries represented.

The Summit delegates were housed in the Waldorf
Astoria, New York. Roads around the hotel were
barricaded and blocked off with men in black everywhere,
talking into their cuffs. The coaches taking us to the UN
(easily within walking distance) each had at least two of
these men. Richard and I thought we were on a film set
for Men in Black but dared not show our humour as this
was deadly serious. On one trip I sat next to a lady who
chattered away and then told me she was the Head of the
Zoroastrian religion. Fascinating, fascinating experiences,
with security measures I have only ever seen in a film.

Upon our arrival at the hotel we were registered and
given our room key, and we made our way to the lift.
It was nine months since I had met Bawa Jain at the
launch of the Earth Charter at the Hague, and then only
for minutes. The hotel was crowded. Richard pressed the
button for the lift to return and we waited patiently. The

lift doors opened. It was still almost full and everyone was going to a higher floor. At the back, stood Bawa Jain, I could not fail to recognise him.

'Diana, Diana, come on in there's room, we'll make room.' he said as he parted the people who compliantly made room for my wheelchair.

He was so enthusiastic and greeted Richard and I by name and welcomed us. He must have met and had contact with thousands and thousands of people whilst organising this Summit and yet somehow he was able to recall and honour an insignificant meeting such as ours. I have great respect for someone who is so focused and tenacious.

During the Summit I met so many of the Spiritual and Religious Leaders, and it was fascinating to see the different approaches from the different Leaders. Some stayed for the whole day listening to all the other speeches and traditions, others came in noisily, attracting attention, gave their dogmatic, unapproachable speech encompassing their blinkered and arrogant attitude and left without a second glance. No respect for another's presence let alone their point of view.

One tiny, frail old man was literally carried onto the stage in all his religious trappings and the voice that came from this skeletal frame amazingly required no microphone to fill the UN Hall! Many of the religious leaders, as I met them at the bottom of the steps leading to the stage (not one to miss an opportunity and having Richard's essential wheelchair driving skills to get me to the front of the Hall) when asked just took out their notes, smiled and handed them to me.

'This says it all. I give them willingly.' was their response. It was at this point I met the representative of the Dalai Lama and presented the Peace Scroll with his remarks included.

This might be a good place to mention that His Holiness the Dalai Lama, although uninvited, was far from absent during this Summit. Bawa Jain the organiser and General Secretary stated that the Chinese Government exerted great pressure on conference organisers not to invite His Holiness. He said UN protocol permitted Security Council members to have such power of veto. The Protocol Office of the UN state no member nation has such power. His Holiness named a delegation of eight Tibetan religious leaders led by the Drikung Kyabung Chetsang Rinpoche, head of the Drikung Kagyu lineage of Tibetan Buddhism a leader who grew up in Tibet and escaped to India in 1975. The others included members from the four Tibetan Buddhist traditions, including two Tibetan women Buddhist leaders, as well as from the traditional Tibetan Bon religion to represent him.

His letter states that in the wake of the controversy arising from the exclusion of His Holiness from the Summit, the organisers extended a partial invitation at the end of July this year. The timing and the nature of the invitation led His Holiness to decline it. He states,

'That he joins with the more than one thousand religious and spiritual leaders and wishes them every success in their deliberations'. He then shares a few of his thoughts,

'I see all the different religious traditions as paths for the development of inner peace which is the true foundation of world peace. These ancient traditions come to us as a gift from our common past. Will we continue to cherish it as a gift and hand it over to future generations as a legacy of our shared desire for peace or will we turn it into another weapon that will snatch away the future of the coming generations?' What a clever insightful man he is.

On another occasion further wisdom was given by His Holiness when he was asked,

'Why didn't you fight back against the Chinese?' The Dalai Lama looked down, swung his feet just a bit, then looked back up and then said with a gentle smile,

'Well, war is obsolete, you know.' Then after a few moments, his face grave, he said,

'Of course the mind can rationalize fighting back … but the heart, the heart would never understand. Then you would be divided in yourself, the heart and the mind, and the war would be inside you.'

What a privilege and experience it was to participate in this unprecedented event. This Summit was brought into realisation because of the foresight of many people and donations from many others with the same foresight and commitment. The Secretary General of the UN Kofi Annan, Bawa Jain, Secretary General of the Summit, Stephen Rockefeller and Ted Turner of Time-Warner, to name just a few. The list is probably endless. This was the first time in history that religious and spiritual leaders of the world's great faith traditions had come together to discuss how to forge a Day of Prayer for World Peace by joining the Summit's more than one thousand religious leaders from over fifteen different faith traditions for sacred ceremony in prayers for peace, tolerance and understanding.

The Summit sent a powerful signal to people of faith around the world that there is no acceptable alternative to the peaceful resolution of differences. The Summit was held at the United Nations as it is a political body that has no involvement in matters of religion, because many of the conflicts in the world today are among different religious and ethnic groups. Instead of wars 'in the name of religion', the Summit was exploring ways to foster peace 'in the name of religion.'

The opening day took place on Monday 28th August, as the Leaders of the great faith traditions filled the halls of the United Nations with prayers for peace. I cannot express the emotion I felt at being seated in the great circle of the United Nations building within the energy that filled that Hall. Richard and I were honoured to be invited and as a Delegate, had access to everything that happened – Kofi Annan was host at a private luncheon as we joined his other guests for this occasion. Many others were there as observers with less involvement in the finer details that allowed Richard and I to be so aware of all that was taking place.

The first day started at the United Nations building with a Meditation Walk through the different religions and cultures. This was led by the Venerable Thich Nhat Hahn, the Vietnamese Buddhist monk who has long been at the forefront of contemplative activism.

This was a beautiful, colourful and exotic display of the costumes and symbols of the world's traditions, stretching from the Christian through the twelve major religions. Obviously the indigenous peoples' costumes including those of Bolivia, the Inuit, and the Native American were the star attractions for the photographers. The indigenous peoples were given a very good representation and their voices were certainly heard and taken into consideration. It was especially good to meet Chief William Commander of the Algonquin, one of the Speakers leading a prayer. He was one of the Native American Elders who was to have been at the Sun Dance planned to be held in Wales at the time of the first Gathering. He was to have brought the sacred Wampum belts – beautifully beaded belts recording the history of the Native American peoples.

The Summit was divided into four themes and it was possible to choose the theme of most interest or relevance to the individual's work and attend those meetings. These themes included Conflict Transformation; Elimination of Poverty; Environmental Preservation; Forgiveness and Reconciliation. Monday and Tuesday were held at the United Nations and Wednesday and Thursday at the Hotel Waldorf Astoria.

On the morning of the Wednesday an Earth Charter Roundtable Breakfast was held with many of the participants from the Summit and eminent people involved with the Charter. At this meeting I was asked to present the Peace Scroll book and say a few words about the Scroll and the work of the Seed of Life Peace Foundation. This brought the Peace Scroll to a wider audience and allowed people to request information for inclusion of their words in the Peace Scroll 2001. To speak to three hundred and fifty people in such prestigious circumstances was a very great honour. I never thought I would visit the United Nations or the Waldorf Astoria, let alone speak there. At this time my feeding pump was housed in a small backpack which I wore all the time. I doubt there has ever been a speaker wearing a back-pack in such an important assembly before.

Later that morning during the Forgiveness and Reconciliation session chaired by Rabbi Jonathan Sacks, I had the opportunity to ask a question about the relationship between the media, the Leaders of religious and spiritual communities, and the ordinary people. My question was related to the media's eagerness to publish 'doom and gloom' material and the general public's willingness to read it. This drew an exceptionally good response from the audience and showed this to be a subject close to many people's hearts.

The end of the Summit came all too soon. It was time to go home and my Millennium experience was complete.

But first, there was the official presentation of the Peace Scroll to the United Nations.

We were escorted to the Penthouse by a representative. As the lift doors opened, a large uniformed guard bristling with weaponry stood up and walked towards us all. Fortunately, our guide explained who we were and why we were here. We were seated in a waiting/holding area in view of the lift. The doors opened, just ten or so feet from us, out stepped two armed, uniformed guards followed by Kofi Annan and Nelson Mandela. The Presentation was to Gillian Sorensen Assistant General Secretary UN to General Secretary Kofi Annan she was a really charming lady. She graciously accepted the Peace Scroll and spent a lot of time arranging her office to get the best photos, with the UN flag and the views overlooking the Hudson river. We were in the Penthouse suite with fantastic views over New York. Richard took many photos with my brand new digital camera.

After this most welcoming meeting and presentation, Ms Sorensen was at pains to stress the importance of the work and philosophy behind the Peace Scroll, after which Richard and I were escorted back down to the Reception Area where we could mingle with more ordinary souls. We went into the grounds to take more photos to add to those taken at the World Millennium Summit for Religious and Spiritual Leaders. The camera was making whirring and whizzing noises and refused to take any more photos that trip. I do not have a single photo of that Presentation in the high echelons of the United Nations, a lesson in humility perhaps.

On our return home Richard and I attended a Peace Concert held in Manchester Cathedral, James Twyman, the world peace troubadour was holding concerts in the UK. He came at the invitation of the Seed of Life Peace Foundation to our small town and held a workshop and then a concert at the Arts Centre here, a rather lovely old chapel, refurbished for its new role.

Whilst in the Cathedral I was introduced to Prince Frederick von Saxe Lauenberg. He said he had heard of my work, particularly with regard to Costa Rica.

Costa Rica is a Central American success story, since the late nineteenth century only two brief periods of violence has marred its democratic development. Although still a largely agricultural country, it has achieved a relatively high standard of living and land ownership is widespread. It has no military, only domestic police forces including the Coast Guard and Air Section. Costa Rica is the home of the United Nations University for Peace

Prince Frederick was interested with other colleagues in organizing an inter-denominational Conference and thought Costa Rica with its non-violent ethos made it an ideal home for such an event. He had many ideas and religious contacts he said and my contacts through the Earth Charter, Millennium World Summit and contacts within the country would help develop his ideas.

After much brainstorming Prince Frederick's original ideas for the Conference changed its direction.

In early 2002, following on from the work with Peace and Conflict Resolution, I felt that the decade of Conferences and Summits had achieved its potential. A new innovative approach was needed.

I had met an American lady at the meeting at St Deiniols with Professor Daffern and as I explained my thoughts we discovered we thought on similar lines. Together we had the passion and will to use our constructive skills and life experiences to create a new approach.

We met up, along with Prince Frederick in Costa Rica where I had so many friends and contacts working in the Peace field.

The name of the new Forum was to be the 'Creative Forum for Conscious Action'. Support from the UN University for Peace and the Earth Charter Secretariat was immediate as the Forum's aim was to bring together people working at the grass roots levels in order to spread their ideas.

The Forum was to incorporate viable, proven working models, not just workshops. These working models would offer an introduction to what is happening at the grass roots levels in communities around the world. It would as far as possible offer a stage for interaction that would create a platform from which to go out into the world and use the expertise offered to influence or even by-pass the decision makers, to work for peace, tolerance, understanding and self-empowerment. It was not in the remit to act as another talking shop for people to propound their views as opposed to someonelse's regardless of consequences. I had seen this at the Millennium World Summit of Religious and Spiritual Leaders and wanted to ensure that this was not present at this Forum. Its remit was to become the beginnings of using successful, working models ready for immediate use as each person left the Forum, not an excuse for academics to discuss how many angels fit on the head of a pin.

The main remit was to enable the ordinary, the lay person to make informed choices and offer the tools and techniques to implement decisions about the future sustainability of the planet through examples of excellence in these established working models. Plans were put in place and a prestigious hotel and Conference Centre was booked (penciled in their diary) in which to hold what was to be a huge Forum. The Opening Ceremony was planned to take place in the National Theatre and the former President Oscar Arias, Nobel Peace Laureate, had agreed to open the ceremony and to open the Forum.

He was elected President on the platform of peace and brought together five of the Central American Presidents to sign his peace treaty in 1987, it was for this that he was awarded the Nobel Peace Prize. He wrote a wonderful personal letter supporting the Forum, now entitled Unfolding Wings – a Creative Forum for Conscious Action, saying he was happy to consider the invitation to speak and open the Forum as dates were finalised. He fully endorsed the constructive community approach based on action, in practical but hope filled ways. Oton Solis, the running President wrote offering help to bring the Forum into fruition.

Prince Frederick with his impressive title opened doors that we ordinary folks could never have done. We met with Ambassadors, Government Ministers, Organisations, Heads of Political Parties, all offering words and letters of support.

Dr Jane Goodall had been the main speaker at that first Peace and Conflict Resolution meeting in Hawarden. She is a wonderful example of such a grass roots project working around the world. She is tireless and committed to the Jane Goodall Institute as in all her work including her Roots & Shoots Programme, who were happy to bring their expertise to the Forum as a tried, tested and established working model. This is an environmental programme now active in 120 countries with over 16,000 groups from kindergarten to university with more adult groups forming. Jane had offered to waive her speaking fee for the opening of the Forum, such was her commitment and enthusiasm for the project.

The Roots & Shoots model is a prime example of how to engage grass roots communities. Jane says roots creep underground to form a firm foundation and shoots reach to the light. They may look weak but they can break brick walls.

Other proven working models included:

Bugrado, a south African educational programme which affirms the individual through mentoring at and by all ages.

Student Judges Promoting Civic Responsibility and Skills in Central America, a judicial programme educating school age children on the values of equitable justice.

Earth Charter Initiative, promoting global ethics for sustainable living.

The Green Light a community partnership programme. At the time a peoples TV station with twelve interactive channels to encompass many aspects of modern life.

Many other projects were wanting to become involved in order to promote different ways of owning civic responsibility, assuming stewardship for the environment, building ongoing community bridges, including through innovative computerized technology.

As the Forum plans progressed they became inspirational with a great deal of support. Out of the blue Sharon, my American colleague, emailed to tell me of her reservations. This was a shock even beyond the shock of the cancellation of the Sundance.

She explained that the world wide financial corruption and lack of integrity in the then recent US scandals, the predicated economic recessions together with President Bush's apparent determination to go to war with Iraq, meant she felt she could not put her energies into furthering this Forum. In her email she quoted a wood sculptor friend of hers, and having been a small time sculptor myself it did hold some resonance and yet, perhaps, I am too stubborn and would have gone on chiseling, hoping to overcome or avoid any flaws inherent in any project, be it a piece of wood or a Forum. She wrote,

'As a wood sculptor friend of mine said yesterday who looked at some cherry wood we have:

'Sometimes you begin a piece. Chisel out the rough form of it and reach a point where you feel that there is something not quite right and that when you continue to put hours and hours into it to try and form the piece, it may split wide open at any moment.'

The word that jumps out at me is 'may', not will only may, surely it is then worth the risk.

I was devastated. I could not possibly carry the work and responsibility alone and felt deeply challenged about why such wonderful things could be allowed to fall by the wayside.

However, I soon realized that the wheels and contacts that had been set in motion were spinning their own web of development and would continue to do so whether my vision of a Forum manifested or not.

When something doesn't happen it isn't the end of the world. So many beautiful and inspirational things spun from the planning and organization, as far as it went, as with the Sundance, the Gatherings that took over from its not happening sent repercussions of linking and hope and tolerance around the world.

I stress something not happening can be the catalyst for even greater things.

Chapter Twenty

Grandma's Garden

The time was coming to move on from the concept of live Gatherings at Dolguog and in 2001 the final Peace Scroll came to fruition, with a Foreword by His Holiness the Dalai Lama. The work of the Seed of Life Peace Foundation continued and to that was added a new dimension – the creation of a Peace Garden and Arboretum at Dolguog, started during the Gatherings.

During the Gatherings people attending would weep at the end of their visit having to leave this wonderful atmosphere and place. So it was decided they would bring a plant from their own garden giving them a physical connection. A little bit of their garden planted in a very special place in Wales. We called it our little Peace Garden.

For some time now Richard and I had been considering our retirement plans and we decided to build a new home. There had been a number of changes in the way the business was run and Richard was now able to take a, small, step back. I say small as he is not someone who will ever truly retire, but will always stay involved with what is going on around him.

Gary and Sharon, who had leased the hotel for a number of years, wrote relinquishing the Lease. It was time for them to move on. At first this was a little frightening and the future not clear, but obviously the universe knew what it was doing and this was the next step in a forward moving saga. Anthony and Tina stepped forward. They both had their degrees in Hotel Catering and Management and were enthusiastic about taking on the challenge. They moved in with little Kiera and baby Taionee in 2001 and have been doing a wonderful job ever since.

In 2002 James and Mandy, after running a small Caravan Park locally, returned to Towcester where Mandy is now the Manageress of the local Doctors' dispensary and James, after working for the race winning teams of Jordan and Red Bull, is now working with the new up and coming Formula One team Virgin F1. Edward married in 2002, acquiring an instant family, as James had done and it was planned that he and his partner Michelle would take over our home in order to be in a position to run the Caravan Park business so that Richard could semi-retire.

This again was an example of something not happening, except this time it exerted an enormously high personal price. Edward and Michelle purchased the Caravan Park and Richard was to act as a 'consultant' to help them settle in and for him to wind down from twenty five years of dedicated commitment to the business and to our customers.

I was again very ill in hospital and Edward and Michelle pushed to purchase the Caravan Park. Richard had not wanted to sell at this stage in his life but with both these stresses and pressures he agreed. Something he says he has lived to regret. Unfortunately it did not take Edward and

Michelle long to decide to leave Wales as their family base and Edward just returns two days a week to work with a Manager at the Caravan Park. Edward and his father were 'joined at the hip' both in work and leisure time so we were grievously shocked that fairly quickly after their marriage and the purchase of the Caravan Park with the subsequent problems that entailed, they chose not to have any contact with us, apart from an occasional short visit more recently from Edward. It was a heartbreaking ordeal but I learnt to accept it by thinking,

'If a fledgling chick failed to leave the nest the bird would not have done its job properly.' So if my chick's happiness after leaving the nest depended on the exclusion of family and friends then all I, as a Mother, could ask for is that her child – even though fully grown and mature – is happy.

I had to view Michelle's children, to whom we had become very close, as though they were pupils at school who came into and blessed my life for a couple of years and then moved on, I missed them but this was how I coped.

Through this dramatic change of plan and Richard's sudden severance from the Caravan Park he channeled his energy into working alongside Anthony and Tina and the hotel and Chalet Park business. It also meant he had time to follow up on all my development ideas for Grandma's Garden.

It was a harsh and difficult price to pay but without this immediate and total severance from our life as it had been; Grandma's Garden would never have been born. Given the choice I would have turned it down, the loss being too great but there was no choice and the garden flourished.

Our move from the Caravan Park to the field of the little Peace Garden was without doubt the catalyst in creating Grandma's Garden and without the traumatic birthing process the Garden would not be here to fulfill its essential and meaningful role in the community and beyond.

Moving from the Caravan Park and our home of twenty six years meant we needed to build again. After a struggle we were given permission to build a purpose designed bungalow to accommodate my needs. It is a dream home, and I joke saying,

'I must have done something good in a previous life to live in a purpose built, beautiful home with inspirational views and in the grounds of my great joy, the Peace Garden.'

As the house was nearing completion one of the Planning/Building Regulations people was inspecting and he asked what we were going to do with the large pile of spoil. When Richard had no constructive response he said,

'Why don't you terrace this area incorporating the spoil within the garden?

This was our Peace Garden. I spent days and nights planning, thinking, analysing my motive and philosophy. We had without question an arboretum of over fifty species of tree and shrub. As sculptures were added the garden quite naturally evolved into its own name, Peace Garden, Arboretum and Sculpture Park. Quite a mouthful.

Whilst the planning and building of our new home was in progress Tina would bring our little granddaughter Kiera to visit.

'We've been to the Peace Garden haven't we Kiera?' she would say.

'No we haven't, we've been to Grandma's Garden.' the three year old would reply.

So against my wishes the family began to refer to it as Grandma's Garden. I still didn't like it. It smacked of ego and 'aren't I a clever girl?'

At this time Community Capital Grant scheme grants were being offered. This was a European funded scheme which aimed to support small-scale community based tourism projects, and in our area it was managed by Powys County Council. These Regeneration grants were for charities and non-profit making organisations. As the admission charge for the garden goes to charity and worthy projects, we already fulfilled the first criteria.

I was due to spend four weeks in Spain to escape the cold wet winter. I took along my lap top, the grant forms and a simple garden design DVD. I spent hours a day answering the questions and designing the gardens. When the garden first started I hardly knew the difference between a daffodil and a rose! I needed detailed plans with explanations of the whys and wherefores and the planting schemes and costs. I wanted to maintain the philosophy of linking cultures and spiritual beliefs from around the world.

The physical dimension of the garden obviously had to be undertaken by those who had the physical ability and I then just became the 'sitting foreman' causing much laughter and even more ragging. Some days I would be wrapped up like a 'mummy' with a heated pad on my knee, in order to make sure everything was being done to my exact instructions. What better healer is there than laughter? When my period of endurance depleted then I came in, sometimes to bed even, but I came fulfilled and happy that I was at least the instigator, the inspiration even, for a dream.

When the garden was complete – at that stage at least (it won't ever be complete as new ideas and thoughts are constantly knocking on the door of my creative process). If I say,

'I've been thinking.' The family all do a runner!

Then it was opened to the public and through the garden visiting season I was 'on duty' answering peoples' queries and taking the money, which as I said is all allocated to different charities and worthy projects. Again this meeting of different, fascinating people who all have a story to tell plays a big part in the continuing ability to at least maintain a certain level of well-being. As time has gone by this is something else I have had to relinquish and work from behind the scenes.

Poems I have written over the years are placed in the seven small sensory gardens and have had an impact that was far out of my initial understanding and realisation. They were placed there in order to encourage people to 'stand and stare' but in fact are having effects at a deeply spiritual level and have meant I have had to produce a booklet with them in for visitors to take away with them. Many requests later when I had not responded and produced the booklet a lady in tears, refused to leave until I promised to produce a booklet for visitors to take home and enjoy the poetry at home.

This confirms how each creative process gives rise to, gives birth to another. A book recording the story behind the garden and containing photos and information for each sculpture, each area of interest, in fact the philosophy of the garden and including the history of the old house, now a Country House Hotel, which is surrounded by the garden, was a direct result of the physical garden and this was closely followed by the poetry booklet.

The philosophy of the garden at the level that can be expressed outwardly is to link cultural and spiritual beliefs from around the world, avoiding religion at all costs. And yet the question I am most frequently asked is,

'Are you a Christian?' to which my reply is,

'If I say I am a Christian and you are of another faith then we have immediately put a barrier between us. Let's accept that certain words ring true between us. Those words, as I am sure you will agree, are Love, Peace, Joy and blessings to all'. I have yet to find anyone who can disagree.

I try to embody a fusion of all and every religion and spiritual belief that I know works for me. It has given me the ability to be happy with who I am and what at this moment my beliefs and principles are, never forgetting that these are fluid as I gain knowledge and experience things in a different light. My beliefs grow and expand with my challenges and the challenges that the world faces in its humanity.

Christ Consciousness is available to all as we learn to embody it. It does not, in my humble opinion, restrict those who do not go through Jesus from seeking and attaining that enlightenment. My Christ goes beyond the Church – it is in the Church but not restricted to the Church. I see the Christ Consciousness in Buddha, Mohammed in all the saints and people who have enlightened us towards higher thinking and higher good. I see the Christ Consciousness in each human being, in a child's smile, a tramp's suffering, an opening flower. I see illness not as a punishment or bad karma but as a challenge to greater understanding and greater compassion. We have the choice as to how we respond to life. I joke and say if I were a card player (which I am not I do not like card games for whatever reason) I would not throw a tantrum and refuse to play if

I was dealt a poor hand. I would pick up the cards and rise to the challenge of playing that hand of cards to the best of my ability. Life is like a hand of cards we can choose how to play it and being human we are likely to get it wrong now and again.

In fact at a creative level I like to work on the philosophy of the garden in terms of it just Being. So many people need to know the name of something – what plant is this, why did you…. What do you mean by…?. Why is Buddha not elevated? Whilst they are searching for answers to their questions and placing names, they are not experiencing. When we are asked,

'Are you happy?' we have to think about it and the connection with the experience of being happy is lost in the search for the word that we use to convey that state of being. We have suddenly lost the experience of being happy. Although science has proven differently, our vocabulary, our concepts, beliefs such as the teaching of sunrise and sunset all leave us with the misconception that we, the earth, are the centre of the Universe. The sun appears to be moving around us, rising and setting. If we stop for a minute, we remember that we move around the sun. We are a speck of dust that in spinning towards and away creates what we name as sunrise and sunset. Because we cannot see or feel it we revert to its name and then find ourselves confronted with the idea and not the truth. Our ideas only become reality when they reflect reality. This is a classic example of when we name something we do not experience it.

Seven is a predominant number in the garden, as in creation, seven spheres of the platonic solid – the Seed of Life, seven days of creation, seven colours of a rainbow, seven musical notes in a scale and seven chakras or major energy centres in the body. There are seven small sensory gardens, and seven rose arches through the rose arbor for example.

The grant was to add seven sensory gardens – 'Gardens for the Human Condition', through which the seven conditions of being human are expressed. These seven gardens are designed to speak through the senses with which we are each blessed.

Garden one – focuses on the senses of sight, scent and touch. A 'sight and light' garden particularly relevant to those with a hearing impairment. The ability to hear – did Joan of Arc, or entities in our religious texts need a physical entity to hear voices and commands?

Garden two – a garden of sound, scent and touch, of particular appeal to those with sight impairment. The ability to see – does this just mean on a physical level or at an internal, spiritual, mental level? Angels, burning bushes, fairies and elementals, are they just imagination?

Garden three – Mother Natures Magic Garden focuses on edible plants such as herbs, fruit bushes, nettles and seeds that succour and heal humanity, with symbols of sun, moon, water and wind to emphasise their necessity to support life.

Garden four – a Garden of Other Dimensions, offers an insight and encouragement to explore fairies, angels, celtic history and Mabonogion mythology. We can commune consciously or unconsciously with the dimensions which science is now proving exist.

Garden five – a Children's Enchanted Garden leads the child along a yellow brick road to discover characters from classic stories and nursery rhymes. The garden has a multi sensory approach using all the senses to stimulate imagination.

Garden six – a Garden of Infinity. This garden came from a challenge to design a garden for people suffering from schizophrenia. I could not just limit it to one mental illness so looked around for help with all mental disturbances. Here is where I found the effect of labyrinths and mazes. A small brick paved figure eight, the sign of infinity, just large enough to walk its shape, allowing the walker to concentrate on the simple but complex task of experiencing limits within life's path and to accept those that are necessary. Where do we begin and where do we end? What is meditation, prayer, the need to be alone? Being lonely is not the same as being alone.

And last but not least,

Garden seven – Humanity's destiny. Humanity is asked to Dream the Vision of man uniting, with a small circle of 'friends' linking arms atop a north, south, east, west circle, representing all the corners of the world. The poem Dreaming the Vision concentrates the mind. Is there meaning to life? Do we have a destiny? As individuals? As a society? A world? A universe? Is there a golden age of peace? Not forgetting that peace is not just an absence of war.

There is a poem related to the topic of each garden to encourage visitors to spend time absorbing the peace and tranquility of each part of the garden.

As visitors walk and experience these seven gardens the potential is there to carry that experience back into the every day world and into the society which we inhabit.

Seven rose arches are to all intents and purposes just a rose arbour walk, but on another level can represent the seven major energy centres in the body – there are in fact millions – known as chakras. As we walk the path through the arches is it possible that at some level the energy centres respond to the intent within that part of the garden. The concept that energy can be manipulated, altered back to its default of well-being?

Grandmother Falling Leaves of the Blue Moon Medicine Lodge, a great friend, told me the following. In Native American tradition, a less well known use for herbs, whether wild or in a garden, is that they are just as healing left as they are. As the wind blows through and plays with the herbs, their healing and beneficial qualities blow them to the four corners of the earth, bringing peace, healing and harmony. In this way the healing essences of the herbs are given to the whole world; the air, the wind, the earth and all elements present. A wind sock or wind flag is essential so that the wind has something to play with, as it is a child by nature, and if it becomes bored it will create havoc with its strength and in its boredom seek something, sometimes destructive in our eyes, to keep it occupied. What a lovely way to think of the plants and elements.

No-one ever owns anything. When we leave this plane we take nothing with us. We can take no-thing only spiritual things. We are therefore only guardians. Guardianship of the land, even a window box, does not depend on the acreage or size of the land in question. A small yard can be a haven for wildlife even in the centre of a busy city. Guardianship is a way of life, a way of thinking, a way of listening to and responding to the diversity and balance of life as we know it. It is important to understand the interconnectedness of all species, whether plant, animal, insect or bird. In so doing we are more able to cultivate a space in harmony with the way that nature devised from the beginning of creation.

We are co-creators and whatever we do in our small plots will extend beyond the sanctuary of that area into the wider world, allowing the wildlife to return to habitats long abandoned. We can rebuild a spiritual relationship with Mother Earth if we work with her ways of wisdom cultivated over eons, instead of trying to impose our new scientific wizardry of genetic manipulation and nano technology thinking that we can improve or override nature.

The garden is an ongoing project – a dream in progress – and is expected to continue its unique contribution to the gardening world whilst benefiting those less fortunate. We can dream a new vision of the interconnectedness of all life where tolerance and understanding for each others' beliefs and differences is a foregone conclusion. A garden can create experiences which allow us to live life through service and action. Understanding that 'I am you and you are me.' 'Do as I would be done by'. How can we be the hearts and hands of God? By creating a vision and living by it. New science certainly has its place as it fits in our world but through service not imposition.

Holy, Holy, Holy.

Great and Gracious Glory.

Man is tending his garden

As he passes through his life.

Is your garden growing, full of life abundant,

Visited by butterflies and nature's spirit world?

Or is it just a-rambling, neglected in its sorrow,

No delicate, sweet flowers with their
pretty leaves unfurled?

Give your garden sunshine, as you smile
throughout the day.

And water it with blessings as you share along the way.

You'll find that as you do this
your life will fill with people

Who flock to see the beauty with their
sense of sight and smell.

This gift of great abundance is yours to claim forever.
Reward for tending, caring, your green
and flowering dell.
Each person's little garden leads right on to
meet his neighbours.
And the neighbour's little garden extends into a park.
The Park, it has no boundaries and it leads into a valley,
And the valley goes on leading to the hills and dales
beyond.
It's here that we can wander midst the creatures
of the country,
Midst the forests and the flowers, midst the birds and
living ponds.
The boundaries are missing and your journey
goes forever,
Through the gardens, parks and valleys.
'Til you come to realise.
You no longer know your garden,
as your garden is extended.
All limitations fade away and you become all-wise.
Wise to joy and merriment, compassion, peace and love.
Unity with all we know, God's garden and the dove.
Wandering, wandering, guided by the Dove of Peace.
Along the winding paths within our garden new.
God is here beside us, above us and below us.
To our right and to our left with us his love imbues.
From here our life is changed forever, eternity is ours.
Gardeners of the world unite and recognise your powers.
Seeds of life are waiting for our patient, tender care,
Responding to our life's work with true creative flair.

Sprouting, growing, flowering, a blossom quite divine -
Each of us producing a fragrant flower sublime.
God's garden is here and now,
it's yours, it's ours, it's mine.

Behind every smiling face, given time, patience and tolerance it will emerge that there is a major challenge, even tragedy, be it health, relationships or finance. These conditions are part of being human and are eased by the energy of unconditional acceptance. Often animals are credited with such a quality but even more profound is the energy of the land, the earth on which we live.

Everything in its original form is in its natural state. Divine energy is omnipresent and as humans we are offered the choice of inviting this energy into our personal space, our mind, our body, our lives. In so doing we are open to receiving infinite compassion, wisdom and nourishment. Connecting to nature is our opportunity to tune into the rhythms of the seasons, the months, weeks, days, each hour of our daily lives. Thus acknowledging this sacred trust, the need to balance the head and the heart in our actions and deeds, by living more closely in harmony with nature we learn to live more harmoniously with each other. Certain spaces and areas of land, even in war torn parts of the world, offer succour and peace to refresh our minds and bodies.

Eventually the rest of the garden challenges our attitude to the earth and our environment, be that physical, emotional, mental or spiritual, or even all of these, then if we believe that intent is highly charged and empowered to have an effect, time spent in the garden empowers us to have an acceptance of who we are. An acceptance of who we are is total healing.

I'll return to the grant application. The grant was for two thirds of the total cost of the project up to a total allowance of £10,000. I applied for the full grant, tongue in cheek, thinking that even £200 would be very welcome, but in for a penny in for a pound. I would try for the £10,000 full grant.

Richard took me to meetings and interviews and the inevitable question of name came up. As I was getting my tongue around Peace Garden Sculpture Park etc Richard jumped in with,

'Grandma's Garden.'

They responded,

'Oh, what a delightful name. You're half way there.'

Outnumbered!

Some time later I was told by visitors,

'We came because of its name. We knew we could bring Grandma and it would be accessible and we knew we could bring children as Grandmas have Grandchildren.' So the name has proven itself and I can now see it as not only practical but a term of endearment.

When the person rang to tell me the grant application had been successful I asked how much was I to expect? You could hear the pleasure in her voice as she said,

'The full £10,000 Diana, well done.'

As the garden has continued to give back financially already more than the original grant, and physically to the community, I was later told it has become their star project and they brought visitors from the EU countries to see its success.

As well as this financial benefit, the benefit to all is unmistakable. I can guarantee that disability is not confined to the near ten million recognised in the UK I can truthfully say that disability is usually invisible.

The philosophy continued to grow alongside the garden. To link spiritual and cultural beliefs around the world, to commune with nature and return to work or daily life refreshed, to learn about conservation and sustainability in an open relaxed way, and last but not least to carry those experiences back into society as part of whom we are.

Lying on its side in the grass in an unattended area of the garden was an ancient standing stone. When we uncovered it, it was inscribed with what Anthony described as medieval grafiti. We decided that this stone should be re-erected and given back its rightful role in the landscape.

On one of Hamish and Ba's visits we asked their advice as to placing it in its most beneficial position. We had hoped to make it the centre stone of a stone circle.

Piezo electricity is generated by some materials such as crystals where an electric field or an electrical potential is created. This produces electrical pulses that are used to mark time. A piezo electrical device was first used in WWI as a submarine/sonar detector, followed by electric cigarette lighters, chemical and biological sensors, auto focus in cameras and much more.

With his usual passion Hamish tuned in to the stone. He explained that stones are embedded with crystals and these resonate and this resonance can be picked up. Crystals are used in computers and watches and can be programmed to carry information. How far fetched is it then to think a larger stone can do the same and carry memories from the past?

Hamish talked of sixteen radials, like the spokes of a wheel, emitting energy. You can't talk to a stone and expect it to answer but you can follow the information it gives out such as the sixteen radials. When Hamish dowsed the monolith in the Hotel he found a strong energy line going between it and the small circular 'temple' in the garden. He then found seven energy lines travelling between the stone, the 'temple' and the Seed of Life symbol that had been cut into the land.

The major line continued past the symbol and down the hill. A further energy line came from the temple down across the land and where these lines crossed Hamish said may be significant. As he marked the crossing point he found a spiral energy coming from that point – sixteen radials branching out from this spiral. We had sixteen energy lines from the monolith, a major line from that to the temple and another major line from the monolith down through the symbol, both meeting further down the hill and crossing, with another sixteen radials at that point. The stone had spoken, this is where it would go. Hamish explained that these energy lines – leys – are male and female and weave back and forward and where they cross are really sacred sites.

The standing stone was placed in position and Richard brought large slate stones from the local quarry to build the circle, in fact an ellipse. Because of the lie of the land and a nearby railway line the shape is not a true circle. It is not placed directly North South East West nor are the stones placed equidistant in the four quarters because it is not a direction finder. The stones are purely markers for the energy lines. As well as the major lines extending from the monolith there were many others, Hamish ceased his attempt at counting when he reached one hundred! However as long as the stone is on the radial, even though not all stones are equidistant, the energy vortex and the earth's magnetic field will resonate. Hamish explained that these sites are cosmic connections resonating to the fields and energies of the cosmos.

Shortly after the building of the stone circle we were visited by a young friend. He and his colleague were in charge, acting as Carers, of a young disturbed youth. He was hyperactive and had quite obvious difficulties relating to what we consider the normal world. The young men took him round the garden and he was eager and full of enthusiasm to explore everything. When he entered the stone circle he ran back out and asked his Carers,

'Why does the hair on the back of my neck stand on end and my hair tingle when I go in there? I feel as if I am floating when I go near the middle stone.'

I have frequently been confronted by these individuals who are not beset by convention or the worries of what people might think, being able to see, hear, tune into dimensions that are not available to most other people. These stories in their millions may only be anecdotal but they powerfully back up the new science of other dimensions, and alternate realities.

I had talked for some time of wanting a wild life pond in the garden but could not come up with a large enough area, the only area left was prone to mild flooding which would of course devastate the pond life.

One morning Richard said,

'I've found somewhere for your wildlife pond. We can turn your stone circle into a huge doughnut shape with a small island in the middle surrounded by water and then enclosed by the stones of the stone circle.'

No sooner said than done. Now the stones, the sky, the trees, reflect in the water creating the most powerful sense of peace and tranquility and yet suffusing the observer with energy and hope for the future of the earth. In less than a year the pond was full of wildlife and indigenous plants. Birds, even a duck nesting on the small island, dragonflies, mayflies, water beetles, pondskaters, butterflies, moths, frogs, newts and even visiting herons. Obviously the natural world felt the energy and made this place a sanctuary of wildlife.

Because of Richard's work as a Director for British Holiday Homes and Parks Association (BHHPA) he has contact with Professor David Bellamy. Each year for the last ten years the business and Garden at Dolguog have received the Gold Award for Conservation from David's Scheme, and in 2004, David himself came to open and dedicate Grandma's Garden. We felt blessed and honoured by his support.

In 2009 a new award was set up. Instead of adding another hierarchical award to the Gold, Silver and Bronze, it was decided to give a Special Award of Distinction. There are more than three thousand Holiday Home Parks in the UK, five hundred of which have been granted an Award for Conservation. The new awards are designed to highlight special efforts to protect and enhance the natural world, with responsibility for careful management more important than the size of the Park. Good neighbourliness, community involvement and centres of education for conservation are all taken into account by the independent Assessors.

Our Assessor came from the Wildlife Trust, looking for the highest standards of conservation practice and awareness. In the first year of the new award, fourteen Special Awards of Distinction were given, with these participants having been deemed to have gone considerably beyond the standards of environmental care expected of winners and made exceptional achievement in areas judged for the competition. Grandma's Garden was honoured to receive one of these special awards. David Bellamy also praised the design of accessibility for all, which was in fact an obvious need for my own access to accomplish the creation of the garden. I'm the lucky one, as I sit in my wheelchair and tell others what to do!

The garden has been and will continue to be the catalyst for others around the world to create Peace Gardens, be they window boxes or large estates. Within the Dolguog Estate grounds there are such old and beautiful trees, forming a natural Arboretum. The small circular temple or summer house that many people found so powerful during the Gatherings has been rebuilt into a beautifully spiritual building, true to its original design.

The whole of the Estate incorporates the use of sense. It encompasses the term sensory garden through its emphasis on the use of sight, sound, smell, taste and touch. Listen to the wind as it rustles through the trees, the grasses, the quivering foliage of plants and seed heads. Hear and see the insects attracted to the strong colours of the flowers, such as the rhododendrons, azaleas, buddleias, poppies etc, whilst remembering that the colours that insects see extends into the UV spectrum, colours which the human eye can not discern. Smell the aromatic flowers and wild plants, extending beyond the general herb garden. Some plants use scent to attract pollinating insects and others use it to act as natural insect repellent, deterring pests from attacking leaves. Taste: the herb garden is an excellent example of this category with its wonderful aromatic and tasty plants used as flavourings in cooking and concoctions such as herb tea and medicinal potions. Last but not least of the senses is the sense of touch. Plants use different textured leaves to protect them from the elements and from attack by pests. Furry or hairy leaves can stop slugs or protect from sun or cold and spines stop herbivores eating the leaves. If you touch some of the plants with your eyes closed you will instantly understand the importance of the sense of touch. Try lambstail, the ferns, berberis, even the trunks of trees.

Grandma's Garden includes sculptures symbolic of the many spiritual and religious beliefs and traditions. A full size bronze stag and doe – the stag representing the Christ consciousness; a pair of bronze verdi gris cranes – the Japanese symbol of peace and longevity; the Budhha for compassion; a large eagle atop a craggy promontory; and many others; natural wood sculptures and small plaques of words of inspiration. The garden is an energy centre; it is being kept simple, a reflection of nature and yet alongside its ancient trees, shimmering river and majestic views it can receive our human offerings, our human creativity to blend and attune to the devas and spirit world, in the form of sculptures, reflections of light through glass, words of inspiration, sound through wind and water, through chimes and water sources.

The garden continues to grow and expand and now includes a stone circle and a thirty-six foot labyrinth of the design found in Chartres Cathedral. This helps walkers to find rest and quiet within themselves, to deal with the patterns of life and our response to it. All of this encompassed within the scenery of beautiful trees, shrubs, bulbs and plants and bounded by the beautiful River Dulas and overlooking the Dyfi/Dovey valley and the Snowdonia National Park. Boardwalks alongside the river give access to, whilst protecting, the wildlife – red kites, buzzards, owls, kingfishers, fly catchers, woodpeckers, otters, badgers, bats, moles and voles, dragonflies, newts and butterflies, flora and fauna too great to mention.

The garden is truly a garden of Eden, a nature reserve in miniature within the concept of garden. How much more special could it be? Recently the Dyfi (Dovey) Valley was officially recognised as Wales' only UNESCO biosphere. This elite status puts it alongside Uluru (Ayers Rock) and Mount Olympus in Greece. A biosphere is a special area in which people work to balance the conservation of biodiversity with its sustainable use.

I have wondered what will happen, as with so many beautiful gardens, when the ravages of time and neglect take their toll. As surely at some point in the far future this will happen for one reason or another. It can be a little disconcerting to think on these lines. The Tibetan monks spend days painting exquisite and complex mandalas with coloured sand. These time consuming works of art are then swept away in an instant once they have fulfilled their potential.

Life is impermanent; by recognising that impermanence in the ritual of the mandalas I am able to relate that to the garden and to life. It is what is now that is important. What happens after is the cycle of life, the acknowledgement of impermanence. Do it today, with joy and without worry for you do not know what tomorrow holds.

'Today is the tomorrow you worried about yesterday'.

I have many stories about the garden, and remember one Sunday lunch time we were driving from our home at the Caravan Park to the Hotel to meet with friends for Richard and them to have lunch. As we drove round I said to Richard,

'Do you know, I would really like an eagle to go in the garden? The Native Americans believe the eagle to be the manifestation of the Creator and it would really fit with the philosophy of the garden in linking spiritual beliefs.' We arrived at the hotel and one of the Chalet owners was there preparing to have lunch with his wife.

'Oh, Diana, just the person I wanted to see.' This genteel gentleman was a Building Contractor and often salvaged things when refurbishing premises.

347

'I've got a couple of carved eagles I thought you might like. They are taking up room in my office. I will willingly give them to you if Richard will bring you to have a look at them and collect them if you want them.' Richard burst into laughter and told him what I had just said.

The following day we set off in the old transit van, I was surrounded by cushions, and two hours later arrived at the office. As we went into the office entrance area I could not believe my eyes. I had expected the trunk of a small tree as a base with an eighteen inch carved eagle perched on top as I had seen for sale on the side of the road by power saw carvers selling their wares. These two eagles: the smaller, I presume female was five feet tall and the larger six feet from head to claw. The eagles were carved larger than life with a four foot wing span and each carved out of one piece of wood. They were spectacular. Richard queried their provenance. Had they come from a demolished church? No, they had come from a Pub! I kept the eagles in the conservatory at our house at the Caravan Park until the Stone Room was complete. Delivery men would stand open mouthed asking if they could buy them. You can't sell a gift and they had a very important job to do.

When I was a child I 'saw' fairies and would often tell stories of the fairy realms seen in the burning open fire in our home. During the Gatherings children would come to tell me what they had seen in the little temple. Fairies, lights, orbs (not their term), together with sounds of music. Their stories differed and it was obvious from their sincerity that they were not all seeing the same things. This was a wonderful validation of my own childhood memories and one day I found a small bronze sculpture of a very beautiful fairy, just three feet tall, awaiting my arrival at the warehouse where I had purchased other bronzes for the garden. She came home with me and was placed a few yards from my front door.

I called Kiera, who was now about five years old. The family was not religious in the conventional sense of the word and she had no experience of church services or rituals. Kiera stood looking at the fairy for several minutes, then solemnly went over to the bird bath, cupped her little hands and filled them with water. She bathed the fairy's legs and then did the same with its arms, body, head and face. All of this in total silence and with great reverence. She then stood back, smiled at me and said,

'The fairy is happy to live here now, Grandma.'

She had baptized this being, seeing beyond its outward expression to its spiritual core. Ceremony and ritual are part of our tradition as humans and Kiera was tapping into the need for sacred ceremony and respect in our lives.

As I was planning the seven small gardens whilst in Spain, I had the idea for a Children's Enchanted Garden. I wanted to bring in the classic fairy tales and nursery rhymes, bringing them to life in order to encourage communication between adults and young children. It was Richard's challenge to build a yellow brick road, so it twists and winds. The idea being that the children would not be able to see around the corners of the twisting path because of the planting and it would be a big adventure waiting for the next surprise. I had told Richard I wanted to put Snow White and the Seven Dwarves in and I knew Spain had got everything from turtles to weird and wonderful objects and even gnomes.

I asked a friend,

'Where will I get some little ornaments of Snow White and the Seven Dwarves?' She thought this was hilarious,

'You won't.' she said. 'I vaguely remember seeing all sorts of weird things up north, but nothing much down here in the south, certainly nothing as specific as Snow White.'

'Oh well it was worth asking.' I thought. I asked another friend with just the same response. Richard just smiled and said,

'They'll be there if she wants them.' We all laughed and left it at that.

Off we went to visit our favourite Garden Centre, to sit in the sun and have a cuppa. We were meant to be on holiday so let's act like it!

We went to our favourite table and stood transfixed. Surrounding 'our' table was Snow White and the Seven Dwarves, each one approximately eighteen inches tall.

I rushed to the Assistant.

'I want to buy Snow White and her Dwarves.' She had no idea what I was talking about. She realized what I meant when she came to the table. They were not known as Snow White or Dwarves they were called Dove Lady, man with spade and so on! She proceeded to wrap them up, taking nearly an hour. When I asked couldn't we have taken them out of stock?

Her reply was,

'No, this is the only set we have. They came in last night and we don't have plans to buy in any more.' Then we had the job of fitting them in the car to get them back to Wales.

Chapter Twenty-One

Self Help

Being human automatically introduces us to challenges. Health is a big one, very few people get through life without experiencing some form of health problem from mild flu to pneumonia, from a broken limb to paralysis, from a short term illness to a chronic life threatening illness.

I had organized four Gatherings; four years being the original commitment required of a Sundance and suddenly was no longer involved in the work that this entailed,

'What can I do to help others fulfill their journey?' had become a way of life and when the Gathering was no longer held, very few came to ask me,

'What can I do for you,' rather than, 'What can you do for me?' This was without judgment or criticism just an amazing awareness that only I could help I. I must look to meeting my own requirements for a time instead of always seeking how I could help others.

Over the years I have learnt different ways of doing things. My Occupational Therapist tells me I am not disabled, I am enabled, working on the principle of necessity being the mother of invention. Or as my Grandmother would have said,

'There's no such thing as 'can't'.

The reason we decided to spend time in the winter in Spain was because the wet and cold made it so difficult in the United Kingdom. I was getting more immobile and the pain was aggravated dramatically by the cold and particularly the wet. Cold you can dress against but wet you can't. In Spain when I got up in a morning a tee shirt and a pair of trousers or a skirt was all that was needed – a couple of minutes. In the UK I needed help to add the vest, the socks, the jumper and to go out was a mammoth task of dressing with hats and scarves and mittens and heated pads.

I had spent years denying I needed help although the Occupational Therapist had done her best to persuade me, if not for my sake then for Richards. One day she said to me,

'Diana, I think the time has come where you can't stay in denial any longer. Look at it this way, if your energy is a pint of milk and it takes half a pint to get dressed and organized in a morning then you only have half a pint left to last the day. If you have help and it only takes a quarter of a pint then you have three quarters to play with through the day.' This made sense and I agreed that indeed the time had come to relinquish some of my hard fought for independence and have help. Her psychology had worked and I had to accept and to learn to be cared for rather than to care for others.

A few weeks after this Richard rang her to say,

'Diana says the darned milkman hasn't delivered today what should she do?'

Learning to say no also helps, but it doesn't seem to be found naturally in a woman's make up and I needed to learn to be what I considered 'selfish' and say that no.

What is illness and what is healing? One day sitting up in bed attached to nebulisers, feeding machines and being given various medications, a conversation ensued between Richard and the District Nurse as to whether I should see a Doctor.

'I don't need a doctor'. I insisted 'I'm not ill.' Richard and the District Nurse gave me a funny look with all my tubes and connections and Richard broke the silence.

'No of course not, she's only ill with one 'l'. I like that way of looking at it and it makes me smile when I think of it.

Mind over matter is a powerful energy, if you doubt this then come play with me for a minute. On the table in front of you is a bowl of lemons. Bright yellow and sensuous. Pick one up and feel its texture. As your hands warm it, bring it to your nose and take a deep breath, smell that tangy aroma. Now, place it on the table, pick up a knife and slice the lemon in half. Watch the juice trickle out on to the table and smell that zesty powerful smell.

Are you still with me? OK, pick up one half of the lemon and suck the juice into your mouth, let it trickle down your chin.

You can stop now. What happened? Did your mouth water? Your reaction was all through the power of suggestion. Mind over matter. There was no matter, your mind created it.

We were in Spain on my fiftieth birthday and Anthony and Tina were insisting I wore the 6 inch diameter '50 today'

353

badge they had given me, as we went out to eat. No-one would miss noticing it, I couldn't escape. We had great fun and even strangers joined in the party. Right, fifty is enough I decided from now on I would go backwards.

Some three years later I found myself facing yet another consultant. He asked my name, age and date of birth. He asked again.

'Forty-seven,' I said, '2nd February 1943.' He pointed out they couldn't both be right. I insisted I was right until he pointed out the mathematical error.

I don't think he thought much of my explanation but I was absolutely convinced I was forty-seven. Six years younger than I actually was. Anthony jokes now that he was born before his Mother!

I was asked by a retired doctor what I did to be able to live with what he called severe RA. I told him he would not want to know if he was a conventional doctor. Eventually he persuaded me to tell him my unusual approach. His response was,

'If walking about with a teapot on your head makes you feel better, go out and buy a teapot.' Drugs, denial and placebo – does it matter if it works for you then do it.

Another older gentleman asked me how I handled my arthritis (his words as I never called it mine – I don't want to be possessive over it!) He was sitting in a comfy armchair holding a large glass of wine.

'What do you do for help to ease the pain in your hands?' This came out of the blue as we hadn't even spoken let alone discussed 'my' arthritis. I knew he wouldn't like what I was about to say.

'If I had a teaspoon of alcohol in any form I wouldn't be able to get out of bed tomorrow morning.' His reply,

'Oh, I couldn't give up my wine, I'd rather be dead.'

We choose how we want to live and then we deal with the consequences. Our life style can and does have a direct impact on our health; smoking, drinking to excess, drugs, over eating, under eating, all have the potential to act adversely on our health, to the point of death. Now, I am going to say something really controversial, you are warned turn away now if you want to stay as you are. What is suicide? If you choose to take part in something that has the potential to kill you, is that not slow suicide? Surely we have a responsibility to care for our health and bodies, whatever that takes. There is a saying,

'If you keep on doing what you have always done then you'll go on being what you have always been.' Unable to see what is in front of your eyes.

When Anthony was fourteen he finally had to have his tonsils removed. This is not an easy operation in older children and adults and takes more time for recovery.

Anthony was in a ward for two with a young man of similar age who was also there for the removal of his tonsils. When they returned from surgery I was waiting and stayed with Anthony through the evening and into the early hours of the morning. I talked to him all this time telling him the good cells were gobbling up and annihilating the bad cells, cleaning and healing the wound, easing his swallowing and reducing the swelling. I stroked his head and whispered in his ear. To all intents and purposes he was in an unconscious state not responding to my voice.

I returned home to catch some sleep when I felt he had settled down and was more restful. When I returned next morning, Anthony was sitting up eating a little breakfast, his room mate was in a pretty bad way, moaning a little, unable to sit up and overcome his pain.

When the doctor visited he said,

'This young man is our star patient. We would expect him to be more like his young colleague for a couple of days. He deserves a medal.' Anthony looked at me and just winked.

Self help doesn't just mean what you can do, but also how you can use others and information to help you make decisions and respond to that information. For many years I produced and edited a sixteen page Newsletter. Jane and I would spend hours putting it into the correct format and then running it off and collating it ready for distribution, not to mention the gathering of the material in the first place. One hundred copies were sent out to subscribers.

Bear in mind when reading what follows that self-help includes taking charge of your own life.

The Newsletter contained articles of inspiration, information and alternative news views. News that the main media avoided for reasons of controversy or even covert censorship. Subjects covered health and alternative health fields, education, weaponry, pharma/farmer controversies such as GM manipulated food. Did you know that Monsanto took a US farmer to court because their GM crop had seeded (albeit wild) in his fields and crops. Monsanto sued him for growing the Monsanto round-up ready seed without a licence. (round-up ready seed is seed that requires the round up weed killer as it grows and is known as a terminator seed as it will not germinate next year) I'm afraid you will have to believe it; Monsanto won and bankrupt the farmer! It is also a fact that 80 per cent of animal feed in Europe is fed on GM feed and there is no responsibility for the producer to label this product.

I wrote a number of articles about a sweetener called aspartame and its adverse effects. Aspartame is the name for an artificial non saccharide sweetener, its E number is E951. It is the technical name for the brand names Nutra Sweet, Equal, Spoonful, Equal Measure, Canderel. It is 200 times sweeter than sugar. In certain markets it is manufactured using a GM modified variation of E coli, not as sweet or tasty as it sounded. Any produce labeled Diet, no added sugar or low calorie should be checked for its ingredients if you wish to eliminate aspartame from your diet. The US figures are easier to come by so hence their use here. Seventy five per cent of adverse reactions to food additives reported to the FDA are about aspartame and ninety different documented symptoms are listed.

Amongst other nasty things, Aspartame includes methanol which breaks down into formic acid and formaldehyde in the body. Formaldehyde is a deadly accumulative toxic poison and is known to be cancer causing. If you research on the internet there is much made of the fact that Donald Rumsfeld became Chief Executive Officer of GD Searle and Company, a world wide pharmaceutical company, and it is claimed that he and Robert Shapiro are solely responsible for using their political muscle to buy off the FDA and get Nutrasweet approved after twenty years of its being turned down due to research finding brain tumours and holes in the brains of rats.

I know a young person with Multiple Sclerosis who cannot touch anything containing aspartame as it exacerbates her condition so dramatically. If in doubt do your own research, your health cannot, must not be compromised. In the 1990's a hotline was set up for pilots suffering, whilst in the cockpit, from acute reactions to aspartame, 600 cases were reported. Aspartame mimics many illnesses not least Multiple Sclerosis and epilepsy and diabetes in its attack on the nervous system.

After reading all the adverse reports and research with these results of holes and tumours in the brains of rats alongside studies funded by the NutraSweet company, and grants given to such as the American Dietetic Association, who state that NutraSweet write their 'Facts' sheets – all this has to pose the question of reliability and validity of the findings. These findings explain why the FDA couldn't give a safe daily intake level.

Despite these results it is a widespread ingredient in food and beverages. We live in a world where it is even added to pharmaceutical drugs such as children's antibiotics, supposedly to make them more palatable.

In the UK products have to be marked 'with sweeteners' or possibly 'contains source of phenylalanine' but I for one would not know what that was or whether it was good or bad. Ninety countries worldwide have found aspartame safe for human consumption despite the overwhelming evidence to the contrary.

I had a phone call from an older lady, who in her seventies had developed severe, life inhibiting epilepsy. She had come across the Newsletter in a waiting room in a small village in the middle of India – how did it get there for heaven's sake? It turned out she was addicted to diet coke and as she came off the diet drinks her epilepsy abated to the point where she no longer needed medication. Correspondence from four other people contained their stories of recovery from different unpleasant symptoms and illness by eliminating aspartame from their diet. Only a small anecdotal study but enough to make us pause for thought.

Codex Alimentarius (Latin for 'food code' or food book') is a collection of internationally recognized standards, codes of practice, guidelines and other recommendations relating to foods, food production and food safety. It was established in 1963 by the Food and Agriculture Organization of the United Nations (FAO) and the World Health Organization (WHO). The term safety has to be read, in my opinion, in the context of how does their safety and testing fare when we acknowledge that 1.6 million people in the UK alone are addicted to prescription drugs

You may or more likely may not have heard of this Codex Alimentarius. Some ten years ago I fought against this and the big boys such as Holland and Barratt helped the smaller privately owned health food shops to overcome this Act being passed. We thought we had won. December 2009 sees this Codex Alimentarius being ratified by the EEC. Most MP's and MEP's either don't understand this Act or think it is benign because it is overseen by the WHO, this is how it will get through.

Fifty three years they have been working to push this Codex Alimentarius through. Fifty three years shows how important the pharmaceutical and agrochemical companies think this is to their business profit and expansion and providing them with life long customers overcoming the damage of such things as GM products. Nature doesn't make mistakes or if it did they have worked their way out of the system. We still arrogantly think we know best and can improve on nature – what a risky experiment.

I give credit to Parallel Community for the following article. Their research shows:

'….. that the Codex Agenda has been carefully prepared over the last 53 years and a colossal investment has been made by a conglomerate of commercial companies including most of the big names in the pharmaceutical industry and the more recently sprouted agri-chemical groups to make the whole project work on their behalf. It is an immensely complex set up and we have attempted to reduce the deliberately confusing data to three simple facts which alone are a threat to our health and certainly that of our children and grandchildren. There are three main aims of the Codex Agenda which will seriously affect us all.

1. GM foods and meat fattened by growth hormone techniques will be sold to us without stating this on the label.

2. Most fruit and vegetables will be irradiated before sale, and harmful pesticides and chemicals will be allowed in our food. This information will not be put on the label. It is claimed that this will improve trade because food would last longer and travel further distances without going off. The process, however, will strip it of most of its nutrients and will effectively ban truly organic food unless we grow it ourselves. We need the trace elements and nutrients from food to support our immune systems in a healthy and natural way. Without them we will become ill more easily, and progressively we will become completely reliant on the drug companies as a result of our depleted immune systems.

The whole idea of transporting foodstuffs for thousands of miles is completely contrary to the ethics of Parallel Community and future planning must be geared to include a high percentage of local production.

3. All high dose vitamins and all herbal products will be made illegal unless the pharmaceutical companies deem them 'safe'. This includes things like Echinacea and Green Tea which will be reclassified as drugs. The

pharmaceutical companies will make sure that the permitted potency levels of vitamins and supplements will be so low as to be ineffective, thus creating a permanently growing market for their own product. At the same time, they will create severe commercial problems for producers of natural health products. Manufacturers of supplements, smallholders, organic farmers, horticulturalists, health food shops and those involved in permaculture will be in danger of being squeezed out of business.

Serious questions have to be asked about the contribution the pharmaceutical and agrochemical companies have made in the current Swine Flu pandemic.

We must also question the part the WHO has played in the merry dance which has resulted in declaring a Stage 6 Pandemic. This is equivalent in seriousness to a major terrorist attack. This, of course, in some places allows military law to take the place of civil law, hence the enforced vaccination of children in some states of America before they are allowed to go to school.

The H1N1 vaccine is toxic and will certainly ensure that these children's immune systems will be affected in such a way that they will become permanently dependent on the pharmaceutical companies for the rest of their lives.'

I find the information above worth considering and including so we are all in a position to act as we wish. We are losing our choice and the draconian measures laid down in Europe are in great and present danger of throwing the baby out with the bath water.

I then heard on a TV news programme (not BBC obviously!) that states in America, California is the example, there is a policy that makes it mandatory for children to be vaccinated in accordance with the state vaccination programme policy. The only way to opt out of this is to take your children out of the school education system and home educate. They have now passed a law that makes home education impossible unless you are a qualified teacher. You think it couldn't happen in the UK? We are already on the slippery slope. Try taking your child out of school for just one day without permission and you face a fine of £100. The question 'how long before that law is extended?' needs to be asked?

Genetic Food!!

Too many sweeties make your teeth rot.

Too much sugar and you're health'll go to pot.

Beans crossed with 'tunias on the menu.

Test tube sheep, casseroled in stew.

Pesticides and chemistry seem to be our lot.

Mixing of the gene pool, animal, plant or what?

No more menus just reserved for food.

E numbers, chemicals these are how we're wooed.

Monosodium glutamate or man made spice?

Witches' brew or chemists' brew, not very nice.

I would like an apple, grown in the sun.

Not ripened on a lorry as he makes his run.

I would like a cauliflower, creamy flesh.

Not dowsed in chemicals to keep it fresh.

I would like a patch, to grow my own.

Sun-filled, rain-soaked and fine wind blown,

Plucked from the soft brown soil

As blessings for all my toil.

Cheap food is never really cheap
If it's grown in soil that's lacking.
Over-used, sanitised to keep the bankers' backing.
Vitamins and minerals are mans' healthy choice.
Proclaim your views across the land
in a loud clear voice.
Free from OP's and fertiliser,
Earth is our Mother and friend and teacher.
Give her her due as you honour her ways
And your life will be filled with many healthy days.
Write to your MP, write to your store.
Show that you care and you want more and more.
Token gestures of organic grown carrots
Won't stop the shoppers as they all shout like parrots.
Good food, clean food, grown for us to eat,
Unadulterated food isn't too great a feat
Irradiated, packaged and stamped for haste.
Give us what we ask for – We Want Taste!

I once took part in an exercise designed to make us
aware of our control, our power over our reality. Over a
thousand people drew on cards with small children's wax
crayons, a picture of something they wished to have or
do in life. I drew a picture of a helicopter, as I had always
wanted to take a ride, but somehow had always managed
to talk myself out of it on the grounds of expense; actually
the truth was far closer to the fact that I was afraid.
As we each drew our picture it was done in a state of
deep thought – back to the day dreaming, meditation
technique – imagining that it was as we wished it to be.

These cards were then exchanged by the thousand plus participants and placed stuck with duct tape to a picket fence around an enclosed field. The participants then went to the field and applied our blindfolds and with specific breathing techniques, to assist our powers of total concentration on our subject – in fact to the extent of entering an altered state of consciousness which in fact is what day dreaming can be – spent the next hours attempting to find our personal card.

As my mobility was so limited I stayed on the outside of the field and sat under a large oak tree and meditated. I mentally landed my helicopter over and over again. After the exercise my helicopter card was exactly where I had landed it in my meditation.

This alone was a most incredible and wonderful experience, even though I tried to convince myself it was a coincidence but when I returned to Wales a few days later and Richard picked me up and brought me home from the airport it became even more incredible.

Sitting on the lawn of the Hotel was a real, live helicopter. I asked the pilot if he would give me a ride – explaining my unusual story and explaining that if I could manifest this then I could manifest anything.

'Absolutely not,' he replied, 'I never give rides.' Later that night he approached me and said,

'I won't give you a ride but tomorrow morning I have to lift over the Hotel to the Bowser to refuel. It's not a ride it's only a lift, OK?' Oh yes, that was certainly OK.

Next morning the rain was sleeting horizontally, the cloud was down to your knees. The phone rang, the lift was off. The pilot had rung the Coastguard and the Met Office and they had told him to hunker down he wouldn't be going anywhere for at least twenty four hours. The rally car racing might continue but his filming of it would not. I got out the card I had made and found it was crudely drawn and the helicopter didn't have a tail! I drew in a tail, focused intently and blew those clouds away.

The phone rang.

'If you get round here – immediately, you can have your lift!' The Met Office had rung and given the pilot a fifteen minute window of clarity to fly out. Richard rushed me round – still in my slippers and they pushed me into the back seat (the front was loaded for single occupancy weight for travel) two minutes round the Caravan Park and back. I disembarked and the pilot flew off.

I floated two feet above the ground back into the hotel kitchen. Where family and staff drank tea and chattered about my luck. After a few moments I said,

'I can hear a helicopter.' Many

'Oh be quiets, you've had your ride.' were forthcoming. I insisted twice more, until the helicopter landed back on the lawn. As the pilot walked towards the Hotel he shook his fist at me,

'I've got twenty five years flying experience and I can't get out of this valley – you are a witch, it only cleared to give you your ride!' At about 9.00 pm that night our doorbell rang.

'Hi.' said the pilot, smiling, 'I think you owe me a drink.' He spent a couple of hours, along with Richard depleting our whisky and then said,

'Can someone pick you up in Welshpool tomorrow?'

'Well, I can, I'm the taxi driver/facilitator. Why?' said Richard.

'Be ready at 8.00 am tomorrow morning and I'll fly you to Welshpool.'

I hardly slept, the next morning dawned, blue sky and wall to wall sunshine. I sat in the front with the clear bubble of the helicopter above and below me. A twenty five minute flight of sheer heaven.

I stress that this was not to prove that we can have anything we desire – be careful what you ask for you might get it syndrome, but to prove that at some deep level and with the right creative thought process we do have a direct influence on our environment and hence our place in the world. Beware of some of the new instant manifestation books, they can be based on greed. I want it and I want it now! This is not the way to work towards a world of peace, tolerance and equality.

The reason behind telling this story is that deprived of our normal senses of sight and touch it is possible to achieve the most amazing things and this challenges the very thought that deprivation of a sense can mean that that person requires healing and is not whole in some way. My experience proved to me that I was in some inexplicable way more focused and able to influence my experience when my senses were compromised and my thoughts were given free reign to be creative and access other ways of communicating with the life process.

I am often asked what have you done to help yourself? Many things I have talked about already. Homeopathy – which did help – but all these years I have not found anyone who could balance the pain of the RA and the difficulty with swallowing. If the pain and mobility improved then the swallowing would deteriorate causing severe nutrition and hydration problems; if the swallowing improved then the pain and immobility became too much to cope with. A balance seemed impossible to strike.

Early on in my difficulties I was challenged to look beyond this life time for reasons of illness. We attended one unusual meeting in Spain and when we arrived there was a gentleman channeling. He was an ex builder, swore like a trooper, drank like a fish and smoked like a chimney. I took this to think it might be a fun evening.

As he went into trance, his face changed completely into that of a very old Chinese man – the transformation was unbelievable except that we all saw it. He pointed at me and said to my surprise,

'Okay, I was hoping you'd ask for a psychic reading but as you didn't I'll tell you anyway – we've been together in a past life and in that past life we were monks together and your job was to care for the sick, for the profoundly sick and ill, suffering from pain and various degrees of illness in various forms.

Nobody could fault the way you cared for these people,' he said 'and this time round you have chosen to experience what they experienced so that you would know what you had done for them.'

I sat there thinking I don't know whether I like that! That wasn't a very good choice this time, was it? But he was convinced I needed to experience what I'd seen in others, and I needed not only to experience their pain and suffering, so I knew what I had done for them, but I had to adapt to the caring of myself by other people, rather than what I had strived for, complete independence. This has taken all these years to try to get anywhere close to and I am still working on it. My life as I have already said is full of 'what ifs?' I don't and never have needed to have answers but potentials and possibilities fascinate me.

Richard and I had studied and acquired the teachings of Reiki I and II, a form of spiritual healing. As a follow up I arranged to attend the Mind, Body and Spirit Conference for a workshop with Matthew Manning, known as Europe's greatest healer.

The venue was packed and not the easiest environment for a wheelchair. The only place to be was at the front in order to see anything. Matthew welcomed us and opened his workshop by asking if anyone had a bad shoulder. He wished to use this person as a demonstration model for his healing technique.

I couldn't raise my arms without using one hand to push the other and elevate it.

'Yes, what are you troubled with?' asked Matthew. When I told him he apologised and explained that I was 'too bad'. He could do little to help in a twenty minute demonstration session with such an entrenched and long term, severe illness. He asked others and started again.

'OK, no luck, so far. Anyone with a bad knee?' Up went my hand again along with the others.

'Not you, I've already explained.' Matthew said, a little confused that I was still trying.

He asked for anyone with other parts of the body, still trying to find someone who fit the bill. As my hand went up for the third time, he looked at me intently.

'What makes you think I'm going to choose you, after so many refusals?'

I didn't expect the response I got to my following reply,

'Because I've been visualising it for the last six weeks.'

The noise that came from Matthew sounded to me to be a groan.

'Sorry folks, it has to be her.'

After the demonstration there was no miraculous cure but I felt lighter, relaxed, something had happened that even now I cannot explain. As I left the stage area Matthew quietly said I must contact him as he thought he could help me and as Matthew doesn't offer 'cures' as such, I felt that this was very positive. For the next two years I rang and I rang but the response from Matthew's secretaries was always the same.

'Matthew is very busy. He is only able to see terminally ill children, or terminally ill parents.'

Three days after the PEG feeding tube was fitted Richard came to the hospital carrying a letter. It contained an appointment to see Matthew in two weeks time. What a coincidence, after all this time for it to happen now when I was so severely ill and weak was truly remarkable The appointments had to be delayed for a couple of months until I was well enough to make the journey. In fact I found it was not co-incidence, my sister had written and it was her letter that Matthew responded to. To this day I do not know what was in that letter that caused Matthew's response.

Self help had so far incorporated treatment with a homeopath, Terry and aromatherapy massage from his wife, Andy. After treatment we went for a meal. Anthony was working in a Bistro in Shrewsbury and he would be our chef. As we sat in the crowded bar area, Terry, the homeopath said,

'I can't find my glasses. Have you got them, Andy?' Andy looked in her handbag confirming to everyone their marriage, in those days partnerships were less common than today so when Andy looked in her handbag it declared a definite marriage. She couldn't find them and said so. Naïve as ever I added,

'When we'd finished Terry I remember seeing them on the bed (massage/consulting bed).' Mouths dropped and people moved away at the thought of these 'loose' couples in their midst. It was during this meal that I had one of the most frightening choking fits I can remember. I had left the table and was in a very bad way clinging on to a chair as I began to black out. Anthony was about to dial

999 when something cleared and I was able to at least get enough breath to stop me from fainting. It took some time to recover my composure and the lovely meal was left untouched.

Self help from others involvement included friends in Spain who had built a large Dome shaped building. It was built to be of the highest acoustic standard. They were both musicians and also practiced toning and chanting.

They were working on what they called sonic massage where the participants are flooded, enveloped with sounds of musical instruments and the human voice. They invited Richard and I to be their first guinea pigs. We settled down in the most acoustically acceptable position on the floor, laid on sleeping bags and covered in rugs for warmth.

The music started, along with the voices of both Michelle and Nestor. The instruments ranged from piano, guitar, wood and wind and even didgeridoo. I have never experienced anything so profound. Its effects produced the following words, which came in the night. They only just begin to touch on that musical experience.

Michelle and Nestor, Thank you.

My first introduction to Sonic Massage, The Dome, Alcalali, 20 January 1998

Like a bride in waiting bedecked by flowers,
I wait in anticipation the harvest that showers.
No habitual thoughts now interfere,
Only ultimate peace and a space so clear.
My senses are heightened and honed so fine,
My body is a physical vehicle, no longer mine.
I am no longer rippled, purely a ripple.
The human element has disappeared,

No longer noticed, just distantly weird
The lights dim down, the stage is cleared,
A passion play waits to be played out.
A tinkling bell rings and a cymbal shouts.
A rushing wind rents and opens a door
For me to pass through as I lose sense of the floor.
No longer do I belong to flesh and blood of man,
I drift in an ocean of feeling as only the disembodied can.
The angel of sound is calling as I journey out in space,
Leaving the blue/green planet to visit another place.
A place of no-time, no-where,
beyond and before such things.
I travel afar so quickly, no time, no thought, no wings.
I integrate slowly and realise nowhere
is the now – here prize.
A gift come down from heaven accepted by the wise.
I dive into space with intrepid desire,
A confidence found in an acrobatic flyer.
My senses reel and I catch my breath.
The personality undergoes its own mock death.
The angel of sound is calling as the instruments massage
my soul,
And way in the distance the wind sings, acknowledging
his mighty role.
A massage of soul and body, the entrance
to a state of bliss.
The rain-stick pattering softly, each patter a gentle kiss.
I think I'm back from the realms of deep space, as the
cymbal crashes its sound,

But it echoes from miles away and reverberates
round and round.

For the first time ever I understand the definition,

Sensational experience has achieved the mission.

The angel of sound is smiling as she plays
her cosmic notes.

I lay in the reverberation as each sound around and
through me floats.

The drums and voices mingle and softly join the song,

And the singing bowls respond again
to the contact of the gong.

Angel of sound is calling as I float and heal in sound.

The universe is with me as resonance abounds.

I have no start, I have no end, the Earth and I are one,

No boundaries or divisions too strong to be undone.

Listen, listen with every cell,

Listening is beyond the hearing of the bell.

Hearing is passive and not always true,

But listening is active and all is new.

Many a human has gone astray,

Requiring a guide to show him the way.

Immersed and enveloped in sound wave patterns

Sound guides his return on a cycle like Saturn's,

Inspiring the chance to start anew,

Altering precepts out of the blue.

Concepts of matter, of time and of space,

Alchemically meld into Alchemists' base.

The angel of sound is calling, it's time to return to me,

But the gift that she has given is to know
that 'I' am 'She'.

My daughter-in-law once overhead me say that I was not afraid of dying and she asked me,

'Do you really mean that? That you are not afraid of dying?" Bless her, she challenged me into analysing what I had said. Yes, of course I am afraid of the process of dying as everyone is, I assume, but actually being dead holds no fear. If we just end, dust to dust, then there is no fear because we won't know anything about it. If there is life after, then I believe heaven and hell in the old fashioned terms are not imposed by some outside force but self imposed so that we can judge ourselves, learn from that and move on. If life after death is entering another dimension, spirit based and bodiless, then I have everything to gain.

I have a number of experiences of being bodiless. I needed to have an endoscopy (camera up my nose and down my throat) not a pleasant experience for anyone but my past experiences meant I was very frightened of the consequences. The doctor packed my nose with cotton wool soaked in cocaine. Because of my vegetarian diet, alcohol free and healthy I was very easily affected by drugs, smoke, perfume etc. I laid down on a hospital trolley bed whilst the anaesthetic effect took hold. The nurse in charge was fearsome. She obviously took no pleasure in her job and was aggressive and unpleasant with the patients, particularly so with me, as the doctor had requested this procedure at the last minute when she thought she was finished for the morning and she grumbled incessantly about the extra time and extra sterilising that she would need to carry out. I can remember feeling very hot and full headed and Richard tells me he called her to come and look at me with my beetroot red face.

"Are you alright Mrs Rhodes? I hope you are not going to cause a fuss when I'm busy.'

'Oh no,' I replied, I'm fine, both of us are.' Richard said her face was something to behold.

'The one here in the bed is very relaxed, a bit hot, but very relaxed. But the one up there in the corner of the room ....' And this apparently came out rather menacingly 'is watching every move you make. So just be careful.' It cured the grumbles I have to say but someone so disgruntled and unsuited to her job could not be cured long term unfortunately.

Meditation is another way to experience being out of body, alongside such things as astral travel, deliberate drug use – other than medicinal, shock and trauma following an accident, and near death experience, this I had experienced as a child.

How often do people, medical professionals included, talk about panic attacks as if they are just in the mind. I wonder how often they relate the difference between mental and physical attack. A mentally induced panic attack can be brought on by a mild hysteria, fear or inability to cope, causing hyperventilation, inducing panic attacks, but there is another more physical cause. I have discovered and experienced that the human body is designed to survive! If something threatens that survival such as choking, then the body's defenses kick in, the adrenaline pumps, the chemicals flow, the flight or fight responses come into action. These physical reactions then cause the mental response to activate creating a circle of threat and fear. Which comes first, the chicken or the egg? Its no good saying,

'Don't panic.' Try telling a room full of people not to look at the blue giraffe with the purple spots as it passes the window and I can guarantee that they will all look at the window. I use Clary Sage aromatherapy oil, which when inhaled helps to release muscle tension and calm the panic response until the life threatening situation comes to an end.

I now have the knowledge that I am not my body. I have qualities of emotion, desire, intellect within me but they are not me. What am 'I' then? What is my essence? What am I if I remove these qualities? I believe from experience that what remains is a centre of pure being. This spiritual centre is what carries out the observing and the responses. My body may be tired, it may be sick, it may find itself in different conditions of health, sickness, financial stability or instability, or relationships, but none of this is who 'I' am. My body is precious, it is my vehicle of experience and action in order to live in the physical world and I must treat it with respect in order to fulfill my role in this physical form but it is not all that I am.

'Once 'I' accept this then I can begin to take control of all those things that can dominate my life. I can direct them and use them as allies and know that 'I' am the centre of control, the centre of consciousness. Suffering is experienced as a threat to what I am. It threatens to diminish and in the end destroy my personal identity. It forces me to become less and less the person I once knew and felt myself to be until I cease to be that person at all. ..... turning the threat into a promise, means what would otherwise destroy me becomes the very means by which I am created. .... Instead of becoming less myself by suffering, I become more myself. Instead of ceasing to live because of what I suffer, I live more deeply, more fully because of it. .... Victory over suffering by its acceptance – not the passive acceptance of hopeless resignation, but the active acceptance of one who has been willing to receive her suffering and absorb it and thus make it contribute powerfully to what she is" True Resurrection Page 144, Author H. A. Williams.

I read this book in 1991 and knew that this had been and to this day is still my philosophy and the way I try to cope.'

Let's move on from out of body and life after death and reincarnation experiences to something I have found even more profound and inspirational. That is the time between lives. A friend gifted me two books by Michael Newton PhD in which the author charts thirty years experience as a hypnotherapist working with clients who spontaneously presented details of the time between lives. This was my epiphany – now I knew where I had come from.

Very early memories are those of knowing I had been delivered into a human body on this earth in error, and I really belonged on a different planet in a different form. Only this could explain the harsh colours, lacking spiritual subtlety, the harsh noises that upset the equilibrium and the crude way in which humans communicated with the misunderstandings of language, body language, words that didn't mean what they said.

Education didn't offer me what I craved, it was crude, just facts to memorise, where was the creativity, the understanding, the melding of souls to exchange the true meanings of each subject? History – I hated it – what is it? It is His Story – not the truth, only the interpretation of one person's viewpoint, and that, certainly in history was a male, patriarchal viewpoint. Now that I am writing My Story I realise how difficult it is to draw back memories and My Story has revealed itself as a Mystery.

As I read these books about life between lives, I remembered what it was I had been missing. Instant manifestation of thought – how careful would we be if this was true in our present physical form? Instant communication without the possibility of misunderstanding or not telling the whole story. Humour – real humour – not at someonelse's expense or negative situations. Learning, of the highest order, held in temples of crystal. Everything I had always felt was somehow missing in our earthlife. One interviewee talks about buildings of ice, which look like ice but are crystal which reminded me of a dream I had which I have never fully interpreted, but is so like the description given by this person.

My dream memory starts with a little girl, and two other girl children, and for some reason she was encouraging a particular person (one of the other children) to run across this stretch of gardens and I knew it was for the pleasure of being able to strike this person down until they weakened. So we set off, three of us, and I was aware what was going to happen and in some strange way was able to control the situation. As we ran through these gardens we appeared to have the ability to fly ((this was taped during the early hours of the morning and at this word I took a shuddering intake of breath as though taking off, quite startling on the recording) short distances over the hedges and things and round and round and about. So I worked the whole situation so that the person who was in danger, but had no face, no personality, I did not know who it was, was protected.

By the time we ran the course, so to speak, this young girl who had set out with the intention of not destroying but overcoming the other child was herself in a state of complete exhaustion and collapsed in a heap beneath a small bush and it was fairly obvious, by this time, that she was not going to recover. She was surprised and devastated by the fact that the plan had gone wrong and had completely turned the tables on her and here she was, sitting there, unable to do anything about it as she sank into her own 'death'.

Watching this happen were two brothers and somehow they had summoned the mother. As the Mother came out of the top floor of a house and began to descend a long, external wooden staircase, watching the whole situation from afar as she did so, she stopped because as she was watching us, the two brothers and I, down came a white cloud shaped like an enormous rectangular blanket. It came down, rolled around the lifeless form of the child, and disappeared from whence it came. We found the child sitting on a white/grey pony and she had turned into a most beautiful 'snow child' dressed as a child would be dressed for the cold frosty weather (which it was there in the area in which she was sitting – but we were quite warm), She was dressed beautifully, as in a multi-million pound film set, in silver and blue, with white fur trimmings and the pony in matching trappings.

In the distance appeared another grey/white pony with a young boy dressed in the same manner. He was riding the grey/white pony down towards her. His pony had two saddles and the one in front of him was empty. The two ponies came very beautifully and majestically together and the boy stood still on his as the girl approached. She said, quite haughtily,

'You needn't think I am going with you on that saddle. My pony is an identical twin to yours and it can take me to the village just as easily by following as by giving up my pony and coming on to your saddle.'

I can't remember what he said but something transpired which made the snow girl change her mind and she got on to the empty saddle in front of the snow boy. They made a very beautiful scene. One of the brothers was saying,

'We can't be angry, we can't even cause any aggression or disturbance over this because what we have seen now is all too beautiful'. You could see that the Mother by this time was in total acceptance of what was happening and the two snow children on the grey/white pony went off past everybody in this, not cold, yet scene of crisp white snow and frost.

They were walking off towards the village that the young girl had mentioned. The words of the brother were,

'It is obviously right that she is going and it is obviously the second time that this has happened to her because she knew where she was going and was happy to go.' How very beautiful she looked, exquisitely dressed, exquisitely formed in this child like manner and when she joined the boy on the pony, although the three remained separate entities, they were so intertwined and so fluid in their movements together they actually were one.

As I sat on the side lines I remember thinking, with a certain amount of heartache, that I had brought this about and stopped evil from happening to the other party and turned it back against itself. So this minor portion of guilt and hurt in my heart had to handle the fact that by turning this evil, however minor it had been, back against itself had transpired/transformed into this very beautiful scene.

My interpretation of the dream seemed fairly obvious to me but I could not explain the frost or symbol of snow children and yet I knew this to be significant. Two days later, however I came across this from Paramahansa Yogananda's book How can You Talk with God?

'It satisfies a deep need in our hearts to think that God may take a human form and come to us and talk with us. Why doesn't he do it for everyone? Many saints have heard the voice of God. Why can't you?

Thou O Lord, art invisible, impersonal, unknown and unknowable; yet I believe that by my devotions frost, Thou cans't be 'frozen' into a form. God can be persuaded to take a personal form by your intense devotion.'

Had I somehow broken through the veils and been given a key to life after death, or even life between lives?

Chapter Twenty-Two

Plas Dolguog – Destiny Threatened

When we were confronted with purchasing Plas Dolguog we had nothing to sell. In other words we had no financial input and therefore had to use the Caravan Park and our home as collateral for a second mortgage. Both of these were in both our names, with life insurance to cover. Upon purchasing Plas Dolguog the Bank decided, due to my poor health and prognosis, I could not be part of the transaction, Richard being the only name on the Deeds, contracts and loans. This was a bit shattering, I was only in my early forties and yet again the prognosis for my life was being questioned.

We had big plans to turn the Estate into a small but superb holiday complex. Privately owned wood built chalets, an extension to the Grade II listed Hotel building and a separate small health and fitness suite and swimming pool. At that time the town didn't have a swimming pool and our idea was to open it to the local people.

We needed a large loan and backing and became involved with a large well known banking group who could find money lenders. We had meetings galore with these people. Money was no object, driving top of the range cars, wearing designer suits and treating Richard and I like royalty. At the time these lenders seemed to get the idea that I was the money and Richard the physical player in this game, and it certainly was a game. (Perhaps they thought why would anyone stay with a wheelchair bound woman unless it was money.) Richard and I had great fun cultivating this because as they were running round this – they thought – moneyed lady, Richard had time to think and keep a straight head with the figures that were being banded about. We have always said that any success in business that we have had was because Richard did the sums and I did the spelling!

After one of these meetings the Company who had found the Lenders informed us that we must pay a certain amount in order to release the main body of this loan and to cover paperwork expenses. This was years before it became a popular scam and even our financial advisors did not pick up the threat. Richard and I were not happy with this arrangement and made enquiries through our Bank. The name of the Bank which was offering the loan appeared genuine, a well known name but on close scrutiny turned out to be something similar to a cloned Bank. All the grants from the Tourist Board and various other financial arrangements had been put in place without any queries on their part as to their lender's integrity, but these ceased to be available upon our learning that the loan was basically non existent. Where was their checking system to ensure financial integrity and viability to ensure everyone's protection? It seems Banks and financial people even then were not really up to dealing with looking after our money.

We picked ourselves up and put our optimistic plans on a back boiler and if the truth were known, the back of a dark cupboard. We progressed with the chalet development but even that was proving to be difficult. Eventually in order to get sales started we did what everyone was requesting which was for the chalet purchaser to buy the Freehold. We had hoped not to sell the land as a wise farmer once said,

'Don't sell your land as they don't make any more'. This at last allowed the development to progress and secure our ability to cover our financial repayments on our debt.

After Anthony left to go to University with Tina, and Gary and Sharon had stepped in as Managers, we, Richard and I, continued to play our role covering the hours that needed covering at the hotel. The economic climate of the country took a downturn and the Bank decided that Plas Dolguog Hotel was now worth one fifth of what they had valued it at originally. An overnight drop of this huge amount meant that our loans were no longer covered. Our only option was to sell up and pay off the debt as best we could but Hotels, Pubs, Restaurants were closing down all over the country and we had little hope of a sale to cover our debt.

The Bank were pushing and pushing and daily harassing me to sign a particular document. This document it turned out was to release my partnership on the Caravan Park and our home. Their original arrangement not to insure me on the purchase of Plas Dolguog left them with a hold on the Caravan Park and our home. What they had neglected to take into account was that that collateral was diminished by 50 per cent due to my partnership, leaving them in the predicament of only having a hold on the other, Richard's 50 per cent.

We did have a prospective buyer and thought we might just survive without going bankrupt, but that was not to be. Fortunately my Welsh was good enough to understand when this family discussed between themselves, in the Welsh language, their strategy. Unfortunately for them they did not take the trouble to realise that their discussions, in my presence, were not as private as they thought, and their manoeuverings were far from acceptable.

We had no option but to go ahead with the prospective sale, having given ourselves a few quiet moments where we acknowledged our belief that Plas Dolguog had a destiny. We were, it would appear, not part of that destiny. So, in a little private ceremony, we formally released it to the Universe in order for it to fulfill its potential in the future.

The Bank gave us two weeks to sort matters out after which they said they would 'pull the rug from under our feet'.

I thought I ought to warn our parents in case the worst happened. Mummy was very sympathetic and concerned and kept repeating that she would pray that we would find the money to keep us going.

'Please, don't do that Mummy.' I begged her. 'Promise me you won't do that.' She was confused.

'Why not? Surely that would be the answer?'

'Yes it would' I said 'but I only know of one way that could happen and be sure to solve our financial problems.'

'Well what's that?' she asked, still confused. My answer silenced us both. 'If Richard where to die the insurance would cover everything. You must be careful what you ask for, as you might get it.'

We had discussed with Gary and Sharon the possibility of their leasing the Hotel but had not been able to agree figures. They couldn't afford the Lease and we couldn't afford to drop our figure. As the sale was falling through, due to the purchasers extra demands, dramatically lowering their original offer and our bankruptcy looming nearer and nearer, we talked again and came to an agreement with Gary and Sharon. They leased the Hotel for some ten years and during that time we were just able to keep our heads above water and service our debts. Certainly better than bankruptcy.

Anthony and Tina after finishing University had spent a year in Australia with the idea of emigrating. Again, the Universe had other ideas and their return meant they were back in Machynlleth when Gary and Sharon decided to move on. Anthony and Tina took over the Hotel with our guidance and all our mutual enthusiasm and hard work. As time has gone by Anthony and Tina have both taken the Hotel from strength to strength. The hotel is now a focal point for weddings, and local anniversaries and functions and is a credit to them both for the dedicated energy and commitment that they have shown.

The hotel and garden complement each other, as people visiting the garden use the hotel facilities and the people staying at the hotel enjoy the garden.

So in June 2002, having been at the Caravan Park for twenty six years, and then leaving to allow Edward and Michelle to take over, we built a new retirement bungalow.

The house as usual was a self build, although Richard was not as young as he had been he was still highly involved in overseeing and managing the work, not to mention laying the odd mixer load of cement or concrete. It was designed to be fully wheelchair user friendly and my involvement was my pet theme of conservation and sustainability researching this to our advantage. This new home gave us the opportunity to walk our talk and incorporated some pretty modern ideas.

Through these systems we have achieved a high level of sovereignty with regard to sustainable and renewable energy use within our home. Apart from the saving to the planet Richard is tickled pink with his free energy, especially when he can go into the basement and see all the dials telling him what is being produced, not only during the day but over the weeks and months. We were quite surprised to discover that all our LED lights (check out how many little green or red lights you have running around your home) from computers, TV, video, cooker, fridge, freezer, power sockets, fire alarms, amounted to approximately forty pence per day in financial terms and even worse in environmental terms. I remember reading somewhere that if all LED lights were switched off we in the UK could close down two power stations. This was all those years ago how much would those lights cost today?

A ground loop, placed a metre and a half down, collects heat from the ground (which in the UK is usually a constant 10 degrees C) and through a heat exchanger raises that to heat our hot water and provide heat for under floor heating for the whole house. A bank of photovoltaic cells produces electricity, enough to power the pumps and working parts of this system and for our lighting and power requirements, which of course are all low energy.

Our personal Kyoto target levels were way above the line producing up to 90 per cent of our yearly energy usage. Our carbon footprint for running our home is minimal. Originally it was forecast it would take twenty years to pay off our grant aided outlay. In fact because of the rise in electricity costs and the fact that it is more efficient than first anticipated we have paid it off in seven years.

By 2007 the Conservatory at the Hotel was leaking like a sieve so grants were applied for to renovate, refurbish, rebuild. The new room is now such a beautiful room with a slate roof alleviating the problem of being too hot on a sunny day and too cold on a cold day. The design of exposed oak beams give it the feel of truly belonging to the old house and the roof incorporates balconies to the bedrooms above overlooking the Snowdonia National Park just half a mile away.

This new function room allowed us to incorporate a special room The Stone Room. After all these years, the monolith that had played such an important part in all the happenings could take its rightful place as a focal point of attraction.

It was wonderful to be able to bring this to life and create a space that could be used on so many different levels. A quiet space to read a book, to sit in and reflect in thought, to clear one's mind, to meditate at a deeper level, all of these processes giving time to quiet the mind, relax and refresh, a space of tranquility and spiritual rest and evolution The Stone Room.

Chapter Twenty-Three

Creativity – It's Effects on Healing

Matthew asked me for my thoughts on this subject and his enquiry brought forth the following. What is it to have a creative thought? What is it to perform a creative act? Firstly I have to decide what creativity is and then ask a more important question, what is healing? Does healing mean that if I am an amputee missing a limb and it regrows again, making me physically whole again then I am considered healed? No, healing is different, it is not the same as curing. What I do know is that if an individual has a debilitating or deforming illness and is able to overcome the pain barrier thus stepping 'out of the box' and defeating the normal bodily response to pain and debilitation then this makes it easier for that individual to step 'out of the box' on other levels.

One of the ways we step out of the box is our ability to dream – day dream, thought dream, enter a world beyond the confines of the body where nothing is impossible and all knowledge and inspiration is housed. This is known as the morphogenetic field, the cosmic consciousness, the akashic records and many other explanations of the field of energy that can be accessed through meditation, deep thought, day-dreaming. And when we allow ourselves to do this we rise above our physical barriers. We choose to do this, as choosing to do nothing is the same as allowing the bad things to proliferate.

When we start the thought process of a creative project, and this need not be a big project – one of mine for instance is to make greetings cards, painting, decoupage, all manner of unique designs, whatever the mood demands, we begin to channel our energy into that thought process instead of other thoughts which may have been controlling our lives to that point. We find that the tools required to carry out our creative process such as artistic ability and physical strength become secondary. The creative energy does not have a specific structure within it, it is our thought processes that bring forth the manifestation of the creative thought process. Without thought there is nothing – No-Thing.

Creativity is not restricted to fields of artistic ability such as painting, singing, playing an instrument even planting and designing a garden. Creation is the most powerful energy in the universe. Creation is the energy that creates worlds. For instance what can compare with the creation of another living being?

There comes a point within our dreaming and creative thought process that we realise that something wants to be expressed and the activity that follows is a direct response to the inner workings of the mind. I was once told that the greatest asset to life was to have an attitude of gratitude. In other words it is the way that we look at the world and our place in it that creates our reality.

An illness or disability, I know this is true for me, prevents one from living life as one has always lived it. In other words we have to start again, to learn to grieve for the person we once were and accept the person we have become or are becoming. Once this difficult process has been gone through then we can become open to our new talents, however simple we perceive these to be.

The world does not require everyone to excel as a painter, a singer, mountain climber, how boring would that be if we all had the same talent? What it does demand however, in order to continue and expand the great adventure of life is that we use our creativity. Some spiritual beliefs talk of being co-creators, I believe that we only have to go back to the example of reproduction, even to the way the world has developed (for better or worse) to know that we are in fact, without being blasphemous, co-creating – extending, probing, pushing the limits and being on the cutting edge of new understanding and technology in every field, to understand that co-creation is true. We are the means by which the great adventure continues to fulfill its potential whether we like it or not.

The only way to overcome illness or physical impairment is to learn, for at least some of the time, to be creative for creations sake, not for necessity or financial gain. When we can access this way of thinking – in fact way of being, why else are we called Human Beings? – then a new potential for healing opens to us. Most Humans have abandoned the Being side of our nature and become Human Doings in order to survive, put bread on the table at the end of the week, purchase the latest gadget, have a better house or car than our neighbour. This is not creativity but merely the need to prove to ourselves that we can fill the hole in our emotional and spiritual welfare through possessions. Unfortunately for most all that happens is that we take a long time discovering that this is not the case.

True creativity is carried out in a spirit of joy and love for the process and the project upon which we have embarked. If we are creative, if we create, then there will be a creation and as we indulge that creative process we are closer to the Creator, whatever or whoever we perceive that to be. Creation is the opposite of destruction. If every act of destruction were replaced with an act of creation what would our world be like? Instead of bombs, construction. Instead of poverty and massive greed, equality?

At a personal level all the above apply to my present physical, mental and spiritual well-being. By most peoples' standards I am not healed and that again raises the question of what is healing? By many standards, including the medical profession, I should not still be alive. In fact I am alive and kicking, albeit within my limits of kickability! There are days when I am unable to overcome the effects of illness and disability but those days are spent in what I consider to be consolidation days. Time out to be spent allowing the body to do its own thing – to recharge and to relax knowing that I love it enough to listen to it when it needs to be heard. These days are spent resting, dozing – in fact daydreaming, often becoming highly involved in the creative process of a desire project and its outcome on a mental level.

Milton Erickson was qualified as a medical doctor and psychiatrist. He inspired the developers of Neuro Linguistic Programming through what they termed the Theory of Excellence. The theory of excellence entailed studying people who were experts in their field or subject, analyzing how they achieved their excellence and then teaching their techniques and disciplines to others. He is a legend in the field of hypnotherapy and one of the most effective psychotherapists ever. He was severely dyslexic, profoundly tone deaf and colour blind. At the age of seventeen he was paralyzed by a bout of life threatening polio. He lay in the living kitchen of his home on a bed, unmoving. When a sibling was born he spent his daily life watching the baby and in his mind mimicking its every move, over and over again. As I have said he went on to overcome the paralysis and become a great man.

Science is now proving that thinking about exercise is almost as effective as getting out there and performing it. I know that this has been true in my case, that my mental processes have played a big part in my ability to function at the level at which I am functioning at at present.

The creative process once it has moved from the realms of thought into manifestation then requires the physical ability to carry it through. Again I have found that whatever I have set my thoughts to can to some extent provide the means needed to accomplish those thoughts. People, gadgets, alternative ways of carrying out normal tasks suddenly present themselves, as though the Universe is saying yes to the process of creativity. If they do not present themselves then there is usually another thought process that allows an adaptation of the original.

Once the process begins, for instance with regard to Grandma's Garden, then it develops a mind of its own. I found, having applied for a grant, that plans had to be drawn up, forms filled in, meetings attended and deadlines met. This necessitated a creative way of allocating, not so much time, as energy in order to fulfil all these requirements. But the advantage of all this was that I was meeting new people, new ideas, new environments, new ways of looking at things, and examining other peoples' ideas and suggestions to combine or reject. All this had the effect of stimulating and enhancing my own creative process and confronting me with the need to discover the passion to find others who could do the things I could not and who could do those things on my behalf

A major effect of this is that whilst the mind is occupied with so many new, exciting and challenging things there is little time left for sitting in a huddle. It is easy to sit in a huddle contemplating the pain, the impairment, the tiredness and the unfairness of life. Which brings me to another point – my paternal grandfather used to say to me,

'I felt sorry for myself because I had no shoes – and then I met a man who had no feet.' The old saying that there is always someone worse off is so true. People find it very difficult to understand that I do not and have not eaten for ten years. If I was told that I could eat and drink anything immediately but I would have to lose my sight – there would be no contest! I am nourished and privileged to live somewhere that has been able to feed me in an alternative way. That cannot be said for two thirds of the world's population who go to bed hungry at night. I believe if you were to ask a blind person the same question in reverse the response would be the same. We adjust to life as we experience it whatever the challenge

My experience of healing then is one of challenge. Who is the healer and who is the healed? A physically whole and healthy body is not necessarily the manifestation of a person who is healed, nor is a less than physically healthy body the manifestation of someone who needs healing. From our three dimensional perspective we judge what is and what is not right and wrong. My interaction, of people with a visual, hearing, sense, mental or physical impairment has proved to me that these people can be the most balanced, happy and free thinking souls that I have ever had the pleasure to meet.

However, I cannot leave it at that because I also know that the healing process can be helped or hindered by other influences. As humans we are not yet all powerful and cannot always overcome external influences of other energies connected to our environment, other people and information and knowledge.

Certain people have the ability to work with others for their higher good. This may or may not include healing. One of these people is Matthew Manning. Without his help and intervention I would not be writing this. I do not begin to understand the energy which he has the power to transmit but do know that it is one of the most powerful and creative that humans know of. My three monthly visits 'hold my head above water' and allow me to muster the energy and thought process, mentally and spiritually to keep that boost running until my next visit.

After the first visit and session with Matthew and as we were travelling home I said to Richard,

'I do not feel any better, in fact I am absolutely exhausted, but at some level I feel as though a switch has been either turned on or turned off, and at some very deep level I am changed and am changing.' This was the beginning of a process that lasted three days and lifted me out of a depression, what I considered to be a clinical depression, caused by my situation. I needed to come to terms with being fed through a tube, overcoming the long standing malnutrition, and the difficulties associated with the pain of the RA extending over so many years and aggravated by the lack of nutrients, not to mention the hospital acquired infections and hospital environment and attitude.

From that day I have continued to rise above the challenges that confront us on a daily basis, whether we – in conventional terms – are healthy or not, and still continue that dramatic improvement in well-being. When I asked the doctor, five years after the PEG was fitted, for my prognosis her reply was,

'You see Diana, you are an anomaly, in our experience people being fed through a PEG feeding tube do not usually live as long as you have done and therefore we are treading new ground.'

This is a testimony to the help I have received from Matthew and others who have supported me on so many levels and I can only express my deep gratitude to who they are. Matthew allows people access to his remarkable gift of offering a way through which they can find a key to unlocking the potential within themselves and accessing a creative healing process that has the effect of enhancing life. The physical body is and can be empowered by a non-physical stream of energy – creative energy – that is what it is possible to harness and with which we can be empowered.

By being in harmony within the body, healing is achieved but harmony is not achieved by everyone in a choir singing the same note, nor by sitting back and not participating in life. It is achieved through realising that harmony and healing are found in stretching the boundaries of possibility, through accepting that members of a choir or orchestra all sing and play different notes to produce exquisite music. Each one balancing, contrasting, synchronising and most of all appreciating the existence of each separate note, that if that single note were played alone it may appear discordant but when included in the harmony becomes one pure focused, inspirational and joyous whole.

Imagination is the playground of the Gods. Do you think when a caterpillar spins its cocoon and awaits its emergence as a butterfly it spends that time holding onto the past, bearing grudges, remembering the struggle? I don't think so. I think it dissolves into a state of forgetfulness and allowing, where its beautiful potential can manifest. Are humans yet capable of following this example? Can we be creative and have the patience and integrity to become our magnificent potential?

Chapter Twenty-Four

The End or the Beginning
of Another Beginning?

When I was at school I was told that a story needed a beginning, a middle and an end. Well, I couldn't find a beginning; it just kept going further back beyond remembering. I certainly found a middle but am having trouble finding an end. Like the beginning I don't think there is one. Even the end as humans think of it, I know is not the end but just another beginning.

Another draw back to writing my story was knowing the criticism and different memories that would arise from those close enough to have their view of the past. I came to a final conclusion on this too; memories are not necessarily the truth as everyone sees it but in fact are the perceptions of those memories. We each have a different view point, a different perception and this is what I have tried to capture – my perception of the stories I remember.

I have also discovered other conclusions to my experiences. So here are some of those conclusions.

Quantum physics and quantum mechanics have proved that information processed by our minds influences the shape of the world in which we live. The observer affects the observed. How did the spiritual masters know this, we are still seeking absolute proof? And how does this affect our daily lives?

We all have challenges with which we have to cope, one of those is the challenge of financial issues.

Money isn't everything but it can certainly help along the way. At the point in our lives when we were facing bankruptcy, because of the Bank threatening foreclosure, I knew what it felt like to have the prospect of losing everything you have worked for put in jeopardy and life and family being left with no home, no income, no prospects. More and more people will face this in the economic climate we are in. Bank policy no longer being policy but idiocy where grown men (generally men) play games of chance and gamboling with what they seem to consider monopoly money.

Of course money does not exist. At one time the Federal Reserve in America and the Bank of England legally had to keep 5% gold bullion of the actual printed money out there. Money was printed with words that said if you present this paper money at the Bank you will be given the value printed on the paper in gold or silver. If everyone presented their money and requested the gold or silver, in other words if there was a rush on the Banks, only 5 per cent would be covered.

Governments, particularly I speak of USA and Britain, print money at will without any backing – quantitive easing in today's terms. And our then Chancellor Gordon Brown along with our then Prime Minister, Tony Blair, sold off our gold at rock bottom prices. In 1991 they sold the country's gold at a quarter of what it was worth in 2009. Three hundred and ninety five tonnes from the National Reserve at an average price of $279 per ounce. Even then a give away price. We have no backing for what most people think is money of value. Money is non-existent, it actually only exists on paper – computer printouts, moving figures, transferring 'money' from one account to another. The only value in the world is labour, the only commodity that can be exchanged at value. All other values are man-made, man decided and depend on the market

We do not need conspiracy theories to realize that when people can no longer pay back their loans, particularly mortgages, they go bankrupt. The banks then have the right to take possession of that wealth – homes, land and businesses. The poor get poorer and the Banks get richer. Unless of course they have just had the fun of a massive gamboling spree using wealth that was not theirs – it is ours or should I say was ours,

The founder of the Rothschild empire said,

'Give me control of a nation's currency and I care not who makes the law.' Ouch!

More and more alternative currencies are being set up around the world. These alternative systems are a form of IOU. There is no law against these currencies as at the end of the day they are just a mechanism of exchange. As individuals, the elderly or incapacitated for instance, may not be members of the mainstream economy any more but they do have skills and time, which in themselves, have value and in a credit crunch much of the population find themselves in the same situation.

An example of this alternative currency is LETS which can help to fill this gap. If I have got something that someone else may want, fresh eggs, baby sitting and someone else has something I want such as painting the living room or gardening, all we need to do is agree a 'price' before hand and an exchange can take place, involving perhaps a circle of people with tokens of a certain value but basically working on a barter system. The taxman at the moment has not yet worked out a way to tax these new currencies, so watch this space.

Money is not evil it is our means of exchange. These new currencies keep the 'money' flowing within the community. They build community, they respond to needs, they build families – not necessarily blood families, and help the poor. Big Business takes money out of the community, it has no remit to include the above, its remit is profit and expansion at the expense of local needs.

Why did Jesus turn over the tax collectors' tables? Because he and others considered usury theft. He may have turned the money lenders out of the temple but we all know they are well and truly back. The bible tells us that God condemned usury, Jesus in Luke 6.35 says,

'Lend, hoping for nothing in return.' And the Qur'an also forbids usury. Al Imran 3:130 says

'O you who believe! Eat not Riba (usury)' Even in modern times because both the bible and Qur'an can be read as forbidding usury, there will always be moral, as well as economic and social reasons for arguing about permitting lending at interest.

Controlling the unit of exchange controls the world and the wealth of the people of the world. I bet many of you, like me, thought that the Bank of England, The Federal Reserve, The Swiss National Bank, the European Bank, if only by inference of name were state/government owned. No, they are not, they are private corporations working for their shareholders and our Government on our behalf bailed them out – with our money – then they could pay their bonuses.

The value of money is not determined by being backed by gold or silver but is printed to cover nine times the value of customers' deposits. How about that, 90 per cent of money comes out of thin air! Borrowing begets borrowing because when money is restricted, by the banks of course, loans cannot be paid back as there isn't enough in circulation. Bang goes your home again.

I am no mathematician, you will have realized by now, and if I can work this out by reading and listening then everyone can and yet we all, the people, continue to agree to it, if only through our apathy and feelings of 'what can I do? It's not worth trying.'

Ultimately wealth must not be confused with possessions. Our obsession with possessions means that we are destroying our primary source of wealth, the earth. The need for non-renewable resources ranges from coal to rainforests. No oxygen, too much carbon equals no life. The oceans, the wetlands, the deserts, all contribute to the well being of the planet. They are part and parcel of our life support systems. Destroying our rainforests, pillaging our coal, oil and minerals may make economic sense but doesn't take into account the cost of the depletion. In many cases, if not all, depletion beyond recovery. These are priceless treasures that we do not pay for. They are not calculated in the overall cost of our craving for profit and possessions. Don't kid yourself, we, you and I, are responsible. Our attitude should be not just <u>who</u> I am but <u>how</u> I am.

Bhutan is a small Buddhist Himalayan country. They have made a collective decision, led by their King, to take a different route. Instead of working for the GDP, Gross National Product, they work for the GNH, the Gross National Happiness. As the King puts it –

'Without peace, security and happiness, we have nothing.' Schools around the country rotate teachers from urban to rural regions to be sure there is equal access to the best teachers. Hospitals give a choice, for non acute problems, of traditional or Western medicine, they have chosen conservation of natural resources and other non economic factors.

Although they themselves admit Bhutan is not a Shangri-La they are well on the way to achieving their aim. They are a country working with the Enlightenment theory of happiness, an expression of public good, public welfare and the contentment of the people and not totally focused on consumption, and production. They have discovered and implemented 'things are not prizes – truth is the prize'.

The second challenge is health and although this has already been fully covered in previous chapters I will make the following observation. Our health care systems are primarily disease-centred rather than focused on whole person healing, and until we return to the holistic approach and move away from the 'bit part' approach we will not be in a position to heal in the context of wholeness.

Richard's mother had a heart specialist, a cancer specialist, a bowel and bladder specialist. It was traumatic for her and anyone attending with her on hospital visits as none of them knew what the other consultants were doing or even what other consultants were using in the drug arsenal with the possibility of complications and interactions. They viewed the body as a machine with totally separate working parts. It isn't a great deal better today in many cases, despite the modern computer based technology, consultants will openly tell you that something is 'not their field'.

Richard's nephew became a paediatric doctor so that, he thought, he would have the opportunity to work with the whole child. It didn't take him long to discover that children's medicine is also governed by the 'bit part' method. He became an anaesthetist and pain relief consultant as this he felt was the only field left where he would be in a position to work with the whole person and use a holistic approach. It is not a coincidence that holistic is spelt differently to whole. Whole, holistic, holy, not just meaning the whole person but meaning holistic as in holy, close to creation/God.

Last but not least, in fact the biggest of them all is Relationships. Relationships, self to self, self to others, society, national, international, global and even space and beyond. You could think that was it, but it isn't. Relationships extend to things, possessions, needs, wants. They extend to the natural world, our relationship as individuals or collectively with animals, birds, insects, water creatures, the weather, the effects of the weather, buildings, open spaces, the rain forests, the elements, and on and on it goes.

Until and unless we accept the effect we each have on everything else, the way we speak, act, look, carry out our daily ways of living, and interpret the ways others behave, we cannot expect to understand why humanity is as it is. All this places life in context.

There has been a shift in social consciousness, a shift in language and thus in thought. It doesn't matter which comes first, one produces the other and the end result is this major shift in attitude. It is no longer politically correct to say 'disabled person', it is now correct to say 'person with a disability'. Guide dogs are now 'dogs for the visually impaired.' We have realised and are realising that the person comes first, the disability is way behind in second place. It goes back to the 'I' not being the body, the 'I' is superior in all respects to the body. We can spend a king's ransom on cosmetic surgery but 'I' will be no more or less beautiful.

I know that part of who I am is everyone I meet and everything I do, and that living in this very special and powerful energy centre in Wales amongst the generous spirited and kind hearted Welsh people has added to my being.

Wales thirty two years ago became our adopted country. From day one we called it home and now thirty some years later can truly feel that we have been adopted in return.

Let's suspend time for a moment and I'll tell you about Wales and our home Dolguog.

Wales is a small country on the western edge of Europe. Although a small country it has its own National Assembly, National Library, National University, National Museum, National Opera, National Botanical Garden and even a National Rugby team!

Come on a journey to a place of verdant green hills; blue/grey/turquoise rivers, glistening over slate river beds; to a land of myth and legend, warrior princes, King Arthur and Merlin; of swirling mists, sacred and pagan religions; castles, stone circles and huge monoliths. The place in question is Wales – the land of the in-between.

Continue your journey to a valley, known as the Lady's valley. In Christian terms, charming and acceptable. Upon research, however, this valley reveals another meaning. At the head of the valley is a settlement, Dinas Mawddwy, which translates as 'settlement of the confluence of two rivers, Maw = the river, ddwy = two. However, look at the word differently and read Mawdd. Mawdd was an ancient Goddess, nurturing, enveloping, the ultimate feminine, in fact known as the ultimate vagina. Indeed the valley resembles a birthing canal, with a womb at its head. In this valley is a residence, written history bears testament to a residence dating back to the 6th century.

Its name Plas Dolguog has been translated by historians as Cuawg's meadow, Plas = Hall or Palace, dol = meadow and Cuawg who was a 6th century warrior Prince.

In the Welsh language the beginnings of words mutate, thus dol = meadow and Guog = a mutated c, and over time the 'awg' had become altered, bastardised even, to 'og', was the explanation given by the academics. A local lady had another explanation. She had been receiving dreams and began to explore the name from the aspect of a linguist, free of convention. Without the need to 'make the name fit' she realised that 'cu' when mutated became 'gu' meaning benevolent or kind, and 'og' was an ancient God. The interpretation then became the meadow –'dol' of the kind 'cu' mutated to gu – (God) Og. Dol – gu – og.

Here we have the coming together of the male/female principle, the balancing of energies to complete the perfect whole linking and fusing in this valley.

Wales is the land of music and song – I don't need to remind the Welsh people that the Welsh language is the language of heaven! The children are groomed and encouraged from an early age to sing, to recite, to stand up and hold their own performing in the Urdd, the junior section of the Eisteddfodau, and having a self worth to know they count.

Have you noticed the difference when people talk to each other as opposed to when they talk at each other? It may sound insignificant but is in reality extremely significant.

Relationships are enhanced by the tradition from many parts of the world of realising that our Elders are a valuable part of our society. The land, the earth on which we live, in its original form is in its natural state. Connecting to nature is our opportunity to tune into the rhythms of the seasons, the months, weeks, days each hour of our daily lives. Through these connections we acknowledge the sacred trust, the need to balance the head and the heart in our actions and deeds.

By living more closely with nature we learn to live more harmoniously with each other. As in the less advanced or so called uncivilised society these poorer – materially that is – people are succoured and held together through family and family values, working and coping, sometimes through great hardship to survive within their social system.

Political power is inherent in each of us so we need to remember that Government is legitimized by the people collectively. It has no natural birthright. Before the Iraq war and during a time of economic collapse, President Bush found the time and felt the need to seal the records of the US Presidents, beginning with the Bush/Reagan era. An act never before carried out in America's Presidential history. During the London protest against the Iraq war, the Not in My Name million or more protesters were called anarchists and hippies by Prime Minister Tony Blair. As enquiries come and go and the extent of his and his governments manipulation becomes more clear and more proven, we know for sure that those middle aged hippies and anarchists were in fact those with firmly held beliefs in morality and integrity and the illegitimacy of a war founded on what appears to have been lies and deceit if not absolute poor judgement.

In 1998 the UN Development Programme's estimate for clean water and sanitation for everyone on earth was nine billion dollars extra. An additional twelve billion dollars would have fed and provided healthcare; twelve billion for reproductive health care; six billion dollars for education.

This forty billion dollars to sort out the world's problems could not be found and yet two hundred billion dollars could be found to build new F35JSF jets.

Even today depleted uranium weaponry is being used. There is nothing depleted about this weaponry it has left vast tracts of land in Iraq also Afghanistan unusable for centuries, the land will be contaminated for hundreds of millions of years.

I heard Marilyn Albright interviewed when she was Secretary of State, she was asked if she thought the deaths of four and a half thousand children a month under five years of age due to sanctions was worth it. She paused a little and then replied,

'It's a very hard choice, but we think the price is worth it.'

I won't tell you any more as this is enough to shock all of us as we sit by and watch the manouverings of war.

War under any guise is undisguised hatred. The world links of so many countries can bring so much more pressure to bear on rogue countries who threaten and posture until war is inevitable. We must look at the reaction to imposing sanctions where millions of children die and yet we continue to sell arms to the very countries to which we send aid. Common sense, which is not so common, must be brought back into politics and big business, and the gods of money and power restrained from the decision making of our future world.

We have an unprecedented responsibility. Historically we do not have records of being in a position before now where we have the nuclear power to annihilate the world sixteen times over. That responsibility is closely linked to our ability to feel comfortable, to remove conflict and aggression, to bring an end to violence, to see an era where war is obsolete. All this is difficult in a civilized country that is not at war how more so for the countries torn by hatred and religious fanaticism.

Peace is not just an absence of war. Peace can only come about when an individual feels comfortable with who they are, regardless of culture, colour, creed or dis/ability.

When I feel comfortable with who I am, then I can begin to feel comfortable with who you are. When I feel comfortable with who you are, I remove the basis of conflict.

When conflict is removed then the need for aggression is removed. When the need for aggression is removed, then the need for violence is removed. When the need for violence is removed then the need for war is removed.

War is not just absent but obsolete. From this foundation we are able to build tolerance and understanding, feeling comfortable with our differences. When this level of comfort is reached we can allow our differences, then we will achieve lasting and sustainable peace. The diversity of all humanity can express itself in all its beauty.

During the Second World War the A bomb was dropped without warning on Hiroshima. We were told this would bring the Japanese up short and end this horrendous war. The second bomb was dropped some days later to make sure the Japanese had got the message. Ask anyone – this is what they will tell you. Not true.

I have visited the Peace Park at Hiroshima. Here you will see, as I saw, a framed letter signed by General McArthur. That letter clearly states that the first bomb was dropped as a statement to the Japanese Government. The second was dropped, monitoring groups and observers in place, so that the different effects of the two different bombs could be observed and assessed.

The Peace Park shows photos of women, children and old people running for their lives, clothes disintegrated, liquid flesh dripping from their arms. There is also a large stone taken from a bridge, a shadow of a crouched person is clearly defined on this stone. A literal photograph as a negative was flash burned onto the stone as the person huddled, sheltering for what he thought was safety. There was no physical trace left of this individual.

The crane is the Japanese symbol for peace, health and long life. A young Japanese girl named Sadako Sasaki was two years old and lived in Hiroshima when the first atomic bomb used on civilians was dropped, on August 6, 1945. When she was eleven, she developed leukaemia, a common disease among children exposed to atomic radiation.

While being treated in the hospital, Sadako was visited by a friend who taught her to fold paper origami cranes. An old Japanese legend stated that anyone who folded one thousand cranes would be granted a wish. Sadako's wish was to be returned to good health and that all children who suffer from war would be healed and that in the future no children should so suffer. Inspired to realise this dream, Sadako began her quest to fold the thousand cranes.

In the following months Sadako managed to fold over six hundred cranes but her disease gradually worsened and finally claimed her life. Her classmates, inspired by her courage, folded the remainder and she was buried with one thousand origami cranes.

The story of Sadako's quest and courage spread all over Japan, and children throughout the country folded Peace Cranes and raised money to build a children's memorial in the Hiroshima Peace Park. In 1958, three years after her death, the monument became a reality. It shows Sadako standing on the mountain of paradise holding a giant golden origami crane overhead in her outstretched arms. At its base is the inscription,

'This is our cry; this is our prayer, Peace in the World.'

Whilst visiting the Peace Park in Hiroshima I witnessed the impact of coach load after coach load of paper cranes arriving and being unloaded. Some sixty years later these are ceremoniously burned in a special sanctuary area, proclaiming and continuing the prayer for peace. All politicians of any country and any party should visit this park as a constant reminder of that experience – experience is how we learn, how we move forward. Relationships can and will eventually function with a 'do as you would be done' by attitude. That is when we will realize true peace – that doesn't mean if we don't all live from this viewpoint others have to lie down and be trodden on. It means tolerance and discrimination not intolerance and judgment.

If I carpet my home in a deep, pure white, wool carpet and don't allow my visitors to come in in muddy boots that is not judgment, that is discrimination. Be discriminate, steer clear of those who might abuse the desire for clarity and truth. I abhor violence and the need for killing. I was vegetarian because I knew I couldn't kill and therefore decided not to ask others to kill on my behalf. And yet if my family were threatened in any way, by a gunman, a mountain lion, a rabid dog, I would find the necessary mental power to kill the threat and save my family.

Hypocrisy has no place in human thinking – killing is killing to what degree are we prepared to go? To wear a mask, as some religious sects ask to avoid breathing insects; to ask others to kill our food on our behalf, to kill others for personal gain or anger? Humans decide their own path but then others must discriminate against the consequences. The individual is part of the whole and cannot at this stage avoid it. We are all part of the big picture.

The world, no doubt the whole of creation, is a hologram. Science now shows us this effect. It is like having a picture of something made of glass. If the picture is shattered you would expect to see a small portion of the picture in each tiny piece. But that is not so, in every tiny smashed piece can be seen the whole picture, when exposed to laser light each part contains the whole. A seed of one plant doesn't grow into a different plant, or the egg and sperm of an animal or human grow into another species. Each contains a blueprint; I see it as a holographic blueprint for the end product. Once the human end product progresses it develops the freedom of choice. What music shall I listen to? What movies shall I watch? What career shall I choose? When I look in a mirror – will I choose to see a frown or a smile? Will I blame others or situations? How do I choose to react to situations for my problems? If I blame my parents, then they blame theirs and so on, then really poor old Adam and Eve get the blame again!

We now are told,

'You are what you eat.' More importantly 'You are how you act'. How we act is who we become, in fact who we are.

We have chosen, our Governments have chosen – and let's not be mistaken people get the Government they deserve by either voting or abstaining. We live in an authoritative patriarchal, nanny state – think of anything you can do without some Government Agency requiring details to give their permission. Building, driving, health, shopping, schooling choice not the least of the choices here are the regulations of catchment areas, whether you can baby sit your neighbour's children or take them to a club.

Walmart, one of the world's largest retailers and who now own Asda, have introduced RFID (Radio Frequency Identification) Its top suppliers are now attaching tiny, minute even, electronic tags to their goods. In the last few years this technology has become affordable and is being used for many things such as animal identification, anti-theft devices, electronic cash cards, and even hospital patient identification for surgery, and keeping checks on and tracing stock and supplies.

It all sounds very benign doesn't it? However, consumer advocates are concerned about privacy implications in the retail and medical applications of RFID as they could also be used to monitor customers, because they continue to remain functional after the goods have left the shop. Person Traffic Units to read these tags can be installed in airports, libraries, elevators, restaurants, shops. Should we also be concerned or are we already fully monitored and tagged with such things as CCTV and mobile phones? The UK is the most watched, tagged, databased country in the whole of the population, certainly of Europe if not of the whole world. We call this Democracy.

Big Brother directs our lives whether we like it or not. Authority is there to keep us in check. But what happened to self discipline? What happened to compassion? to consideration for others? to freedom? The only true freedom is through self discipline. You choose the world in which you wish to live. You choose the answers to the previous questions. You decide to say No to things in your life that will aggravate your peace and equilibrium. Don't wait for someone else to create the rules and regulations of authority. Mother Theresa said,

'Don't wait for leaders, do it person to person.'

We talk about civilized behavior as though this is a high ideal. Look at so called primitive societies and animal groups and see the moral codes within their societies. Even animals can and do display compassion and consideration for others in their community. I think of elephants where a baby elephant has many surrogate mothers in its many aunties.

There is no such thing as a civilized society. It is a misnomer. How can any country engaged in the processes of war, crime, abuse and greed be classed as civilized?

Humans have an inbuilt system of survival – we seem incapable of true honesty about ourselves. I heard a psychologist say the other day that there are different kinds of lies. White lies, which are kind, forgivable lies, yellow lies which are lies of cowardice or fear, green lies which are lies of jealousy and black lies which are evil. It cannot be denied that lies are lies, it is only the degree that appears to matter.

Look around and make your choice, have the self discipline to choose – if you don't take in the horror movies, the excessive alcohol, the aggressive and degenerative lifestyles on offer then your world will not be colored by these to hinder evolutionary progress. Self discipline and self enquiry can awaken the path, and I stress the path, to enlightenment. To follow the path requires hard work and dedication.

The Indian Guru, Dr Pillau taught and practiced Conscious Living – to be fully present in every moment of life. He carried this through into conscious dying. Nine months before his death in his eighties he announced the date and time of his death. A few days before the predicted date he sat on his pallet and went into deep meditation, he died at the exact time he predicted, fully present, fully at peace.

If I could begin to achieve his example I would know I had begun to understand that the meaning of life is to discover the meaning of life.

I feel what I have just said is a lecture. It is not because I am surrounded by people who have chosen the way they want to live. I seek those around the world who also make this choice. Seek out the media, the TV, the radio, whatever and wherever you can find people like you who have taken that step of self discipline and live lives of compassion and consideration. You and they do outweigh the others it's just that you don't make the news or hit the headlines as often.

The ultimate choice is of consideration for others, animals, the planet, knowing that this is the world in which we can all live. Our incarnational expression manifests in many different forms, where preconceived beliefs and teachings can limit the fulfillment of the soul. If we accept we are challenged to expand our reality, to release our need to control, we will find that deep metamorphosis of the butterfly.

We have not inherited the earth from our fathers; we have borrowed it from our children. Life is a gift, a present. We leave this gift to our children and grandchildren. That is why we call Now, The Present.

My final conclusion is who you are.

God Within

If when you look in the mirror, you could see what I see,
when I look at you –
you would know the truth of all being.

As I look into those eyes, beyond the physical,
I see a beautiful, shining, radiant God. Why do we try or
need to mask this truth?

Our living is our means by which to discover who we are,
to recognise our God.

If we gaze at the sky, looking at the clouds we will never
see the snowdrops,
the primroses tenderly growing at our feet.

If we continually seek God in some form of religion
or dogma,
we will never look close enough to ourselves.

Always seeking someone else's thoughts,
someone else's views,
someone else's approval, we trample the snowdrops
of our being.

Take time to look into your own eyes.

Nurture the snowdrops and primroses growing there
and realise that you are that radiant,
glowing God whom you seek.

Without judgement, just allow, just be.

No forgiveness is needed,
because no wrong has been done.

Our God loves us so deeply that we have free will,
free choice – to experience all.

All experience entails feeling – feeling is emotion.

Emotion is the most powerful energy.

Through feeling and emotion our experiences,
all our experiences,
give us the opportunity to grow, to expand.

The more our thoughts expand,
the more our God consciousness expands,
the more God expands.

God is infinite, God is forever.

Forever expanding, forever experiencing,
forever loving, forever unjudging.

Just allowing to be.

As we expand in experiences, in feeling, in emotion,
we come closer to our Godhood,
to the ultimate Joy of Being.

To be what Is – now. In the instant, in the moment.

Not tied, limited by the past. Holding us down
with judgments, what ifs?

The limited view, of always looking over the shoulder.
Not limited by the future.

Always planning, judging, organising,
gazing so far ahead for comparisons of past and future,
that, we yet again, trample the beauty lying at our feet.

Take the moment, the sacrament of the holy moment.

Live it as Joy, live it as God, live it as You.

Unjudged, unlimited, unconditionally loved.